UNDREAMED SHORES

The Hidden Heroines
of British Anthropology

FRANCES LARSON

GRANTA

Granta Publications, 12 Addison Avenue, London W11 4QR

First published in Great Britain by Granta Books, 2021
This paperback edition published in 2022

A CIP catalogue record for this book
is available from the British Library.

1 3 5 7 9 10 8 6 4 2

ISBN 978 1 78378 334 2
eISBN 978 1 84708 333 5

Typeset by M Rules

Printed and bound by CPI Group (UK) Ltd, Croydon, CR0 4YY

www.granta.com

Dr Frances Larson is the author of *Severed: A History of Heads Lost and Heads Found*, which was a Book of the Year in the *Spectator* and the *TLS*, and *An Infinity of Things: How Sir Henry Wellcome Collected the World*, which was a *Sunday Times* Book of the Year and a *New Scientist* Best Book of 2009. She is a research associate at the Pitt Rivers Museum at the University of Oxford.

'*Undreamed Shores* captivates, fascinates and haunts ... Superbly researched and winningly written' Boyd Tonkin, *Arts Desk*

'Absorbing ... With this tender and luminously written work, Larson has convincingly vindicated [the women's] careers' Rana Mitter, *Literary Review*

'*Undreamed Shores* is an extraordinarily well-crafted, many-layered, and captivating book, in which the author makes the amount of research that underlies its chapters seem effortless.' Felix Haas, *World Literature Today*

'Meticulously researched' Martha Macintyre, *Inside Story* (Australia)

'Larson is an elegant writer not given to hyperbolic gush ... [S]he animates her subjects by careful reading and close observation, and she draws out their complexities with delicate sympathy. I found myself gasping at the sheer nerve of these women ... Poignant' Charlotte Gray, *Wall Street Journal*

Also by Frances Larson from Granta Books

Severed: A History of Heads Lost and Heads Found

For Mia and Una

Contents

Illustrations

UNDREAMED
SHORES

Introduction

The past is my field site. I am an anthropologist who travels to places long ago rather than to places far away. Anthropology is predicated on travel, on embracing distance in an attempt to collapse it again. It is about reaching across boundaries and becoming strange. It is the study of translations, interludes, peripheries, and fragmented meanings. It is about confronting yourself through the unfamiliar presence of others.

As a graduate student, I had neither the inclination nor the courage to go abroad. One of my friends went to Zanzibar to study the souvenir market; another had already done research in Papua New Guinea by the time we met as doctoral students at Oxford. But our tutors did not necessarily expect us to travel: for our generation, anthropology was no longer limited to the study of distant shores. The whole notion of an isolated, exotic anthropological field site was in a healthy state of disarray by then anyway. One of my contemporaries decided to study local church bell-ringers; another explored the world of online video-gaming communities from the comfort of the college computer room; and I travelled into the past.

To reach my particular part of the late nineteenth century, I had to commute into London by bus each day and swipe my card at the door of the Wellcome Library archives. There I lost myself in the vast and chaotic private collections of Sir Henry Wellcome, the pharmaceuticals magnate and, more importantly to me, a fanatical collector of anything and everything.

It was in this archive, surrounded by stacks of documentation generated by Sir Henry's avarice, that I first met Winifred Blackman. Born in 1872, Winifred had gone up to Oxford to read anthropology eighty-six years before me, in 1912, and through dogged determination and persistent pestering, she had managed to squeeze a few hundred pounds out of Sir Henry in the 1920s to fund her research in Egypt. That was no small achievement, for a woman. Men, I soon learned, found it easier to win Sir Henry's support.

With the privileged perspective of a historian, I could see the casual prejudices Winifred faced – more clearly, perhaps, than she could have seen them herself. Henry Wellcome funded many anthropologists over the years, both male and female. The women had to provide him with letters of reference, résumés and written research proposals, then they had to sign contractual agreements stipulating that they would deliver every single artefact they laid their hands on into Wellcome's collection. Sir Henry's staff told Winifred what she must buy for him, they carefully examined all her field collections, and after each season in Egypt she was made to wait for months to hear whether he would continue his financial support.

By contrast, her male contemporaries were simply given a cheque and sent off on their travels in eager anticipation of the treasures they would undoubtedly find. They enjoyed a far freer rein and did not have to concern themselves with any references, résumés or research plans. In short, the men were all men together; the women were useful up to a point.

Winifred Blackman played a cameo role in my doctoral dissertation and I thought little more about her, but during my next research project, writing a history of the collections at the Pitt Rivers Museum in Oxford, I met some of her contemporaries. Blackman, it turned out, was one of a handful of women who had come up to Oxford University to study anthropology on the eve of the First World War.

Oxford was unique in training a group of female anthropologists in the opening decades of the twentieth century. At Cambridge, there was only one comparable student: Winifred Hoernle, a South African who came up to read anthropology and psychology in 1908 and went on to become a lecturer in anthropology at the University of the Witwatersrand. The next female student who studied anthropology at Cambridge and established a career in the subject was Camilla Wedgwood. She arrived at Newnham College in 1920 and did fieldwork in Manam Island, off the north coast of New Guinea, in 1933. Meanwhile, no professional female anthropologists were trained exclusively at the University of London until the 1920s, although the London School of Economics then became home to the pre-eminent anthropology department in the country. Oxford was ahead of its time. Twenty-seven women (and 103 men) registered for the diploma in anthropology at Oxford between 1907 and 1918, and five of those women – the subjects of this book – became Britain's first female anthropologists.

From the earliest year that a qualification in anthropology was offered at Oxford, the course attracted extraordinary women determined to travel to remote and inhospitable countries. The five whose stories I tell here led groundbreaking research in their fields. Katherine Routledge commissioned her own boat and sailed to Easter Island, one of the most isolated communities in the world. Maria Czaplicka risked her health to trek more than three thousand miles through a frozen Siberian winter in search of nomadic reindeer-herders who had never before seen a European woman. Winifred Blackman spent nineteen consecutive field seasons living with the agricultural peasants of Upper Egypt. Barbara Freire-Marreco went to work in the pueblos of New Mexico and Arizona. And Beatrice Blackwood, ignoring all advice, travelled into the New Guinea interior to live with warriors who still made their weapons from wood and stone.

Their travels were sensationalized in the press. 'Woman Lives for Year with Savages. Never Felt in Danger, Even on Fringe of Cannibal Land' and 'Girl Risks Life at Forbidden Rites' ran the headlines when Beatrice Blackwood returned from the Pacific in the 1930s. Blackwood disliked publicity, she felt it detracted from her research, but her peers sought media attention insofar as it could give a platform to their work and further their academic ambitions. Maria Czaplicka neatly pasted all the press clippings relating to her career in a large leather-bound scrapbook. It was more than a hundred pages long by the time of her death. Today, it is a crucial record of her work.

These five women were not simply adventurers; they were intellectual pioneers, members of the very first generation of professional anthropologists who set out to study human cultural diversity as part of a coherent, self-conscious academic community. Only a few dozen students – male or female – had studied anthropology at any British university when they embarked on fieldwork. The discipline was tiny and consisted of a handful of academics who all knew each other personally.

In 1910, there were just three university posts in the subject: Cambridge University and the London School of Economics both had a lecturer in ethnology, and at Oxford there was a reader in anthropology. Those studying anthropology at the time were largely taught by academics from a range of related subjects, like psychology, linguistics, human anatomy and sociology. The parameters of the discipline had yet to be firmly established, and field methods varied. There was very little money for research. Jobs were scarce, and there were plenty of men to take them.

The women in this book would have wanted to be remembered for their professional achievements alone, but before they were adventurers and intellectual pioneers they were women, and as women they faced entrenched prejudice and constraint at every turn. At the end of the nineteenth century, middle-class girls and boys were born into different worlds. Winifred Blackman's brothers, for example, were privately educated, while she and her sisters stayed at home and did needlework to pay the bills. She never went to school, but she read voraciously and attended Oxford later, as a mature student.

Once at Oxford, most women were seen as potential research assistants at best, or threatening impostors at worst. In British academic and professional life they were expected to be peripheral, clerical and grateful. Only a few hundred had ever attended Oxford University before the First World War. They were not admitted as members of the university, and although they could sit examinations, they were not permitted to take the degrees they had earned until 1920. Women were almost entirely invisible, frequently disdained, and usually inconsequential to the men they studied alongside. A small number worked at the university as typists or assistants. To trade subordinate occupations like these for the forests of New Guinea or the brutal expanse of the Arctic tundra in the name of academic inquiry was an astonishing achievement.

On her return from Siberia, Maria Czaplicka was given a lectureship at Oxford. It was a significant accomplishment in itself, but it was only temporary. Maria was a good teacher, but she lost her job when the male lecturer she had replaced came home at the end of the war. Despite universal admiration from her colleagues, she was never given a permanent academic position and she struggled to make ends meet.

Money troubled Katherine Routledge in different ways. She was born into a wealthy industrial family, but her fortune cast a shadow over her research. One colleague thought she and her husband were 'well-to-do people who do their work as a form of amusement'. They were 'not endowing science, but pleasing themselves'. Routledge had married a man who shared her intellectual interests, but their marriage gradually fell apart. Despite her private wealth, she had no recourse when he secured a High Court order to take control of her assets.

Winifred Blackman, Maria Czaplicka and Beatrice Blackwood never married. They knew women who had given up an academic career for marriage, like Barbara Freire-Marreco, who met a mathematician during the war and married him in 1920. For professional women, marriage was inevitably a watershed that reset relationships and priorities. (Female employees of Sir Henry Wellcome's pharmaceuticals firm, Burroughs Wellcome & Co., were fired on marriage, which was standard business practice at the time.)

All five women, then, were defined and constrained by their womanhood. No doubt being female sharpened their faculties as well as restricting their freedoms. It certainly tested their resolve. If anthropology is the art and science of being an interloper, then these women were perfectly, and sometimes painfully, primed for the job.

Initially I knew them for their scholarship and for their ethnographic collections, which were shipped back to Oxford in crates and added to the reserves at the Pitt Rivers Museum, where I now worked. But they remained peripheral to the histories I was writing then, of great men and great institutions, just as they have been peripheral to those histories for a hundred years, since they met at Oxford.

This book seeks to change that.

Anthropology did not simply promise Katherine Routledge, Barbara Freire-Marreco, Maria Czaplicka, Winifred Blackman and Beatrice Blackwood a professional opportunity: it provided an escape. Fieldwork offered these women a temporary relief from the strictures of English society, or at least it offered a new context – a new place, a new culture – in which to negotiate their own identity. The anthropologists in this account endured isolation and physical hardship in cultures very different from their own, but they found freedom far from home. They went from the periphery into the unknown, and I doubt that any of them felt fully at home in England again. Instead, on their return, they fought for recognition in a university system ruled by men, and their professional aspirations strained their personal relationships. They defied the social expectations of their time with brilliant, and tragic, results.

I

No Civilization Between Us

Katherine Routledge in British East Africa, 1906

Katherine Routledge spent many years trying to escape the forbidding red-brick family mansion on the outskirts of Darlington where she grew up. She was born Katherine Pease, and her family presided over a small empire of collieries, quarries and mills in northeast England. She had once dreamt of marrying a barrister or an MP and presiding over a busy household of her own. In truth, her high spirits rarely chimed with her family's provincial habits. She was regarded as an impulsive child: too unpredictable, too demanding. When, in her mid-twenties, she told her widowed mother that she wanted to go to university, it was a radical suggestion. It was 1891 and only a few hundred women had ever gone on to higher education in England. Katie's decision to abandon her domestic duties would be talked about all over town, but she had become such a 'tactless' and unhappy young woman that her mother agreed to her Oxford application.

Wilson Pease, Katherine's younger brother, sympathized with his sister's lot in life. 'Darlington certainly is not a congenial place for anyone with any brains or literary tastes,' he wrote in his diary when he heard of Katherine's plan to study. Wilson described Woodside, the family house, as large, cold, dismal and depressing. When, by some unfortunate oversight, he found himself there for more than a few weeks at a time, he liked to joke that he had become the 'daughter at home', paying bills, posting parcels, helping the cook, and performing other mundane niceties that made up 'a somewhat monotonous existence' (and this from a man who happily spent his life squandering his inheritance on holidays, dining out and playing golf). After a month or so at Woodside, Wilson would claim that he had yet to hear a conversation worth writing down. For Katherine – who actually was the daughter at home, and far more ambitious than her brother – the dreary domesticity of Darlington was intolerable.

Katherine Pease, far left, and Wilson Pease, seated, with their cousins, July 1891. Wilson's future wife, Caroline Joanne ('Joan') Fowler, stands next to him in the centre of the group; they married three years after this photograph was taken.

In 1891 Katherine went up to Somerville College, Oxford, to read History. Educating women was still considered radical, subversive, even dangerous, by the many in middle-class England who thought that it risked undermining women's true calling as wives and mothers. An education, it was argued, would render them either unwilling or unfit for their domestic duties. It might damage their feminine constitutions, which were too frail and too irrational for the rigours of academic study. Since these delicate female students would lose any interest in pleasing men, educating women also threatened the male establishment. Anxieties ran deep, and they endured: when women were finally granted their degrees at Oxford in 1920, an anonymous letter to *Isis*, the student magazine, warned that men's freedom to enjoy university and make male friends was under threat and that they would now stop coming to Oxford and would apply to Cambridge instead. For decades, educating women was thought to be both unnatural and unsafe.

To get around these prejudices, the first women's colleges at Oxford were presented as harmless finishing schools, in which education was both an extension of home life and an enhancement of it. Students at Somerville were expected to kiss the college principal goodnight, eat apples at the dinner table with a knife and fork, and address each other using their full title, as, for example, 'Miss Pease'. The use of first names was unusual and subject to the ritual formality of a 'proposal'. Receiving a proposal from a friend was a matter of great excitement among the students. They paid calls, left visiting cards and issued invitations to each other, while work was organized around formal meals in the dining room, afternoon teas, and drinks served in the drawing-room. Some students found these traditions suffocating, but others, living away from home for the first (and perhaps only) time, were comforted by the routines. And little could diminish the joy of sleeping out in the college gardens on summer nights, punting on the river, or staying up late in a friend's room drinking cocoa.

Wilson Pease visited Somerville in 1891 with the air of an intrepid anthropologist observing an exotic tribe: 'The students were more presentable than I had expected,' he noted in his diary. Women, he felt, having forfeited their privileged position in society as the objects of men's adoration, must be prepared to accept the consequences. 'When women come down from the pedestal of quiet refinement and hustle in the crowd of men, they must not expect to be worshipped,' he wrote. Wilson felt unsettled and preferred the old state of things, but he could not bring himself to deny women like his sister the opportunity to think for themselves.

That summer, Katherine was finding her voice. 'We have discovered that Katie is "the backbone" of our family, she always has a decided opinion when we cannot make up our minds about anything,' Wilson wrote. At Oxford, Katherine was quick to learn but rather erratic in her work, and her tutors took her to task for not grounding her arguments in the evidence. Meanwhile, at home, her relationship with her mother was strained.

After university, Katherine returned to Woodside and took a job teaching at Darlington Training College. Wilson thought she taught 'uncommonly well'. She hardly looked at her notes at all despite addressing her students for one and a half hours at a stretch. There was often, however, 'a slight bother to trouble about' at home. Katherine was restless. Wilson thought her unhappiness came from a craving for something new that would never be satisfied. Mrs Pease made light of her daughter's depression, telling people dismissively, 'It's in her that ills her', a phrase her own father had used when she was young. Katherine spent a few unhappy years in Darlington before her mother agreed to rent her a small, high-end flat on the tenth floor of Queen Anne Mansions in Westminster where she could live, for at least part of the year, on her own.

In London she became involved with the South African Colonization Society, based in Victoria Street, just around the corner from her flat. Founded in the wake of the Boer War and run by a group of wealthy female imperialists, the society aimed to move respectable, capable young women to the colony, and prided itself on contributing to the 'civilizing' effects of Empire and the reconstruction of the country. Katherine travelled to South Africa in 1902 under the auspices of the society, and spent five months assessing the job prospects for young British women in various schools, offices and shops in the country's major cities. She marvelled at the wild expanse of the veldt, and at the hills and flowers that reminded her of the south of France, or perhaps, she imagined, of how it might be in the East.

Memories of that trip would play their part in her courtship with William Scoresby Routledge, whom she met in London in 1905. Katherine was then a clever, wealthy, unmarried thirty-eight-year-old looking for a new adventure, and Scoresby was forty-seven, a colonial drifter just back from two years living in a remote outpost of British East Africa. They quickly came to talk of returning to Africa together, but Katherine's family was concerned about the match. Mr Routledge had no profession, his private income paled in comparison to the Pease family's wealth, and he seemed aloof and judgemental.

Routledge was an Oxford graduate who had never completed his medical degree in London. For the past two years he had been living at Nyeri, on the slopes of Mount Kenya and on the very edge of British occupation. When he first arrived in East Africa in 1902, a handful of British men, under Subcommissioner Sydney Hinde, were forcibly bringing the Kikuyu people who lived there under their control. Hinde oversaw the construction of the first roads in the area, and when Nyeri was chosen as the site for a new government station Scoresby secured a small plot of land for himself. He organized for a trench to be dug around it, and put up a few huts with grass roofs and open sides. This became his home while he spent his time shooting game, taking photographs, collecting objects and writing notes about his new neighbours, the Kikuyu. The Nyeri homestead transformed Scoresby Routledge, by virtue of circumstance and because he had no more pressing job to do, into an amateur anthropologist.

Anthropology had emerged in the late nineteenth century as an academic discipline concerned with charting, categorizing and understanding the world's cultures. Early anthropologists were preoccupied with data and were eager for detailed reports of 'primitive' people's beliefs and ceremonies, as well as information about their clothes, houses, food and artefacts, and descriptions of their appearance. The Kikuyu were little known and ripe for anthropological study. In truth, almost any observations Routledge made about them would have been valuable.

In 1904, his photographs appeared in the academic journal of the Anthropological Institute, *Man*, as illustrations for an article about Kikuyu tribes. That same year, now back in London, he was elected Fellow of the Anthropological Institute and his academic ambitions grew. When he met Katherine he talked of taking her with him to British East Africa, where they would collect plant samples for the Royal Botanic Gardens at Kew and artefacts for the British Museum.

Life in Africa promised a new start for them both, and an opportunity to shed the expectations of British society. In Nyeri, it mattered less that Scoresby did not have a job, and Katherine could escape the strictures of the social circles in which she had grown up. There were, in effect, no social circles in Nyeri. Mrs Routledge would be the only white woman for miles around. Nairobi, home to some six hundred white settlers, was a six-day trek away, and Nyeri was the northernmost British outpost of the East Africa Protectorate; as Katherine saw it, there would be 'no civilization between us and Egypt'. On the homestead she could wear the same loose cotton clothes every day, tend to her garden, learn Swahili and go for long rides. Marriage, in these circumstances, gave her new freedoms. If Mr Routledge did not have the proper credentials as far as the Pease family was concerned, then that was partly the point.

Katherine's family would probably have agreed with one of Scoresby's relatives who said, bluntly, that Scoresby had found himself 'a rich wife who wanted to travel'. Wilson Pease, who was tasked with enquiring about Mr Routledge's prospects in the months leading up to the marriage, declared that the responsibility left him with 'black lines under the eyes'. It did not help that Katherine, who was usually so decisive, seemed uncertain. When she 'at last made up her mind to accept him' in May 1906, her agitated efforts to arrange the wedding drove Wilson and his wife Joan to distraction. On the day itself, in August, there was a huge thunderstorm and it poured with rain, which Wilson considered to be a bad omen, while Katherine's mother kept to her room and did not attend the ceremony.

Within four months of their wedding, Katherine and Scoresby were on board a ship bound for Mombasa, en route to Nyeri. A twenty-four-hour train journey took them to Nairobi, where they practised putting up their tents – one each, connected by an awning, under which they often ate – plus stable tents, servants' tents and tents for supplies. Then, it was a five-day trek north-east to the small administrative post of Fort Hall, accompanied by seventy porters carrying their belongings, and from there two more days to Nyeri. The homestead that greeted them consisted of a group of thatched huts with cement floors and open sides, surrounded by a moat. They pitched their tents underneath the roof of the main building, creating a veranda in front. Here they lived for two years. Katherine tended a vegetable garden and kept goats; Scoresby hunted game. Together they rode their horses out across the grassy uplands in the late afternoons, and sat on the veranda around the fire in the evenings.

The Routledges were living a frontier life. Even Nairobi, established by white colonists less than ten years earlier, was a crude outpost with only a few permanent buildings. Beyond one or two central streets, a sprawl of tin huts and tents housed the town's growing population of European hunters, Africans looking for work, and Indian shopkeepers, 'all selling a little of everything at very poor quality and at very expensive prices', Katherine reported home. She was one of very few white women in Nairobi for the short time they stayed there, and beyond the town, as they began their trek north, they saw 'no traces' of British occupation. In Nyeri there was only one British resident, a government administrator, and no land other than Scoresby's had been given to Europeans. The nearby hills were home to Kikuyu huts, circular and thatched with grass, and their banana and maize plantations. Zebra, wildebeest and antelope ran thick across the plains, and Katherine fell asleep at night listening to the cries of hyenas. When they rode out, Scoresby went first in case 'there is a lion in the way', and they employed four Swahili camp policemen to guard their home-stead day and night.

Katherine found 'this gipsy outdoor life' bewitching at first. 'There is plenty to do in the neighbourhood, if we are energetic, in the study of primitive existence ... [however,] if one lays in nothing but numberless fresh impressions and interests, the time will not have been wasted,' she wrote to her family. Before long, though, the Routledges began researching the lives of the Kikuyu with more purpose. Scoresby pursued his interests in technology, watching people working iron, making fire and building huts and bridges over the mountain streams, while Katherine visited their homes, talking to the women in broken Swahili about marriage and children, and finding out what she could about the Kikuyu political system, using her Swahili servants and young Kikuyu helpers to interpret and check facts for her when necessary.

The Kikuyu matched the anthropologist's ideal of a 'primi-tive culture' perfectly. For a group of people to be deemed truly primitive they had to be untouched by other cultures, and the Kikuyu lived in a remote rural location and had little contact with people from towns and cities or from other countries. Their technological traditions were simple and unmechanized, which was thought to be a good indicator of how pristine their way of life remained. They made fire by rubbing together two pieces of wood; they rolled lengths of string from strips of chewed tree bark and animal sinew; they panned iron ore from the streams and smelted it in clay-lined holes dug in the ground that served as ovens; they cultivated the land using hand tools, and har-vested clay from the marshes in wicker baskets to make pots. They looked the part, too. They wore goatskin garments, and decorated themselves with metal chains, coiled-wire jewellery, strips of leather, feathers and wooden beads.

Kikuyu political organization was another sign of their credentials as 'good primitives'. Anthropologists considered blood
ties to be the most basic determinant of political affiliation
possible in human society, and the Kikuyu were organized into
groups based on families living together in homesteads. They
were also thought to be naturally bellicose, superstitious and
sexually prolific, all of which were classic primitive traits (no
matter that the same traits were ubiquitous in civilized society).
In short, Scoresby had hit upon an anthropological goldmine
when he first visited Nyeri, and studying the Kikuyu turned the
couple's privileged expatriate existence into academic capital.

Katherine revelled in the 'sensation of rest and space and
freedom, [and] of in some mysterious way, "coming once more
to one's own"' which she found at Nyeri, but this new sense of
herself did little for her marriage. If, after two years there, the
Routledges were still in love with Africa, by 1908 they were
no longer as deeply in love with each other. Early that year
Katherine wrote to her brother, 'I am so wretched ... and so
tired,' and he responded by reminding her, unsympathetically,
how far she had come: 'Any husband is better than none,' he
counselled. 'Most old maids are miserable.'

The Routledges arrived home in the spring of 1908 determined to
write up their research. Their book *With a Prehistoric People: The
Akikuyu of British East Africa* was published in 1910. In it, Scoresby
and Katherine clearly distinguished their separate contributions.
They each wrote their own preface and their own chapters, and
carefully explained their division of labour throughout. Katherine
added her own commentary in appendices which she signed with
her name, and when they used the first person in the text they
clarified with a footnote: 'W.S.R.' or 'K.R.'. Even their photographs

were individually initialled. This was a strikingly transparent editorial approach for a married couple, and it did not go unnoticed in the press. Indeed, almost everyone who reviewed the book remarked on the contributions of Mrs Routledge, since no one could overlook them.

In *With a Prehistoric People* Katherine convinced her readership that, as far as anthropology was concerned, 'there is work which, if it is to be done properly, must be done by a woman' (so wrote a reviewer for the *Manchester Guardian*). It was an extraordinary achievement. No one reading her chapters of the book, which she had written in a very personal style, could avoid the conclusion that she had obtained information from the Kikuyu women – about marriage, children and domestic life, and about their feelings and reflections on their lives – that could not have been acquired by a man. It was not simply that the Routledges, working together, had covered more ground than Scoresby could have alone; rather, Katherine had shifted the entire landscape of their study and opened up vistas that a man would never have noticed or explored. When it came to studying women's lives in savage society it was clear that 'the lady anthropologist has this field entirely to herself', and Katherine had made the most of it.

She wrote with verve and revelled in the opportunity to disrupt British upper-middle-class assumptions. The Kikuyu, for example, were polygamous: most Kikuyu men had two or three wives, and some had six or seven. But the women, far from being resentful or feeling enslaved by their husbands, as British readers might assume, found the idea of monogamy cruel in comparison. 'Only one wife to do the work!' they exclaimed in astonishment when they learned that Katherine had her husband all to herself. Far from feeling subjugated, Kikuyu women pressed their husbands to take more wives to help them run the household. And Katherine came to respect the Kikuyu marital system, despite her Christian beliefs. In fact, she pointed out, the women led 'incomparably easier' lives than many women in Britain. They were happier, they enjoyed more leisure time, earned greater respect in old age, and suffered no anxiety when it came to providing for their families. They never questioned their value to society, and, they insisted, they never married anyone they did not want to marry.

Katherine boldly pointed out these advantages to her readers and they had little choice but to accept her opinion, since none of them had ever met a Kikuyu woman for verification. 'Her reports are probably the most minute, intimate, and accurate which have hitherto appeared about the position of the female savage in any country,' one reviewer opined.

It was unusual at the time for an anthropologist to spend a year working in the field. As a discipline, anthropology was young and largely populated by people in related professions, such as museum curators, medics and academics in other subjects, who all brought different interests to their work. Few thought it strictly necessary to spend time with the people they studied. The British scholars who had tackled anthropological questions during the late nineteenth century had relied on travellers' reports, and letters from missionaries and colonial officials stationed abroad, for descriptions of foreign cultures. They collated this evidence at their desks and theorized about the broad brushstrokes of cultural history, piecing together an elaborate jigsaw puzzle using infor-mation from many different sources to chart cultural diversity.

This 'epistolary anthropology' meant relying on collaborators who had little, if any, academic training and whose observa-tions were incidental to their professional responsibilities. The Routledges, by contrast, had not only set out to describe the Kikuyu culture, they had spent almost two years on the job.

This kind of 'intensive study', the academic community agreed, was not only admirable, it was the future of anthropology.

Katherine and Scoresby's book was commendable, but it was not revolutionary. They were not the first to embark on an intensive study of a 'primitive' people, and they were certainly not professional anthropologists. Their achievements were limited by the fact that they had not received any training, beyond reading one or two of the more popular books on the subject. Cautious reviewers agreed that there was a lamentable lack of detail in some sections of their work. One or two academic reviews were critical, pointing out the authors' obvious unfamiliarity with technical concepts like exogamy and totemism, but at least the Routledges had been honest about their ignorance. They had pointed out the weaknesses of their research, said what they were not sure about, and explained how they had obtained their information. If they were unaware of technical concepts, at least they did not rush to sweeping conclusions.

While preparing their manuscript, the Routledges had sent those chapters dealing with Kikuyu spiritual beliefs to the acknowledged expert on 'primitive religion', Robert Ranulph Marett, the newly appointed Reader in Social Anthropology at Oxford. He reviewed their material and his report appeared as an appendix in *With a Prehistoric People*. Marett was cautious in his conclusions. He had to be, since the Routledges did not know much about the theory of religion, and he could rely only on what they might or might not have seen and understood. But Marett also knew an opportunity when he saw one. He was looking for students to take Oxford's new diploma in anthropology, and Mrs Routledge was the perfect candidate. She was wealthy and able, but unqualified, and she knew it. In the autumn of 1911, Marett persuaded Katherine to enrol.

2

There Were No Women

The Oxford University Diploma
in Anthropology, 1911

Katherine's years of study at the University of Oxford had cultivated her independence, and brought the conflicts in her character into sharp relief. After her first year at Somerville, in August 1892, she declared to her family that it had been her 'misfortune to be born a woman with the feelings of a man'. A few months later, knowing the reaction it would elicit from the wealthy families of Darlington, she had provocatively attended a Christmas fancy-dress ball as 'an undergraduate', wearing a red dress and an academic cap and gown. Her relationship with Oxford had been born of a determination to be different. Now, twenty years later, she was married, a seasoned traveller, and a successful author. Her attitude towards the university had become pragmatic and distracted.

Katherine registered as a student for the diploma in anthropology in the autumn of 1911, but she did not spend much time in Oxford in the months that followed. Her studies were part of a wider set of preparations that were already well under way. She was in the midst of planning a second expedition with Scoresby, this time to Easter Island, and she was often in a shipyard on the Kent coast, supervising the construction of the ninety-foot sailing boat, the *Mana*, that would take them there. In June the following year Marett wrote urging her to attend her final exams, and telling her which books she must read for 'cramming purposes'. 'I hope you will face the music,' he wrote. 'It mustn't be said of your sex that it won't come up to scratch!! And both my other two ladies are showing the white feather more or less, and No. 4 (Miss Fischer) has "cracked". So I count on you!!'

There was a record number of women taking the anthropology diploma at Oxford that year. Nine men and four women had enrolled on the course, the largest intake of students in the five years that it had been running (only two women had taken it previously). The men were almost all Oxford graduates in their early twenties who had been persuaded by Marett to extend their studies for a year; many of them went on to pursue careers in the Colonial Office. Anthropology was one of a cluster of diploma courses established at Oxford in the opening decade of the twentieth century, in new subjects like geography, education and modern languages, that gave vocational training outside the purview of the university's traditional degrees. They were open to people outside the university, and many were taught by progressive tutors who welcomed female students.

Women were not yet allowed to be members of the university: they could not matriculate or take degrees; they could not serve on faculty boards or as examiners; and they could not join Congregation or Council, the university's governing bodies. They were, however, permitted to attend lectures, albeit at the lecturer's discretion, and sit examinations. Women at Oxford were still interlopers in a male world: a tiny minority, present only by invitation and dependent on the goodwill of men.

Two of the women Marett mentioned in his letter, Martha Fleming and Anna Fischer, have all but sunk without trace, although according to the course register Fleming had previously worked in education at the University of Chicago, and Fischer had a PhD from the University of Prague. As Marett predicted, neither of them took their exams that year. The fourth was Maria Czaplicka, a Polish student in her late twenties whose upbringing could not have been more different from Katherine's. Maria had no money, no family outside Poland, and she spoke only broken English. She had been the first woman to win a travelling scholarship from the Mianowski Fund, a private foundation supporting scientific research in Poland. She grasped her opportunities in Oxford fiercely and fell in love with the city completely. While Katherine missed lectures, Maria could think of little else.

Maria Czaplicka immersed herself in all that Oxford had to offer. She enjoyed collegiate life and accepted the university's habitual eccentricities, and she worked fiendishly hard. Her dedication and intelligence were, according to Marett, 'quite out of the ordinary': 'She is keen almost to a fault – I mean, almost to the point of disregarding what she owes to herself in the way of recreations.' As her English improved, Maria's aptitude and sheer determination convinced Marett that she had the potential to be a professional anthropologist.

Before she arrived at Oxford, she had spent a year attending seminars on the subject at the London School of Economics, where her peers regarded her as a serious student who worked hard on her English and spent her time reading in the British Museum library. Another Polish student, Bronislaw Malinowski, had started at the LSE that year and they became friends. Malinowski would go on to become a towering presence in British anthropology. He was a brilliant writer, teacher and theoretician, and his fieldwork in the Trobriand Islands during the First World War helped to redefine the discipline in the twentieth century.

Malinowski was the same age as Czaplicka, and they both arrived in London to study anthropology in 1910, Czaplicka from Warsaw, and Malinowski from Krakow. Both had a sharp intellect and wit and were fired by academic debate. In Czaplicka, these attributes could seem indelicate: an acquaintance remembered that she used to 'throw her weight about' in seminar discussions. And when, one day, Malinowski and Czaplicka pretended that they were engaged 'and sat holding each other's hands and demonstratively called each other <u>Daarling</u> [sic]' to fool their friends, the effect was unnerving because it was so out of character. Malinowski enjoyed practical jokes and wore his formidable intellect lightly, but Czaplicka seemed too ambitious and highly strung to be pulling pranks.

At Oxford, in any case, there were fewer opportunities for her to socialize with men than there had been in London. The few hundred female students lived in new women's halls on the outskirts of town, and were barely acknowledged by their male peers. Precariously poised between conservatism and radicalism, women at Oxford were allowed to attend lectures only in chaperoned parties and on condition of silence. They were obliged to walk around the city in groups and refrain from speaking to male undergraduates, even their own brothers or cousins. They were not allowed to have meals in men's colleges until the 1960s. '[T]his sex *apartheid* seemed very odd to me,' wrote the economist Mary Stocks, who left the LSE and moved to Oxford in 1913, two years after Czaplicka. Stocks was surprised when an Oxford student attended a tea-time meeting of the university's Fabian Society with a chaperone: at the LSE, men and women mixed far more freely. Czaplicka was philosophical about her new home. 'Oxford and Cambridge do not generally recognize women yet, but I cannot complain,' she told a journalist a few years later.

Oxford University had been an exclusively male institution until the 1870s, and it was only in 1877, when the rules on celibacy changed, that fellows were allowed to marry. The following year, the Association for Promoting the Higher Education of Women in Oxford was formed to provide lectures for female students, but progress was painfully slow. For decades, women were treated with suspicion and horror by the male establishment, and proponents of their education urged a strategy of meticulous inconspicuousness that lasted well into the twentieth century. Women at Oxford were expected to be dutiful, grateful, and all but invisible. Such was their success at this that Harold Macmillan, who went up to Balliol College in 1912, could later state bluntly that Oxford was an 'almost monastic' society at the time, where the undergraduates were not conscious of the women's colleges or the women students, and for practical purposes '[t]here were no women'.

Considerable effort went into making female students invisible. They were exhorted to dress with a 'cloistral simplicity', and wear clothes that were tasteful but plain: neither too drab, nor too showy. Vera Brittain, who went up to Somerville in 1914, wrote that it was 'deeply attached to its standards of scholarship and totally indifferent to ugliness and dowdiness'. (Katherine Routledge had donated a mirror to Somerville when she studied there in the 1890s, so that she could at least check her skirts.)

One tutor there, Vera Farnell, remembered struggling to persuade Dorothy Sayers, who arrived in 1912, to remove a pair of large red and green parrot earrings and her wide scarlet head-band before attending a lecture. Such duties were not unusual for Farnell and she did not relish them. On one occasion the fashionable student in question turned to her and cried, 'I won't, I *won't*, I WON'T be a dowd!' But women were not permitted to rock the boat. 'We have many privileges, but no rights,' the principal of Somerville, Emily Penrose, wrote to incoming students in 1907.

There were nearly a hundred students at Somerville when Czaplicka arrived in 1911. They lived in two large houses – each with its own dining-room, to preserve the intimate domestic atmosphere – and several cottages, all sharing generous grounds of two acres with a kitchen garden, bicycle sheds, tennis courts and a porter's lodge, in semi-rural north Oxford. The carriage drive and gardens were shaded by mature trees, and bordered a field that filled with buttercups in spring. A housekeeper and her staff attended to the women's domestic needs: they came into each student room at 7 a.m. with a large can of hot water to fill the washstand, and returned every evening to pull out a zinc bath from under the bed, fill it, and stoke the fire. They stocked the students' coal bunkers, some of which were neatly hidden in window seats, carried endless teapots in and out of drawing-rooms, and prepared a succession of meals of cold meat, cheese, bread and soup.

The mediocre food fuelled tennis and hockey matches, or boating on the river – although women were not allowed to race boats until the 1920s, and then only one after the other, since rowing side by side was deemed unladylike. Amateur theatricals were popular, and gave students the opportunity to take leading male roles. And Somerville was famous for its Parliament, a formal debating society modelled closely on Westminster, where debates were conducted strictly on party lines and members addressed each other as 'the Honourable Gentleman'.

Women's halls like Somerville were private worlds, accessible to men only by invitation, and run very successfully without them. Within their walls, women learned to behave like men, exercising their authority, aggression and assertiveness often for the first time. They learned how to act together, and how to win. Even the smallest expression of these new skills could be shocking. On a visit to see his sister Katherine at Somerville in June 1893, Wilson Pease had been taken aback when one of her friends shouted out in delight, 'Swop [sic] got a first!', while they were walking down the stairs together. It was something 'no man' would dream of doing in the presence of a lady. 'I think this incident remarkable as showing that women, now allowed to be noisy on occasion, will have to learn what those occasions are,' he wrote primly in his diary.

Women's second-class citizenship at Oxford came with its compensations: because they existed largely under the radar, they developed a relatively autonomous culture of their own. Their halls housed intimate, supportive communities that pushed women to challenge society's expectations of them, albeit a risky business that had to be kept under wraps. As soon as students walked out of the college gates, they were expected to perform the part of the subservient woman perfectly. Emily Penrose firmly believed that women would consolidate their gains within the university as a whole only through a judicious policy of deference and discretion.

Maria Czaplicka, who joined this nervous, radical, anachronistic British middle-class community in the autumn of 1911, was an unknown quantity. The secretary at the LSE had written her a letter of recommendation, assuring Miss Penrose that Czaplicka would make 'a delightful inmate of a residential college' and possessed 'a considerable amount of personal charm'. 'The only hesitation I could possibly have would be in regard to her age and the fact that she has been entirely her own mistress for several years,' Miss MacTaggart added. By 1910, most of the women entering Somerville were in their early twenties, some were still teenagers.

Czaplicka, who was nearer thirty, Polish, with no family in Britain and studying independently at a graduate level, must have seemed very different, and perhaps slightly mysterious to her peers. Sybil Ruegg, who had come up to Somerville that autumn to read English, wrote in her diary a 'nice little story about the Polish lady', who had confused the word 'comb' with the word 'corn' when she asked where to buy hair accessories. In a College photo taken in May 1913 'the Polish lady' sits with her peers, wearing a different style of dress from the other students, observing the camera with a steady gaze, and set slightly apart in her own space.

Foreigners like Czaplicka were a cause for concern to the Delegacy for Women Students (the committee that oversaw women's education), because it was assumed they were 'accustomed to different and more independent conditions of University life' and might disregard social mores. Czaplicka, however, had no time for anything but her work. Her unceasing intellectual energy had secured her place at Oxford and she was not about to forfeit her chances now. Far from being a foreigner set upon undermining the university's genteel

Members of Somerville College, Oxford, May 1913. Maria Czaplicka sits to the left of the central pillar wearing a dark dress; Emily Penrose sits in the centre wearing a white blouse and pale necktie.

status quo, Czaplicka was an immigrant seeking its intellectual freedoms.

There had been few freedoms in Warsaw, Czaplicka's hometown, which was then part of the Russian Empire. For decades, Warsaw's residents had been forced to speak Russian, abandon their own customs and give up their intellectual aspirations. It was almost impossible for Poles to get a Polish education, and women, in particular, were denied access to university. As a consequence, Maria had to attend the Flying University, an illegal underground organization that offered students classes in Polish, in private homes around the city. Locations were often changed at the last minute to avoid detection and arrest. Czaplicka had struggled for years to make enough money for her studies, working numerous jobs and trying to manage her debts as best she could. 'I was impossibly overworked,' she remembered of her life in Warsaw, 'with various secretarialships [sic], substitutions [supply work], lessons, lectures etc. All those paid poorly or not at all.'

Now at Somerville, she settled into her own room, wallpapered, furnished in walnut and chintz, with a polished wooden floor, and the unusual and hopelessly ineffective 'shuttered' fireplace that was a unique feature of the college. Servants cooked her food, cleaned her room, lit her fire, and brought her hot water to wash. Here she found unprecedented space to study; and anthropology, her chosen subject, was one of the few to be taught by a group of men with a liberal, progressive outlook who welcomed women to their classes.

Across the university, women faced least resistance to their ambitions in the newer departments that were struggling for money. Anthropology was trying to find a foothold amongst the more traditional disciplines, and it was both underfunded and undersubscribed. Robert Marett was always on the lookout for students who might be persuaded to pay the course fees for a diploma that offered relatively few vocational opportunities, and certainly none that were lucrative. Women were less likely to be concerned about their future earning potential than men. But anthropology, as Katherine Routledge's work on the Kikuyu had shown, was also an inherently egalitarian subject, since – in theory – it was concerned with the cultural life of women as much as the cultural life of men.

When Marett read Mr and Mrs Routledge's *With a Prehistoric People*, he was convinced that 'only a woman can study the condition of women in primitive society'. Later on, during the war, he would make an impassioned call for the inclusion of women in all aspects of anthropology – as students, as fieldworkers and as university lecturers – since women's lives could never be fully accessible to 'the mere male'.

Marett was not alone in his support of female scholarship. One of his colleagues, and a fellow founder of the anthropology diploma at Oxford, the classicist John Myres, regularly spoke in public, sometimes at suffrage meetings, using historical and cross-cultural evidence to support his argument that women were as intelligent and as capable as men. Marett, Myres and their colleagues used their positions at Oxford to open the door to a significant number of women. In doing so they risked compromising their reputations in a masculine culture that was routinely hostile to the opposite sex. The fact that Oxford anthropology was popular with female students made it easier to dismiss as a marginal subject. Nevertheless, by the end of the war they had taught 103 men and twenty-seven women in the eleven years since their diploma course began – an impressive proportion of females for a small subject.

Czaplicka – and presumably Katherine Routledge too, occasionally – attended tutorials with Marett in his rooms at Exeter College, where they discussed religious and social institutions in different cultures. Marett, in his forties, was the same age as Katherine. He was charming, energetic and erudite. He saw the good in people and inspired great love in his students, and Katherine and Maria both became very fond of him. One of Marett's male students remembered that his tutorials were highly informal. He made occasional suggestions for reading, but he seemed wholly indifferent as to whether his pupils followed them or not. No wonder he was faintly surprised and concerned by the 'ardour' with which Czaplicka met the increasingly challenging tasks he set her; she never blanched when asked to complete detailed analyses of complicated questions that required the critical use of many diverse sources of evidence. On the contrary, she wrote her essays in an 'ingenious and systematic way' and returned them to him asking for more.

Czaplicka, Routledge and their fellow students also attended the peripatetic lectures of Henry Balfour, the curator of the Pitt Rivers Museum, who strode between the museum's display cases shuffling handfuls of letters and press clippings while teaching his students about basket-weaving in Nigeria or hand axes from New Guinea. Balfour, in his late forties, had devoted his life to the Pitt Rivers Museum and its contents. He reigned over a kingdom of treasures, tucked away behind an arched doorway at the back of the Oxford University Museum of Natural History, where he had taught himself to knap flint, make fire from two sticks of wood, shoot bows and arrows, and play musical instruments from around the world. His knowledge of the material world was unsurpassed, and it was fed by an expanding network of alumni who travelled the globe, sending back letters, artefacts and research papers to furnish Balfour's museum and fuel his mind. It was these notes that Balfour grasped by the handful as he led his students between the glass cases, from one continent to another, opening cabinets as he went, to take out stone tools or a skull, a hunting trap or a blowpipe, or to demonstrate how a fire piston worked.

Marett and Balfour taught alongside Arthur Thomson, the Professor of Human Anatomy, who ran practical classes at the University Museum in which the anthropology students measured bones and learned about human evolution. Thomson was a great organizer and an artist, who drew brilliantly on the blackboard and spoke so clearly that he had to remind his students to take notes, saying, 'This may seem simple to you now, but you'd better write some of it down.'

Tutors and students of the anthropology diploma in 1910. Seated are, left to right, Henry Balfour, Arthur Thomson, and Robert Marett. The students standing behind them are, left to right, Wilson Dallam Wallis, Diamond Jenness, and Marius Barbeau.

These three men – Marett, Balfour and Thomson – were affectionately known to their students as 'the triumvirate' and they held sway over the teaching of anthropology at Oxford for nearly thirty years, until Thomson's death in 1935 and Balfour's four years later. Between them they provided the core training, although the syllabus was astonishingly wide and students attended lectures in almost every university department, including geology, physiology, philology and law. Over the course of a single year, they also learned archaeology, zoology, anatomy, sociology, government, ethics, religion, arts and industries: in short, nothing should be excluded since anthropology was the study of man in all his – or her – guises.

That year, 1911, for the first time, a woman gave a series of lectures to students on the anthropology course at Oxford. Her name was Barbara Freire-Marreco; a former diploma student herself, she had been invited back to lecture that autumn term. Quiet, dignified and in her early thirties, Freire-Marreco had grown up in Woking, Surrey, the devoted daughter of a wealthy Anglican accountant and his wife (her unusual name came from her paternal grandfather who was Portuguese). Like Routledge and Czaplicka, she had won her place at Oxford thanks to a sheer determination to be different. Her father had been reluctant to let her go to university, but when she taught herself enough Greek in six weeks to pass the Oxford entrance requirements he could think of no further objections. She went up to Lady Margaret Hall in 1902 to read Classics, received the Sedgwick Latin prize in 1904, and gained Honours in her Latin and Greek exams the following year.

One of her tutors was John Myres, who became her mentor and friend. When she failed to win a research fellowship at the university in 1906, Myres encouraged her to study for the newly created diploma in anthropology instead. She was one of the first two students to take the diploma examination, in 1908 (the other being a man), and she was the only one to achieve a distinction. Now, she was a research fellow at Somerville, and thanks to an invitation from Myres, Marett and their colleagues, she was one of the first women ever to give a course of lectures to a mixed audience at Oxford.

Freire-Marreco's topic was 'The Self-Government of the

Pueblo Indians under Spanish and American Administration',
and she was qualified to speak on the subject because she had
undertaken field research. None of her Oxford tutors had done
anthropological fieldwork, but by 1911 the tradition of epistolary
anthropology, which supported these desk-bound theorists, was
coming under increasing criticism. Freire-Marreco herself had
written about 'a very dangerous division of labour' between
'literary anthropologists' who were extremely knowledgeable
but never left home, and amateur observers abroad, who did
not always appreciate the meaning of what they saw. She was
not alone in pointing out that, although valuable work was being
done, 'it was not scientific in any strict sense' because half the
people doing it had no first-hand experience and the other half
had no training in the subject.

During the opening decade of the twentieth century, anthropologists were employed in British universities for the first time,
and many of them had trained as scientists. Alfred C. Haddon,
the first lecturer in ethnology at Cambridge, started his academic
career as a zoologist and marine biologist, and his closest colleague, William H.R. Rivers, was a successful psychologist as well
as an anthropologist. Charles Seligman, who became lecturer in
ethnology at the University of London in 1910, was a physician.
These three men transformed anthropology from the armchair
pursuit of academics at home into a field-based scientific study.
Between them they had conducted research in the Torres Strait,
Borneo, New Guinea, India, Sri Lanka and Sudan, and they were
particularly focused on the question of method. They worked
to systematize field techniques, so that the next generation of
anthropologists would gather information more thoroughly and
consistently. Not only was fieldwork better done by trained anthropologists – anthropologists were better for having done fieldwork.

Freire-Marreco had not planned to go abroad when she took up her research fellowship in June 1909. She had intended to work in libraries rather than travel, but her ideas quickly changed. 'People have been telling me how wrong it would be to enjoy an anthropological scholarship without fieldwork, and I begin to believe it,' she wrote to Myres after just a few weeks back in Oxford. So, with the encouragement of Haddon, Rivers and Myres, she went to work in the pueblos of New Mexico and Arizona during the winter of 1910–11, where she learned one of the Native American languages, Tewa, and researched local systems of government.

Barbara Freire-Marreco blazed a trail for those who followed. Her work held an important lesson for Maria Czaplicka, whom she taught in the autumn term of 1911 and who was to become her friend: it showed that a woman could be an anthropologist at Oxford. Freire-Marreco's success as a graduate student, as a woman who had travelled alone to study 'primitive' people and as a research fellow who lectured at the university, gave Czaplicka and her peers hope for more. There is no record of what she said during her lectures, but it is unlikely that she told her students the whole truth: that at times her research in the pueblos had felt ineffective and frustrating, and that it had failed to fulfil her hopes of being a 'real anthropologist'.

3

A Little More Like Savages

Barbara Freire-Marreco in
New Mexico, 1910

Barbara Freire-Marreco had recently arrived in New Mexico and things were not going to plan. She was struggling to find a suitably 'savage' group of people to study: some were not savage enough, others were too savage, and none were particularly willing to talk. 'It seems that this is one of the most difficult fields in the world, and if I had known anything of it beforehand I would never have come,' she wrote to Emily Penrose in August 1910.

Freire-Marreco was 'in the field', but she was far from alone. She had joined a camp run by the School of American Archaeology at El Rito de los Frijoles, a rocky canyon of sheer cliffs, pinewoods and streams near the Rio Grande, to the west of Santa Fe. A team of American academics and graduate students was digging here for the summer, living in tents and employing Native American workmen from the nearby pueblos. They worked under the directorship of Edgar Lee Hewett, an anthropologist and archaeologist who was to take Freire-Marreco under his wing and guide her research.

Students at the School of American Archaeology summer camp, El Rito de los Frijoles, New Mexico, 1910. Barbara Freire-Marreco stands at the far right; next to her is Maude Woy, a history teacher from Denver. Edgar Hewett stands in the centre wearing a jacket.

She spent her first few weeks in camp learning the Tewa language from some of the workmen, but it was Native American life itself that she was really interested in. She planned to visit one of the nearby pueblos for a few weeks at a time, where she could rent a room, learn about local culture and return regularly to report back to her colleagues at the camp. The problem was, which pueblo to choose? The Rio Grande settlements were all thoroughly Americanized – 'You should see the Indian workmen here in camp poring over the Smithsonian Reports!' – while in the more remote communities there was real resistance to

American intrusion and anyone who talked to a visitor about their culture was putting their life in danger.

Concerned for her safety, Barbara's parents had stipulated that she must always be in reach of 'white people', which was likely to cause some logistical problems given that she was trying to find a suitably untouched culture to study. She hoped to visit the nearby settlement of Santo Domingo, home to the Keres people. 'There they are a little more like "savages",' she wrote to one of her Somerville tutors, but after a few weeks in New Mexico she was feeling less ambitious. Native American communities like the Keres invariably remained isolated because they were hostile to strangers. She had to balance the requirements of her subject, which demanded that she study a remote cultural group, with her own safety. What is more, she had only a few months to produce results, so she could not spend much time developing relationships with her hosts. As the weeks ticked by, she began to realize that expediency would have to take precedence over any desire for an adventure into the unknown.

In the end, Freire-Marreco chose to live in Santa Clara, a pueblo where people were less threatening, if no less guarded, when it came to outsiders. The residents of Santa Clara were extremely polite, but they were just as determined as the more intimidating Keres to frustrate their visitors' inquiries. They knew about anthropology and academic publications, and they realized that people with more power and political influence could retell their stories elsewhere, regardless of their own feelings on the matter. They were not about to open their hearts to an Englishwoman simply because she asked politely.

Freire-Marreco was facing the deep distrust that had shaped pueblo relations with newcomers for generations. Several Native

American pueblos lay in the fertile valley of the Rio Grande, where it cut through the high, arid plains of New Mexico. They were fortress-like settlements, made distinctive by their golden-red earthen architecture. The houses of smooth adobe – sun-dried mud-brick and plaster – had packed dirt floors and flat earthen roofs. Some had no windows or doors on the ground floor, so visitors had to climb a ladder to gain entry through a trapdoor on the first floor. Each pueblo had a central plaza, sheltered by buildings on all four sides, which provided the focal point for dances, meetings and daily life.

Pueblo communities, which dated back as far as the thirteenth century, had borne the brunt of colonial intrusion and aggression since Spanish and Mexican settlers first brought Catholicism to their land in the seventeenth century. In 1846, as a result of the Mexican–American war, the territory had come under American rule for the first time, and fighting between Anglo settlers and Native Americans increased. In the decades that followed, diseases ravaged the pueblos and wiped out three-quarters of the population. As Native American communities declined, the number of settlers burgeoned. When the railroad cut its way through New Mexico for the first time in 1880, it brought an unprecedented influx of immigrants and goods from other parts of America and also Europe. In just forty years, the population of the territory trebled.

Barbara Freire-Marreco arrived in New Mexico as its leaders were pushing for statehood, which would be granted eighteen months later, in January 1912. Knowing that many in the United States saw New Mexico as an uncivilized backwater, Anglo settlers were intent on defining themselves in opposition to their pueblo neighbours, and they increasingly treated Native Americans as inferior and in need of supervision.

Schoolteachers, field matrons, clergymen and government superintendents, all intent on assimilation, were shaping pueblo life in greater numbers than ever before. Pueblo children were forced to attend 'Indian schools', where every detail of the way they moved, spoke, washed themselves, wore their hair and clothes and played together was controlled. They were discouraged from joining in traditional dances, and those who were at boarding school were not allowed to return home for religious observations. Some parents encouraged their children to learn the Anglo skills they needed, but others kept theirs at home.

Pueblo land was also constantly under threat. Reservations, including the Santa Clara Reservation which President Roosevelt had established in 1905, put Native American land and grazing rights under US government control. There were painful legal disputes dating back to the eighteenth century, and the government routinely ruled against Native American claims to their land, with little regard for their sacred sites; it created reservations that disregarded ancient territories, and allowed Anglo settlers to graze their livestock on pueblo land.

Ironically, these forces of cultural assimilation also roused in Americans a sharp sense of loss, and they began to focus on preserving the cultural heritage of New Mexico in a more systematic way. People believed that Native American culture was on the brink of extinction and it became central to a romantic image of 'old New Mexico'. Photographs of pueblo towns, Native American ceremonies and archaeological ruins appeared in magazines and brochures and on postcards, promoting New Mexico as a tourist destination. At the forefront of this popular interest in pueblo life was Freire-Marreco's mentor, Edgar Hewett, founder and director of the Museum of New Mexico, which had opened in 1909.

Hewett's work involved complex, contradictory objectives. He served as an advocate for pueblo communities, but his own goals did not always align with theirs. His archaeological surveys of the region, including the summer camp where Freire-Marreco worked, served an economic purpose too. He saw the potential of ancient pueblo sites as tourist attractions and wanted to transform them into famous landmarks that would bring visitors to the territory. He was intent on establishing a national park, which would, ironically, encroach on pueblo land and sacred sites. In such situations preservation could be a cloaked form of appropriation, and for Hewett and his contemporaries Native American culture was an asset that needed to be managed.

There was an insurmountable conflict at the heart of Hewett's work, because his genuine academic interest and his desire to share information about pueblo culture also threatened to debase it. Pueblo people knew, from long and painful experience, that the only way to protect their beliefs was to keep them secret.

It was hardly surprising, then, that Barbara discovered cultural life ran 'just below the surface' at Santa Clara. People felt none of the deference that she seemed to expect and that might have led to more open and honest conversations; on the contrary, they were 'proud and secretive, and very much on an equality with white people, in their own estimation at least'. She was disheartened, but all she could do was wait patiently to build their trust.

Initially, she divided her time between the Santa Clara pueblo, where she rented a room for a few days at a time, and the Rito de los Frijoles summer camp where she studied with the Native American workmen, asking them questions about their culture and particularly their systems of governance, and learning the Tewa language. When the camp broke up in September, she moved to Santa Clara and lived in a disused house – little more than two wood and canvas structures linked by a porch made of branches – that had been put up originally 'for some tourist'. Around two hundred and seventy people lived in Santa Clara, in one- and two-storey adobe dwellings laid out around the central square, which served as the spiritual and political heart of the pueblo. The floors of the houses were made from wooden planks or packed earth, and ladders led to the upper levels and onto the flat roofs above. The Santa Clarans grew wheat, maize and beans. They hunted rabbits and fished in the canyon creeks, and they kept sheep and cattle on the surrounding land.

That autumn, Freire-Marreco joined the women in their daily tasks, cleaning wheat, tending their gardens and picking fruit, doing embroidery and preparing family meals. She sat quietly and listened to their conversations, and invited people to her house, learning as much as she could about their marriage systems, their religious rites, and their structure of government. Whenever there was a wedding or a dance she went to watch and took notes; she wrote down folk stories, and made detailed lists of Tewa phrases and vocabulary.

She did all her own chores and cooking, which for a while was quite a novelty: '. . . really you never know what the pleasures of hospitality are until you do your own cooking! What a useful member of a reading party I shall be ever after this! I think I shall hire myself out in College to conduct camping parties and wash, bake and cook for them.' She had never had to do these jobs at her family home in Woking, where her parents employed a cook, a parlourmaid and a housemaid. As the weeks went by, her hands became sore from husking maize, drying melons and splitting peaches for the winter, but she was gradually making friends. She asked some of the local women to teach her about their medicines, she joined in 'endless needlework' with them and gave advice on babies' health; ' ... next thing I know I shall be teaching Sunday School!'

Freire-Marreco laughed at her homely state of affairs, but in this instance becoming a domestic woman was in the interests of science, for it was only 'by sinking the ethnologist in the polite visitor' that she could start to break through the people's reserve.

In her correspondence she expressed surprise at how unforthcoming her hosts could be, as though she half-expected the Santa Clarans to grasp her intentions, respect her status, and valiantly meet her requests for information. She certainly did not expect her work to be so slow, or so circuitous, and she quickly experienced the fear that every anthropologist feels in the field: that she would have nothing to show for her time abroad. All the lofty theories she had read at Oxford, about collective psychology and comparative religion and the history of political institutions, seemed reduced to nothing in this world of housework and preserving fruit. But she knew that *doing* things with people, and sharing their everyday lives, although slow as a research technique, was more reliable than simply asking people to describe themselves.

Many of the American academics she met relied on 'informants', whom they often paid, to provide information about their culture and local traditions. One of these informants, Santiago Naranjo, who worked with Hewett and his staff at the School of American Archaeology camp, gave Freire-Marreco a lot of help learning Tewa and provided information about local customs. Naranjo was a prominent Santa Claran who would later serve as

governor of the pueblo. He was a skilful politician and acted as
an intermediary between his people and the Americans. Naranjo
had befriended Hewett, showing him ancient and sacred sites
around Santa Clara and, in return, lobbying for Hewett's support
when pueblo land rights and ceremonies were under threat. He
navigated two, often antagonistic, worlds, and cultivated different personas depending on which one he currently occupied. He
dressed like his fellow villagers when he was in Santa Clara, but
they knew when he was going off to Santa Fe because he put on
his silver earrings and tied up his braids: the finishing touches
to his image as an authentic 'Indian' in American eyes. Almost
inevitably, people on both sides were wary of his motives. Many
Santa Clarans thought him vain and greedy, and questioned his

Santiago Naranjo, seated far left, with (left to right) Manuel Tafoya, Leandro Tafoya,
and Victoriano Sisneros. Freire-Marreco took this photograph in Santa Clara in 1910;
Santiago, Leandro, and their families were her closest friends.

loyalty to the pueblo, while Americans saw through his affectations and suspected he made up stories about pueblo culture to hide the truth.

Barbara Freire-Marreco had a love-hate relationship with Naranjo. She knew that he was one of the most knowledgeable and obliging Native Americans in the area, who in the early days of her stay had supplied all her information; but she also felt deeply uncomfortable about having to rely on a paid collaborator, with little means of judging the veracity of what he told her, which was, in any case, partial – and, she soon found out, politically motivated. After a few months at Santa Clara she realized that Naranjo was keeping hidden from her religious rites that had been suppressed during centuries of aggressive Christian missionizing. She knew why. 'Though it is disappointing from the ethnologist's standpoint,' she wrote, 'I feel bound to respect his resolution ... [since] all the virtue of uncivilized rites lies in secrecy.'

By the end of her stay, she and Naranjo would know the limits of their relationship. He would even joke about it, reminding her to rely exclusively on his help, 'for if you ask another man, there is always a danger of your coming to something important'. Of course, she had never relied exclusively on Naranjo. From the start, she had known that paying for information went against her training and opened her up to 'treacherous and mercenary' people. She had been determined to study her subjects 'in their natural setting', as she had been taught. In the early days, though, she had worried she would never crack the Santa Clarans' suspicious reserve, until she made an unexpected breakthrough.

In August 1910, she happened to mention to one of the men in Santa Clara that her grandfather owned a green parrot: '[T]he effect was as if I had said that I was heir to a gold-mine.' Feathers from the green Mexican parrot were essential for religious dances in the pueblos, but since New Mexico's incorporation into the United States as a territory in 1846, which had affected trade with Mexico, they were scarce. People told her that there was a village fifty miles away where someone owned a single live bird and sold its feathers at fabulous prices.

Freire-Marreco immediately saw a gap in the market and decided to fill it. She wrote to everyone she could think of – to her family, her tutors at Oxford and colleagues at Somerville, her American colleagues at the Smithsonian Institution in Washington, DC, even to London Zoo and commercial dealers in Mexico – asking them to send her parrot feathers. First to respond was Frederick Hodge, head of the Bureau of American Ethnology at the Smithsonian, who sent her a parrot skin at the end of September, and in early October a parcel of parrot feathers arrived from London Zoo. As she sat with her pueblo hosts that evening, on blankets around the fire, gloating over the precious package of plumes from England, she felt she was finally making some progress as an anthropologist and as a friend.

Despite all her doubts and frustrations, Barbara had fallen in love with Santa Clara. In one of her earliest letters to Emily Penrose, she confessed, 'I love the Santa Clara people and could live there for the rest of my life with pleasure.' It was the pressure of 'doing' anthropology – 'the job that I am now making a failure of' – and the need to make valuable academic discoveries that weighed her down. In November, she went on an excursion with the School of American Archaeology to the Fort McDowell Reservation in Arizona for a month, leaving Santa Clara with some regret now that she had begun to make progress, 'but I know I <u>must</u> go somewhere where publishable information can be got'. In Arizona, the Yavapai people at Fort McDowell competed with each other to give her information, and with only a few months left in America she had to prioritize this kind of openness.

After a month in Arizona, Freire-Marreco returned to Santa Clara and worked there until her funds ran out in February 1911. Santiago Naranjo had been made governor, which gave her new insight into the pueblo's political institutions, her primary research interest. Her last two months in Santa Clara were her most productive, but the gap between *knowing* people there and *theorizing* about them in the abstract always seemed great. The more her affection for them grew, the harder it was to achieve any academic perspective. 'It is hard to think of them as material, as they are too real,' she wrote to John Myres. A few months later, after she had tried to explain the English tradition of fox-hunting to a family she was staying with, she joked, 'I love the family too well to do much anthropologising on them; but it is great fun to see them doing it on me!'

She knew that the limited understanding her new friends had of fox hunting, from her inadequate explanations and their unfamiliar reference points, was hardly more reliable than her understanding of their complex cultural traditions. The more she got to know them, the more aware she became of the limitations of her knowledge. And all the while her own life in the pueblo seemed so much more real and vital than any ideas she might have formed about the lives of her hosts.

She had left home the previous year feeling confident. Now, about to return to England, she felt incompetent. The field had taught her that fieldwork is a fragmentary experience. At times she had lost faith in the whole business. 'It has not made an anthropologist of me,' she wrote to Haddon, detailing her inadequacies with characteristic cheerfulness. She had gone out expecting subjects who could be neatly described, but she had met real people who baffled and fascinated her in all their concrete ambiguity. The more real they became, the more fake she herself seemed. '<u>Real</u> anthropologists get thro' twice as much in the time: I wish there had been a better man to take advantage of the opportunities.' The failings, she insisted, were all hers: 'They really did try to teach me to <u>think</u> Indian.' But for all its shortcomings, the experience had been irresistible.

As she left New Mexico that February, she wrote to her patrons at Somerville. Again, she was strikingly honest about the limitations of her work: she had not had the energy or the perseverance to do justice to her training; she had been too timid and inexperienced; she had not had enough time, and she had faced too many practical difficulties in the field ... 'But O what a time I have had ... What scope to live and be a real person!' Anthropological fieldwork may have been a crude tool when it came to learning about other cultures, but it was an excellent way to discover yourself. As she headed back to England after eight months in America, full of insecurities about her intellectual achievements, she could hardly believe her luck: 'You <u>have</u> given me the time of my life!' she wrote to the Fellowship Committee at Somerville.

Barbara Freire-Marreco had arrived in America expecting to work, and left having learned how to live. Perhaps New Mexico had always been a dream, conjured and lost before she had even docked in Liverpool. She was determined to go back.

4

Miss C

Maria Czaplicka Plans an Expedition, 1913

Barbara Freire-Marreco met Maria Czaplicka at Oxford in the autumn of 1911, and they became lifelong friends. 'In friendship she was loyal, candid, and delicately kind,' Freire-Marreco later wrote of Czaplicka, but the two women were very different in temperament. Czaplicka's vivacity was 'infectious'. She was witty and fun and devoted to her friends, but there was sometimes a dark edge to her energy. Her passions were 'unresting', her moods could swing dramatically, and she worked so hard that her colleagues worried about her well-being. Freire-Marreco admired Czaplicka's vigour, and offered her in return a sense of equilibrium.

Freire-Marreco, a 'well-bred' woman with a quiet, efficient disposition, was five years older than Czaplicka. She was more familiar with Oxford, having first come up as a student in 1902, and had valuable experience of field research; but professionally she had less at stake than her Polish friend.

Barbara's career developed firmly within the boundaries set by her prosperous parents in Woking. She sought their approval for every decision she made, and returned home whenever they requested her presence. Every term she spent in Oxford was the result of careful negotiations with 'my people'. She forged a space for her work as best she could within the limits of her role as daughter of the house. Czaplicka, by contrast, had left her family behind in Poland. Far from home, she was freer to devote herself to her career, but with that freedom came greater pressure to succeed. She had to survive on her own. Her mother had little money, and although she occasionally sent Maria cash in emergencies, it was not enough to live on. She had to support herself.

By the summer of 1912, Czaplicka had finished her diploma course and her money was running out. She needed to find a job, and Freire-Marreco wrote to her colleague Frederick Hodge at the Smithsonian Institution to see if he could help. She told him that Czaplicka wanted to 'make progress in anthropology, which she means to make a lifelong career'. She described her friend as decidedly original, very industrious and well regarded by her tutors, and she outlined her qualifications and language skills – as well as Polish and English, Czaplicka spoke Russian, French and German 'like a native', fair Czech and some Spanish. She was willing to take either office work or fieldwork: anything that would set her on a career in America. Could Hodge give her a job in the ethnology department?

He wrote back to say that he could not help. Smithsonian employees had to be American citizens, and although he had sent Freire-Marreco's letter on to colleagues at the University of Pennsylvania Museum and the American Museum of Natural History in New York, they could not offer her anything either. Czaplicka must have known that Freire-Marreco's letter had little chance of success. There was more hope of her getting a position in Oxford, where Marett was making plans for her to take on a new research project.

Maria Czaplicka in 1916. This photograph was the frontis-piece to her book, *My Siberian Year*.

After teaching Czaplicka for a year, Marett was deeply impressed by her intellect. He wanted her to work under him on a project translating Russian studies of the indigenous Siberian culture into English. A whole body of Russian research on the subject was inaccessible to English-speaking anthropologists, and Marett knew that Czaplicka's exhaustive, methodical approach was suited to work of this kind. A few days after Freire-Marreco wrote to Hodge at the Smithsonian, Marett wrote to Emily Penrose at Somerville, asking her to do everything she could to secure Czaplicka's finances for another year and keep her in Oxford.

Emily Penrose was to become one of Czaplicka's key allies. She was a classics scholar in her late forties who had become principal of Somerville in 1907. Some students remembered her as stern and socially awkward. Vera Brittain, in 1914, thought her 'alarmingly suggestive of a tiger about to spring', but Penrose was universally admired for her intellect and her skills as a politician. She must have been drawn to Czaplicka, because time and again she found money to keep her in Oxford when there was hardly any money to be found. Somerville, like all the women's colleges, existed on a shoestring, without endowments, wealthy benefactors or state support. It was the largest of the four women's colleges in Oxford but it had only a hundred students, simply because it could not afford to expand, or house any more. Now, despite the strains on the college finances, Penrose persuaded Somerville's Council to grant Czaplicka a small stipend of £30, and she became known as a 'research student'. With the help of a further grant from the Reid Trust in London, she was set on a path not to America, but to Siberia.

Czaplicka wrote her book, *Aboriginal Siberia: A Study in Social Anthropology*, in just eighteen months. It was a triumph of translation and synthesis, with a bibliography thirty-five pages long. Marett was delighted with the manuscript and submitted it to Oxford University Press for publication on her behalf, but the editor, R.W. Chapman, rejected it at first. Chapman, after reading a few sample chapters, thought that she lacked first-hand knowledge and critical power, and suggested that her research was better suited to an academic journal, 'if there is one that could find space'.

Marett, determined to stand by his student in the project he had masterminded, immediately asked Chapman to reconsider, and sent him letters in support of Czaplicka's work from the presidents of both the Royal Anthropological Institute and the anthropological section of the British Association for the Advancement of Science. In the face of Marett's appeal, Chapman decided to find a Russian speaker who could 'check the lady's use of her authorities'. He asked the archaeologist D.G. Hogarth to review the manuscript and, although Hogarth admitted that he started out 'with a prejudice against her', Czaplicka's work won him over. He decided her book was worth publishing – despite the fact that it was 'of course, not literature, not even, if you like, a book' – primarily because the valuable Slavic texts she dealt with would otherwise be inaccessible to English-speaking scholars.

Siberia was little known, but vast and evocative. Hogarth had assured Chapman that there was much that was 'quite new' in Czaplicka's book despite it being 'second-hand', since so little had been published on the ethnography of Siberia in English. In *Aboriginal Siberia*, as well as describing the geography and social customs of the region, Czaplicka suggested her own classification of Siberian peoples; she discussed their shamanistic practices and looked systematically at the evidence for 'arctic hysteria', a condition in which people entered a trance-like state, or suffered from hysterics, because of the extreme cold and darkness of the winter months. The book was welcomed as a vital foundation work (it is still considered essential reading for English-speaking students of Siberia today), but it was primarily a work of reference, and for Czaplicka it quickly became a preparatory study for her own expedition.

By the autumn of 1913, Czaplicka had begun organizing a field trip to Siberia. She intended to study the nomadic reindeer herders who lived above the Arctic Circle to the east of the great Yenisei River. Relatively little was known about the people living in the expansive territories of north-central Siberia. There had been Russian and American-led expeditions, including the Jesup North Pacific Expedition, which surveyed the cultures of far-eastern Siberia during the early 1900s, but none had been to the central regions. Czaplicka wanted to find communities that were still untouched by industrial life, which would mean travelling north for weeks, first by boat down the Yenisei, then by sledge over the snow, across the sparsely populated frozen wilderness in search of small groups of herders living in reindeer-hide tents.

She would not go alone. Czaplicka planned to travel with a friend of hers, an American named Henry Hall. Hall was crucial to her plans, but he is a shadowy figure in her story and little is known about his early life or his professional motivation. Born in Jamaica in 1876, he was eight years older than Maria. He had emigrated to America in his mid-twenties and worked as a teacher in New York City for eleven years before moving to London, where he studied anthropology at the London School of Economics. He never took a university degree, and although he went to lectures at the LSE he was not officially registered as a student there and must have attended on a casual basis. Whatever the nature of their first meeting, by the autumn of 1913 he and Maria were living at the same lodging house in Bloomsbury: 58 Torrington Square. Maria was finishing *Aboriginal Siberia* in the library at the British Museum, and Hall was studying at the LSE. That winter they worked together to secure their trip to Siberia for the spring of 1914.

Czaplicka and Hall presented their collaboration as purely professional and hid the fact that they were living together from their correspondents. Czaplicka wrote to her friends in Oxford and London using her Torrington Square address but to Hall's contacts in America using her Somerville College one, while Hall maintained his own correspondence with them from Torrington Square.

Marett was uneasy about Czaplicka's friendship with Hall, whom he had not met (Marett believed, mistakenly, that Hall was a professor of mathematics). Neither of them had any money to travel, so Marett suggested financial backers to Hall, but it is clear from his correspondence that he did so for the sake of Czaplicka and the expedition. He told Hall to apply to the director of the University of Pennsylvania Museum in Philadelphia, George B. Gordon, because he had heard that Gordon might have money for expeditions in exchange for contributions to his museum collections. Czaplicka had already promised to collect Siberian artefacts for the Pitt Rivers in Oxford, and now Hall promised to do the same for Gordon.

After several months of correspondence, Gordon agreed to give Hall $1500 (approximately £300), even though Hall had no qualifications and Gordon knew very little about him. No doubt it helped that Marett wrote to endorse the expedition and that Hall presented it as a joint venture with the University of

Oxford; in fact Czaplicka had been given only a nominal £25 by Oxford, and the rest of her funding was still in doubt. Marett, meanwhile, admitted to Gordon that he did not know Hall, and explained that they were trying to find other people to join the expedition because 'Miss C (who is fairly young and pretty) can't go off by herself with a solitary man, however respectable, to live on the Siberian tundra.'

That spring, two women agreed to join the expedition, to Marett's relief. Maud Haviland was an ornithologist who had grown up roaming her stepfather's estate in southeast Ireland and was a good game-shot. She was practical, independent and passionate about birds. In her book about the Siberian trip, *A Summer on the Yenesei*, she wrote that she joined the expedition late, having been won over by Czaplicka's intelligence, energy and 'most winning address'. The fourth member of the group was Dora Curtis, an illustrator who planned to sketch their travels and the people they met. Curtis would turn out to be 'the life of the party', a good cook, always positive and everyone's friend. 'A better comrade for such a journey it would be impossible to find,' wrote Haviland later, and Czaplicka agreed that Curtis was a most helpful member of the team. Haviland, meanwhile, would spend most of her time in Siberia striding across the tundra shooting birds and was little interested in the ethnological questions that preoccupied the others. According to press reports, two additional men were originally included in the team – G.A. Whyte, who was to have made 'physiological observations', and a man from the school of forestry at a Scottish university – but at the last minute they withdrew.

The group had to leave England before the end of May in order to reach the Yenisei River, their route north through

Siberia, as the winter ice was breaking up. The Yenisei was open for only five months of the year so it was imperative that they left in time to make the most of their summer above the Arctic Circle, but by early May, Czaplicka still had not secured her funding. She had been hoping to receive money from two scientific societies in Moscow but they had let her down.

Could Marett have done more to help her? By appealing to wealthy men's colleges at Oxford for support he had successfully raised nearly £200 for one of his male students, Diamond Jenness, who went to do fieldwork in the D'Entrecasteaux Islands off the east coast of New Guinea. He did not do the same for Czaplicka, believing she was more likely to raise funds from those interested in 'the cause of the education of women'. In desperation, just a couple of weeks before their departure date, Czaplicka appealed to her alma mater again. On 9 May, she wrote a letter to the secretary of the Mary Ewart Trust at Somerville, which had funded Freire-Marreco's travel to New Mexico, to ask if they would support her. Emily Penrose was one of the three trustees, along with Charles Buller Heberden, principal of Brasenose College, and Charlotte Green, vice-president of Somerville Council. These three met informally on 18 May, and agreed to grant Czaplicka £200. Charlotte Green took it upon herself to personally advance half of the money to the Russian Bank for Foreign Trade in Czaplicka's name, because they knew she was due to depart in less than a week.

This last-minute decision meant that Maria Czaplicka did not know whether she would be able to start out until just three days before she was due to leave England. Hall, Haviland and Curtis spoke no Russian and were completely reliant on her contacts: without her, they would have had to abandon the entire venture.

It must have been nerve-racking waiting for news – at times they must have given up hope. Czaplicka had spent months working to get the expedition under way, buying equipment, planning routes and contacting Russian officials, with no guarantee that it would actually happen. Then, suddenly, she was on her way.

Czaplicka departed London on the boat train from Charing Cross about a week before her travelling companions, so that she could visit St Petersburg to meet government officials and receive letters of introduction for their onward journey. In Moscow, she met up with Hall, Haviland and Curtis and together they spent five days on the 'unspeakably tedious' Trans-Siberian Railway, travelling east to Krasnoyarsk, where they would leave the train and continue north on the Yenisei by boat. After just one night in Krasnoyarsk, 'surely the dustiest town in the world', they boarded a little paddle-wheel steamboat, the *Oryol*, filled with fishermen and their families heading to their fishing stations for the summer.

They spent three weeks 'crawling down stream' on the *Oryol*, stopping frequently to put fishermen ashore with their barrels, nets, and the planks of wood they used to build temporary summer shelters along the river. They travelled for fifteen hundred miles on the boat, and as the days passed, the dense pine forest thinned, the trees became smaller and the patches of snow between them larger, until there were only a few larch trees barely ten feet high to be seen in the marshy tundra. The river widened, blocks of ice piled up on its banks, and the water and the land spread out vast and flat before them. Travelling north had the strange effect of reversing time. 'It was as if for every day, spring was retarded for one week,' Haviland wrote as they went back into winter, leaving towns and villages behind and seeing only the occasional *balagan* – a low, turf-roofed fishing hut – along the way.

At every stop, Haviland hiked through the trees or across the snowy marshes to find nests and eggs and to shoot birds, some of which she skinned for her collection, and others, common ducks and geese, she gave to Curtis to cook for dinner on the boat. Czaplicka, Curtis and Hall visited locals in their homes whenever they could, to ask about their lives and customs. Curtis sketched the people she met, and Czaplicka, with her 'talent for strange tongues', set about learning two of the local languages: Nenets and Samoyedic.

Alongside the three vivacious female members of the expedition, Henry Hall makes little impression. Haviland barely mentioned him in her book, although she described her female companions fondly: in *A Summer on the Yenisei* only occasionally does the reader realize that Hall is still there, getting a raw deal on accommodation and speaking 'nothing but English'. Czaplicka carefully edited him out of her later book as much as possible, and so she gives us no reason to doubt his peripheral part in the proceedings. In fact, she and Haviland both enjoyed telling the story that, on first meeting, Siberians often thought their visitors must be a group of *suffragettski*, banished to Siberia by the British government. Even the jokes excluded him, and Hall slides out of view in this group of radical women travellers.

In a neat reversal of their lives at home, during that summer in Siberia Czaplicka and her female companions not only took the limelight but took control as well – apparently with Hall's consent. To the Siberians they met, Haviland, with her gun, was known as 'the boy'; Curtis, with her pencil, was 'the writing woman'; and Czaplicka, who took charge of the team's medical supplies, was given the semi-spiritual status of 'the healing woman'. Hall was simply 'the man'. Czaplicka jokingly called him 'the only "mere man" of the party'.

For all intents and purposes, Maria Czaplicka was the man. She had organized the venture and she led throughout. To take responsibility in this way, she found, was both a burden and a thrill.

5

The Threshold of Infinite Space

Maria Czaplicka in Siberia, 1914

Maria and her team were lost in a storm, five hundred miles north of the Arctic Circle. The winds were blowing at thirty miles an hour and the air was hazy with diamond-hard snow that stung her face 'with a maddening hail of pin-pricks'. The sun had not risen for weeks, and she had been trying to find Orion's Belt among the stars. It was not easy. She was strapped, semi-recumbent, to a light wooden sledge pulled by a team of reindeer. The ground here was stony and only partially covered with snow, so the sledge constantly tossed and jarred against the ground and threatened to pitch its contents off completely. They had been travelling like this for ten hours.

Maria was lying under furs, wrapped in woollen shirts, a whipcord coat and breeches, windproof overalls, oilskins and a sheepskin coat which, she noted, was 'heavy, clumsy, of a particularly evil odour, the crude black dye of the skin comes off on your face and hands, and if it is rained on, nothing could be more stubbornly and obtrusively wet'. It did not help that the reindeer quite liked eating it when they got the chance. Her legs and feet, stretched out in front of her, were particularly exposed to the cold. They were clad in dog-hair stockings underneath woollen stockings, and two pairs of reindeer-skin boots: the inner pair, a soft fawn with the hair facing inside, the outer pair made from the tough leg skin with the hair on the outside. Her boots were stuffed with straw and blotting-paper to absorb the moisture, and inserted in a buckskin foot-bag. She wore dog-hair gloves inside reindeer-skin mittens. A thick cake of ice had built up on her scarf where she had pulled it across her nose and mouth, and the white fox-fur trim of her hood did little to keep out the piercing snow. Maria hoped that her stargazing would 'distract my mind from the struggle between the two great questions that racked it: Was I going to be violently and ignominiously "sea"-sick, or would my cold-tortured anatomy be jolted to splinters first?'

Suddenly, her driver pulled up his team, and the two sledges behind braked rapidly in their wake. The reindeer collapsed in exhaustion: 'It seemed that the wind blew them flat.' They were on a high open moor with no trees or hills to protect them from the gale. The men conferred, and soon Maria realized that they were lost. This was an alarming situation. They were travelling between family tents, or *chum*s. In the winter, the indigenous people spread out across the Arctic tundra with their reindeer herds in search of grazing. Their solitary *chum*s could be scattered many miles apart. But at each stop on her journey from *chum* to *chum*, Maria took on a local driver who knew the white wilderness intimately – she had become 'accustomed to put unhesitating confidence in our tundra pilots'.

Maria Czaplicka's team in Siberia; the print has been overpainted for publication, and Czaplicka has written on the back, 'Our train in the tundra'.

Had there been more snow on the ground, they would have dug themselves into a snowdrift and waited for the storm to pass. Or they might have pitched their expedition tent (modelled on those used by Scott in the Antarctic only three years before), but they had become separated from the sledge that was carrying it. They were alone.

Maria pulled her numb legs out of her foot-bag and hobbled over to the next sledge, where her guide and interpreter, a woman called Michikha, was screaming with rage at the driver. Maria tried to calm her, and the two began to walk together up and down in the snow. Michikha's anger seemed 'so indecent, so paltry, in the face of that awful rage of the elements which would soon shout us all down into silence forever'. They rummaged, painfully, through the furs on the back of one of the sledges and found Maria's Thermos bottle – 'Happy thought!' – it was full of hot cocoa. They had not eaten for twelve hours. Slowly, with aching fingers, working together they unscrewed the bottle and poured out a mouthful of cocoa for Michikha, but by the time Maria tilted the Thermos for a second cup the contents had frozen solid.

The storm was making the stars, their only guide, skip and dip from sight. Their driver took one of the sledges in search of landmarks, while the rest of the team waited on high ground with the exhausted reindeer. Maria's heavy clothes seemed to provide no warmth, she was sore from the rough ride, and most of all she was hungry. Her tormented imagination now settled on the reindeer. She began to question Michikha about the best way to butcher a deer. She scanned them lying together in the rocky snow. Which one would provide the tenderest meat? Would their pocket-knife be large enough to make the kill? 'I became obsessed with the thought of the warm, reeking flesh beneath the shivering hide of those unfortunate reindeer. Now I understood how the Tungus [today known as Evenks] could drink with a relish the blood of a freshly slaughtered deer, and tear the smoking raw flesh with their teeth.'

She chattered on incoherently, ignoring Michikha's impatient objections to her questions. When eventually the driver came back and announced that he now knew where they were, Maria felt only desperate disappointment: 'What about the reindeer?' she demanded, and as they inserted themselves back into their travelling positions 'all my thoughts were absorbed by one regret: now I should not get my draught of warm, delicious blood!'

As the sledges sped over the frozen ground again, Maria fell into a cold, restless sleep. Her next memory was of being pulled from her seat and roughly bundled into a warm, smoky tent, with a fire in the hearth at its centre. As she sat motionless in the warmth, her hosts did slaughter one of their herd and in time she began to eat the meat, roasted on the fire in small pieces, while watching Michikha, 'a ghastly study in red and yellow', as she gnawed at large portions of raw flesh and rubbed the hot reindeer carcass on her cold feet, so that she seemed to 'drip with gore from top to toe'. Nobody spoke until these unexpected guests had warmed through and eaten their fill.

Maria's hosts were astonished by her arrival at their *chum*. They had never seen a white woman before. To the dark-skinned Evenks, Maria's fair hair was incongruous: how could such a young woman have such old hair? Her eyes were strangely 'straight'; she apparently had no children or family; she carried so much paper around with her and yet she seemed to know so little about the workings of the world: she could not even get the marrow out of a reindeer bone to eat. Why did she ask so many questions and why did she travel in such dreadful weather, when all sensible people stayed safe inside their *chum*?

Maria sometimes asked herself the same questions. That winter, she and Henry Hall had separated from Dora Curtis and Maud Haviland so as to begin a journey of more than three thousand miles by sledge across the Arctic tundra. Travelling from tent to tent, living on little more than reindeer meat and tea, they went in search of people who had never seen a European. All their hopes had rested on this expedition, but there were times when they wished they had never come. Czaplicka pushed them on. Hall himself later acknowledged that they worked 'under difficulties which the skill and resourcefulness alone of Miss Czaplicka enabled me to overcome'.

The previous summer, when they were still with Haviland

and Curtis, had been challenging enough. They had spent it all together at Golchikha, a small settlement with two permanent log huts for traders and a handful of temporary fishing shanties, some 450 miles north of the Arctic Circle on the Yenisei River. From here they visited neighbouring fishing stations and kept an open house for fishermen and traders who came to the river to work. Hall, Czaplicka and Curtis talked to the locals, taking notes on their language and customs, measuring and drawing them and acquiring artefacts, while Haviland went out across the tundra to track and catch birds.

It was physically demanding. The land all around their huts was marshy, with thick tussocks of coarse grass, and at every step one foot might be balancing on top of a grassy tuft while the other was sinking into the bog. Usually, they ended up wading through it, knee-deep. Curtis thought it 'the most difficult ground in the world' and was astonished by Czaplicka's fortitude: 'I have known her walk thirty five versta [23 miles] with only a piece of bread and some chocolate to sustain her and at the end appear unfatigued.' Their hut was damp, with a turf roof that leaked. On the first morning, the women had woken to find cockroaches swarming through the room and inside their sleeping bags, and had shrieked in horror, but within a few days they were so accustomed to their insect housemates that they casually squashed them in their felt-slippered feet as they went about their work.

Outside, the river was turbid and coffee-coloured, filled with driftwood and vast blocks of ice. Even in late June the air was infused with the sound of melting ice: a strange hissing and rustling, splitting, cracking and groaning as pieces came apart, collided and drifted downriver. The weather was fickle, and howling gales could transform into tranquil summer days in a matter of minutes. The sheer expanse of the horizon played tricks on the mind. Sometimes the late sun sat so large over the land, flushing the ground pink, that Czaplicka 'forgot the world was round, and had a queer feeling of approaching the threshold of infinite space'. Even in winter, in the desperate desolation of a snowstorm – a *purga* – deep in freezing physical isolation, the unearthly beauty of the air could produce a sense of ecstasy that blotted out the pain. On clear nights, the northern lights shot and pulsed through the sky in spectral colours. It was in these moments of beauty, Czaplicka wrote, that the far north, 'veiling her cruelties ... chose to live on in your fancy and to enslave your heart'.

She pushed herself to the limit, psychologically and physically, throughout her Siberian expedition, and the strain had shown early. During their initial journey from Moscow to remote Golchikha, first by rail and then by steamer, they had lost their luggage numerous times, missed trains, and had to change their plans at the last minute. Within days of embarking on their fifteen-hundred-mile river journey, in reaction to the stress and enormity of her undertaking Czaplicka became alarmingly ill. She was in great pain in her back and sides, and confined to her cabin, unable to eat. Curtis and Haviland nursed her 'night and day' for a week with hot pumices and massage, as they did not know what was wrong and had nothing else to give her until, on 15 June, the boat at last reached a settlement substantial enough to accommodate a doctor. On that very day, Czaplicka's health improved. The doctor was reassuring and said that her condition was the result of overwork, irregular meals and a chill. According to Curtis, who worried about Czaplicka driving herself too hard, 'She occasionally had pains again. I think from what the doctor said they were partly nervous, but massage relieved her.'

If Maria was feeling the strain, she hid her moments of fragility from as many people as she could. On 10 June, while in the midst of her nervous illness on the *Oryol*, she had dictated a letter to Emily Penrose in which she pretended she had to attend to 'practical matters' that prevented her from writing in her own hand. She admitted only that the white nights were having a strange effect on her nervous system, signing off, 'I wish you would not be disappointed with me in this work I have undertaken.' Knowing the disquiet her companions felt as they took down her dictation, it is possible to see self-doubt in Czaplicka's desire to please. But in a businesslike letter packed with travel plans, Penrose was given no indication of the drama that was unfolding.

Just a couple of weeks later Czaplicka's resilience was put to the test again in no uncertain terms, on a boat trip across the Yenisei from Golchikha. The episode haunted her friends long afterwards.

They were returning from a visit to a fishing station downriver. A small twitchy fisherman with bad teeth, one Vassilli Vassillievitch, who was addicted to vodka, was rowing them back home along with a powerful, red-haired 'local Titan' named Nill. The boat, carrying seven people, was sitting low in the water, but the journey started well and they travelled for two hours sheltered from the wind by a breakwater of ice. As they rounded the breakwater, however, the full force of the weather coming across the snowy tundra hit them hard: the river foamed and roared, and slabs of ice pounded in the waves around them. Soon their boat was filling with water. They took to bailing, at first with the only wooden scoop they could find in the boat, and then, in desperation, with Hall's boots; but after four hours of frantic bailing they were drenched, freezing, scared and exhausted – and only halfway across the river.

By now Czaplicka had collapsed. She was so violently sick that she vomited blood, and Dora Curtis had to give up bailing to support her. The river kept pushing them back, and it took ten hours to reach the far shore: having departed at 5 a.m., they did not land until three in the afternoon. As they climbed out of the boat the wind died down and the sun came out, giving them a 'halcyon evening' for their pains. They had not eaten or drunk all day, so they made a fire on the riverbank, ate, dried their clothes and rested, and Czaplicka began to recover her strength.

Although she was able 'to endure more than a normally strung person', she did not admit her limitations. At the end of the summer, Haviland and Curtis were due to leave her and Hall to face the winter alone, and they worried about her safety. The other women had never intended to stay. As Czaplicka pointed out, there would be little to interest an ornithologist during the winter months, and Curtis, the artist, would have found few subjects for the number of miles travelled at such great risk. So at the end of August, they boarded a steamboat and started for home. The four companions spent their last afternoon together walking along the shore of the Yenisei in silence, only too aware that while two of them were facing the isolation of an Arctic winter, to reach England the others would have to cross a Europe at war.

Confused reports of war had reached them on the 26th, just a few days before Curtis and Haviland's departure, and the news had left them uneasy. All they had been told, from some men who had landed their boat that day, was that Britain and Germany were at war and that other European countries were in the ominous process of forming alliances. They were stunned and bewildered. 'We could only stare at each other helplessly and exclaim: "War in Europe!"' It would be weeks before they knew anything more. The first letters Czaplicka received from England arrived on 3 September, but they had been written at the end of May, only a few days after their own departure for Siberia. Having left their homes with no thought of war, they struggled to comprehend the news.

Maria worried for Poland and her family. Her mother was in Warsaw, and she had no idea whether her country was involved in the conflict. She feared it had been occupied by Germany. She considered returning home and joining the war effort herself, but she was on the verge of the most important phase in her career, the culmination of everything she had worked for since arriving in Oxford, and an opportunity to go north that might never come again. With neither the transport to travel home nor enough money for it, she and Hall resolved to stay. They would head into the frozen tundra as planned and cut themselves off from all communication with the wider world until the spring, even though, as she wrote to Penrose on 6 September, 'I find the anxiety and uncertainty almost unbearable'.

Maria was short of funds and warm winter clothing, and Dora Curtis was not reassured by her impressions of Henry Hall. 'I do not look upon him as a capable person,' she wrote. 'In fact during the many experiences we had I think he proved very much the reverse. I should be easier in my mind if she had someone of resource with her.' Curtis feared that Hall would not look after Maria. On the contrary, she would have to look after *him*. She believed that Maria's determination rendered her vulnerable, and worried that she would neither eat properly nor rest regularly to conserve her strength. To make matters worse, they did not have the right equipment or clothing for the winter, or enough money to buy it.

Maria Czaplicka and Henry Hall with some of the objects
they collected in Siberia, 1915.

It was now October, and Czaplicka's friends in Oxford and
London were trying to determine exactly where she was, and
whether she had the cash she needed for the months ahead.
Curtis urged Emily Penrose to send her funds 'to buy the proper
fur garments necessary', and Maria herself admitted to Penrose
in an unusually candid letter that she was 'terrified to think that
I may find myself without money'. It did not help that letters
took weeks to arrive. The banks in Siberia had been failing
since the outbreak of war, and it was hard to trace transactions.
Nevertheless, Penrose successfully transferred £50 to Maria in
early November, the last instalment of her travel grant from the
Mary Ewart Trust at Somerville.

By this time, Czaplicka and Hall were travelling north together, accompanied by the 'thoroughly immoral old rascal', Michikha, whom Czaplicka referred to as 'my Tungus woman' or 'my dame de compagnie'. No one at home would hear from them until April 1915. Their aim was to find 'the real Tungus' who lived to the east of the lower Yenisei River, as it flows out to the Arctic Sea. The Evenks were reindeer breeders, fishermen and hunters, who followed their herds for miles through the snow in search of pasture. Travelling by sledge in the dark for hours at a time, Czaplicka and Hall soon learned that the first, welcome, sign of a nearby *chum* was a column of sparks rising into the sky from the smoke-hole, which promised hot tea while sitting on deerskins by the fire within. Welcomed by every family they visited, they always ate first, sharing reindeer meat off the bone and rubbing their hands clean with wood shavings when they had had their fill. Then, they talked.

Czaplicka often found herself answering more questions than she asked, since her hosts rarely had unexpected guests and they had certainly never had visitors like these before. In a reversal of roles, she became the subject of the Evenks' anthropological enquiries, as they tried to make sense of where she had come from and what she was doing here. She gave up trying to tell them that she and Hall came from 'widely separated tundras', and struggled to explain how they made money when they had no reindeer or fox skins to trade. The Evenks could not imagine a *chum* several stories high, or how Czaplicka could live in a *chum* without any children. Her lack of children was a constant talking point, but not, apparently, her lack of a husband, a subject which she never mentions in her book. People in Siberia must have assumed that she and Hall were married. It was a conceit they were free to indulge in, now that they were travelling alone, and would have been an understandable one, given the challenges of cultural translation they faced every day.

Although they were not married, their close relationship was essential to their success and strong enough to endure the intimacies their work demanded of them. They stayed, during the depths of winter, as guests in the *chum*s they visited, reliant on the Evenks for their food and warmth and retiring to their own sleeping bags around the fire when they were too tired to keep talking. When they could not rely on local hospitality, they shared their own tent. It was modelled on the one used by Captain Scott at the South Pole, although it was lined with wool and separated into two sections, giving a degree of privacy.

Maria's single-minded ambition suited them both while they were alone in the limitless snows, and Hall was content to follow her lead, but there is no doubt that she needed him too. At the beginning of April 1915, on their way back south for the summer, they reached Turukhansk, a small town on the Yenisei, and took their first opportunity to send letters home. Czaplicka wrote a short postcard to Penrose, which remains the only evidence of her reliance on Hall. They were, she said, 'safe and well though it was a hard trip and I had a hard time with my dame de compagnie, especially when Mr H. had a severe cold'. It is an odd remark for such a short note. Hall's illness must have put her under strain. Michikha had an unmatched 'capacity for thorough-paced double-dealing'. She constantly demanded rewards for good behaviour, and tried to manipulate situations and make life generally disagreeable. Czaplicka even began to suspect that Michikha was plotting against her in the hope of inheriting their equipment and provisions.

By June, in the relative metropolis of Krasnoyarsk, Michikha had left them, and Czaplicka and Hall worked at the museum

and collected artefacts from the surrounding region. Maria told
Penrose that she was living in a small private room she had found
through friends. She did not mention Hall's living arrangements.
They spent their second and final summer together exploring
the fertile southern plains of central Siberia, where they traded
their sledges for large wicker carriages, like giant baskets on
wheels, pulled by stocky steppe ponies. With no seats, they
were hardly more comfortable for the passenger than the sledges
had been. 'The baskets are half-filled with straw,' Czaplicka
wrote, 'on which you sit with legs stretched out straight in front
of you, and ponder, so far as pondering is possible between
bumps, on the hopeless ineffectiveness of straw as a substitute
for springs.' She had become so acclimatized to the cold she
found it hard to stand the heat. In July they went to Moscow,
and from there they started for home.

Maria Czaplicka travelling in a wicker carriage through south central Siberia during
the summer of 1915.

Maria's journey had been divided into three parts. She had learned the traditions of the seasonal fishermen who worked around Golchikha in the summer months; she had travelled amongst the solitary indigenous reindeer herders of the far north; and she had visited the settled labourers of the vast, empty steppe country in the south. She met now-forgotten characters in this scattered community: Dens, the drunken prince of the Karasinsk Enets, who fed his sickly child vodka to restore his strength; Hunta the mischievous storyteller and part-time priest; the great shaman Bokkobushka who saw into her future; and Chunga, the herdsman whose fortunes and family were destroyed by a curse. She met 'A' and 'K', political exiles, banished from Russia and Poland for life but practising their skills, as meteorologist and doctor respectively, in their wilderness home. She witnessed the unhappiness wreaked by criminal exiles, the 'gamblers, drunkards, thieves, and degenerates' who mixed freely with their unwilling hosts. She saw caravans of immigrants from Russia and Poland, 'destitute and infirm', gradually descending into poverty.

Through Czaplicka's encounters with these people, recounted in her book *My Siberian Year*, a vision of culture at a time of great change comes to life. The completion of the Trans-Siberian Railway in 1904, the population's steadfast dependence on vodka, and the awkward mix of migrants, exiles and natives find a personal resonance, and Maria emerges as a brave and humorous woman with a striking disregard for her own discomfort. She endured pain, hunger and exhaustion in her determination to document the people of Siberia. And, in return, she found a form of freedom.

Siberia had a strange levelling effect on its population: gentlemen, savants and criminals all became 'peasants'. People were judged by what they did rather than where they had come from. Maria was accepted into this mix, and she enjoyed the candour of her friendships with her hosts. 'As I review my mental portrait gallery of native friends, I find ... that those to whom my heart warms most in memory are characters whom my moral judgment cannot with the best will in the world hold up as worthy exemplars of conduct even from a native point of view.'

She always joked about her 'voluntary exile' in Siberia. In the far north, she and Hall had lived in a surreal landscape, part reality, part fantasy. A world with no reference points: neither physical features, nor the usual social norms. The sun and the horizon disappeared, time and distance lost their meaning, and the extreme mental and physical pressure left them in a trance-like cycle of torpor and rejuvenation, hunger and feasting, alienation and intimacy. The abnormal environment, Czaplicka wrote, was calculated to warp the mind and left its trace on even the strongest constitution. The alternative reality of her Siberian year had been inescapable, brief, and all-consuming.

For the Siberians she met, Maria's foreignness was as remarkable as her gender, and the two combined to make her difficult to categorize. She was liberated by her strangeness and found a sense of autonomy in her exile. Back in England, she would gladly have accepted a return to these physical hardships if only they could have freed her from the professional challenges she was to face.

6

The Riddle of the Pacific

Katherine Routledge Sails to Easter Island, 1913

Maria Czaplicka left Siberia in the summer of 1915, just as Katherine Routledge, ten thousand miles away in the Pacific Ocean, was savouring her final few weeks on Easter Island, having lived there for almost eighteen months. Both women had travelled in search of the most isolated communities in the world. Oxford, where they had met as diploma students and where Robert Marett and Emily Penrose waited to hear of their progress and safety, could not have seemed further away. But while Maria had pushed herself to the limits of endurance in Siberia and had been emancipated by her travels, Katherine's experiences had been far from liberating. During her year-long voyage to Easter Island the claustrophobia of life aboard a small sailing boat had put her marriage under intense pressure and left her struggling to assert herself over her male crew. She had endured disputes, desertions, illnesses, mechanical failures, storms and weather delays on a journey that often felt interminable.

The Routledges' expedition to Easter Island was a bold undertaking. Following the success of their book on the Kikuyu in 1910, they hankered for more 'epoch-making' results. A curator at the British Museum, T.A. Joyce, had recommended Easter Island as a possible field site. Not only had the difficulties of getting there prevented anyone from doing long-term research, but once the work was under way, Joyce explained, 'you would do more with a spoon there than [with] a spade elsewhere'. There had been two short surveys of the island in the 1880s, one by a German team and the other on behalf of the Smithsonian, but each had lasted only a few weeks. The Routledges proposed an exhaustive eighteen-month investigation. They would be away from home for more than three years.

Very little was known about Easter Island. Called Rapa Nui by its Polynesian inhabitants, it was, in the popular imagination, a place shrouded in mystery. Occasionally a ship visited and its crew would return to describe the unwelcoming rocky coastline, the lack of fresh water, and the complete absence of trees. Easter Island was no tropical paradise. On the contrary, it was a remote and 'wretched' place. There was no safe anchorage, no wood for fuel, and it was nearly always windy. There were no streams or lush vegetation to enrich the soil and provide fruit, seeds and nuts to eat, as on other Polynesian islands. The land was barren volcanic rock, difficult to cultivate. The inhabitants were said to be lazy, 'incurable thieves' with no code of honour, who struggled for their existence.

The questionable reputation of the islanders provided a neat counterpoint to the majestic stone statues that had brought the island its fame. On the coastline and in the foothills stood hundreds of these *moai*, colossal monuments depicting ancestor figures, several metres high and each weighing more than ten tons. Their presence there defied reason. The present-day islanders had no strong artistic tradition or engineering skills and, it was said, knew nothing about how the statues had been made or moved into position.

How could a place so austere, and a people who lived so simply, be responsible for such incredible works of art? Visitors speculated that there had been an earlier, more powerful race living on the island – hundreds, if not thousands, of years ago – who had left the sculptures behind. Some said that these ancient islanders must have been giants, ten or twelve feet tall. Others suggested that Easter Island was the last surviving tip of a vast submerged continent, where once huge numbers of people had worked to install the *moai*; but even with a large team of labourers it was hard to fathom the effort required to haul hundreds of these monuments into place using only basic tools and techniques. A handful of wooden tablets, inscribed with tiny characters, had been found in caves on the island, and scholars believed that this 'script' might hold the answer to who had settled the island and carved the statues. If more of these *kohau rongorongo* – 'talking wood' – could be found, perhaps the mysteries of Easter Island would be solved.

The Routledges commissioned their own boat for the expedition, and no expense was spared. The *Mana* was built in Whitstable, with a schooner rig and auxiliary motor power, electric light and steam heating. She had oak decking and brass fittings. She sported a small chart room, a deck-house and a saloon, a pantry, a bathroom and cabins, all finished to the highest specification. Before departure, every cubic inch of space was packed with provisions: coal, water, oil, tents, buckets, basins, kitchen utensils, sails, ropes, anchors, medical supplies, photographic gear and surveying instruments, rifles and ammunition, tins of tobacco, mosquito nets, pillows, blankets ... 'Never was a boat equipped with such care, or so many conveniences,' wrote one of the *Mana*'s crew as they prepared to depart from Falmouth in March 1913. The *Mana*, according to her captain Henry James Gillam, was splendidly built and 'very handy', but with eleven people on board the living space was confined and, once they were under way, relationships were soon showing the strain.

The *Mana*, moored at Charua Bay, Patagonian Channels, Chile, December 1913.

The Routledges' intellectual aspirations paled in comparison to the challenges they faced managing their crew. There were six professional sailors on board, as well as a cook and a steward, who had answered the Routledges' advertisement for deckhands. O.G.S. Crawford, a twenty-six-year-old Oxford graduate, was taken on as an archaeologist, and a geologist from Cambridge named Frederick Corry was due to join the boat in Chile. All of them found the Routledges difficult. Crawford said the couple showed an 'utter absence of any courtesy ... especially Mrs R'. They were arrogant, exacting, petty and pretentious. On top of that, Scoresby Routledge thought himself a seaman, whereas everyone else thought him a fraud who could not control his temper.

Crawford's relationship with the Routledges was particularly strained. He reached breaking-point after just six weeks at sea, while the boat was in Las Palmas, the capital of Gran Canaria. He had joined the expedition as a scientific expert and strongly objected 'to being sent ashore with a list of things to be bought by Mrs Routledge'. Crawford was indignant at being treated like 'a cook's boy'; and what is more, a cook's boy who had to present Mrs Routledge with accounts for items like fruit and vegetables, which cost only a few pence. Such was his rage that he threatened to resign his position and return to England unless the couple promised him more autonomy. Having little choice in the matter, they agreed to give him three or four consecutive days off each week to explore. Mollified, Crawford held his fire. 'I hope we shall get along somehow,' he wrote to his family once the dust had settled, but he asked them to send him £20 nonetheless, just in case he decided to resign and had to find his own way home.

The Routledges needed Crawford. He had studied geography

at Oxford, had a diploma in anthropology and was trained in archaeological techniques. His expertise gave their expedition professional credibility. Nonetheless, they had hoped that he would accept some of the everyday tasks on board with good grace. This was not unreasonable: Crawford had been officially taken on as 'purser' on the understanding that he would work off his debt, since he could only afford to pay half the agreed £100 contribution towards his living expenses when he joined the expedition.

While Crawford found Mrs Routledge demanding, Katherine was struggling with her own responsibilities. She had hoped to employ a steward who could take charge of the complicated food provisions during the voyage, but they had never found a reliable candidate, and since Scoresby had nothing to do with such domestic issues, preferring to concern himself with the ship's engine and technical equipment, the job fell to his wife. The situation was not easy for Katherine, whose position in the ship's hierarchy was awkward and ambiguous. It was her expedition as much as it was her husband's – her private income had paid for it and they had organized it together – but the other men did not relish taking orders from a woman. The situation was made worse when it came to buying food, because Katherine was instinctively parsimonious. The costs of the expedition had escalated quickly, and she knew that boats like the *Mana* were a renowned target for unscrupulous hawkers at every port; she was determined not to be swindled by harbour traders.

In hindsight, it was a recipe for disaster. Crawford later admitted that although half his reason for joining the expedition had been to gain valuable experience in the field, the other half had been to have 'great fun'. 'With anyone but the Routledges it would have been [fun], but as it was obviously not going to be, at least 50% of my reason for continuing vanished.'

A few days after his row with Mrs Routledge, when the *Mana* was sailing from the Canary Islands to Cape Verde, it was her husband's turn to pick a fight. Crawford was on night watch, leaning against the rigging in the early hours of the morning, with Captain Gillam at the helm. Scoresby, who had a habit of coming up on deck in the early hours, caught sight of Crawford and chastised him for sitting down while on watch. The young man was furious. Not only did he deny sitting down: it was, he retorted, none of Routledge's business whether he was sitting or not, since Gillam was at the helm. Routledge's petty, patronizing reproach was the last straw. Crawford resigned and told Scoresby he would leave the boat at the next port, St Vincent.

Katherine must have been devastated when she heard what had happened, but her attempt at reconciliation was awkward and inadequate. Crawford remembered that she read both men 'a prepared sermon on temperamental clashes between strong characters', to which Crawford uttered 'words which were only just within the bounds of good manners'. They sailed on to St Vincent in stony silence. The Routledges kept to their quarters and the crew spoke to them only when absolutely necessary. Such was the atmosphere on board that Crawford thought the Routledges might forbid him to land and hold him hostage, but in the event Scoresby shook his hand politely when he left the *Mana*, while Katherine stayed 'sulking' below.

Crawford wrote to his family: '[T]here is not a soul on board whom the Rs have not exasperated beyond bearing', and he was undoubtedly right. His departure was neither the first, nor the last: the *Mana*'s voyage was punctuated by desertions.

Before the boat had even left their home village of Bursledon in Hampshire, for Southampton in December 1912, the Routledges' entire crew had deserted them because – according to Katherine – they were afraid they would set sail before Christmas and miss their family holiday. Assembling a new team set them back several months. The expedition also lost two navigators before leaving England, as well as a young astronomer, James Worthington, who had hoped to document a total eclipse of the sun: he resigned, in part, because of 'the obvious incompatibility of temperament etc etc etc'. The Routledges promptly sued him for breach of contract, just as they had sued the company that built the *Mana* over the design of the boat's bulkheads. Later, a steward deserted in Buenos Aires; another steward, a cook and an understeward (who stole Katherine's family recipe books) disappeared at Punta Arenas in Chile; and a third steward absconded in Talcahuano.

Desertion was to some extent an occupational hazard because seamen were regularly tempted by opportunities in ports along the way, but the Routledges did not give their employees many reasons to be loyal. Stewards worked a long day, from 5.15 a.m. until 9 p.m., divided into short intervals for the completion of specific tasks like cleaning, laundry, management of the stores and food preparation. At any moment, with no warning, Mr or Mrs Routledge might upbraid a crew member for careless work.

The stories of their habitual disrespect towards their employees are almost unbelievable. When Scoresby was sent a birthday cake by relatives in England, which was delivered to him in St Vincent, he opened the package to find that the cake had gone bad. No matter, he simply told the steward to give it to the crew. They immediately guessed there was something wrong with it, 'or we should not have seen a crumb of it', and sure enough, when they examined it they saw that it was only fit to be thrown in the sea. It happened later with cheese; whenever the Routledges were sent food that turned rotten, they gave it to their crew. Meanwhile there were constant complaints about the poor quality of the meals in general, and the fact that the Routledges kept the best food for themselves.

Scoresby and Katherine worked hard to maintain a hierarchy on board, between the sailors and the academic expedition members. They had designed the *Mana* with a separate saloon for the exclusive use of those who had joined the trip as scientific experts, but given that after Crawford's departure there would be no scientist on board until the geologist Frederick Corry joined the boat at Punta Arenas in October 1913, in effect it meant that the Routledges ate and lived separately from the others. The fact that they enjoyed larger quarters and better meals did not help the atmosphere on board when relations soured, and Katherine bore the brunt of these resentments, since she had the most spacious cabin and suffered less at times of stringency. When Scoresby decided to ration the water – irrationally, in the men's opinion – she was given a double allocation, a fact that did not go unnoticed by her shipmates.

Despite the couple's outward appearance of lofty arrogance, their marriage was under strain and their crew knew it. Only a week after Crawford's departure, there was an incident that proved how humiliating this could be for Katherine. She wanted the men to tidy up the boat. Knowing they would not take kindly to her criticism, she asked Scoresby to talk to the captain about it. Scoresby did as he was told, but reluctantly. He came up on deck and, like a resentful child, informed Gillam that his

wife had sent him, that she was unhappy with the decks but he
did not know why, and then he stalked away again.

Neither man had any intention of respecting Katherine's
opinion. Shortly afterwards, she appeared on deck herself. She
walked straight up to Gillam and told him what she thought of
the state of the boat, but he replied that it was not her place
to address him like that. She was outraged, and he laughed at
her. Scoresby refused to defend her and stayed out of sight.
Later, the men saw Katherine sitting alone in the deck-house,
crying into her handkerchief. With glee Frank Green, the
engineer, related the incident to Crawford in a letter. The only
reason Mrs Routledge had complained in the first place, he
said, was because the boat's canvas hatch covers were hanging out to dry and they did not look 'pretty'. Not only were
the crew lining up against her, but her husband was lining up
with them.

In her book *The Mystery of Easter Island*, published six years
later, Katherine referred to herself in the third person as 'the
stewardess' when describing her duties on the *Mana*. It was
an ironic commentary on her ambiguous position as a member
of the expedition. She had managed the venture, and now she
had written a book about it, yet she was always and inescapably
'the stewardess' on board. Once, the boat's cook, whom she
later grew to like, informed her that as a cook he held a superior
position to the stewardess in the ship's books. Sure enough,
Katherine checked the stores, organized the provisions and
occasionally cleaned the cabins, tasks that Scoresby would never
have done. And when during a particularly violent storm, all
hands were on deck to stow the sails, Gillam and Scoresby sent
Mrs Routledge below. 'It has been made painfully clear to me,'
she wrote in her diary, 'that my presence on deck when things

are bad is an added anxiety; this is humiliating, and will not, I trust, apply to the next generation of females.'

Had Katherine's relationship with her husband been happier, indignities like these might have been minimized, but the dynamics of the Routledges' marriage were corrosive. It was, after all, Katherine's family money that had bought the boat, the equipment, the provisions and the permits, and paid the crew. The expedition had cost thousands of pounds, and Scoresby had only a modest inherited £300 per annum to his name. When Crawford wrote that Mr Routledge's wife was the dominant partner in the marriage, it was not intended as a compliment to either of them.

Living on a small boat with ten people tried everyone's patience, and sometimes Scoresby's temper got the better of him. He had a reputation for being a bully, and the men took to calling him 'Lightning Willie' behind his back because of his unpredictable temper and impulsive demands. On one occasion he accused George Smith the steward, and Shepherd the cook, of being 'wasters' for using more than their ration of water, and when Smith answered back Routledge struck him, only to be reminded that 'his morning's work was a very serious offence in the eyes of the law'. Realizing the possible legal consequences of his outburst, Routledge apologized.

He was also capable of underhand behaviour. While the *Mana* was in harbour at Buenos Aires he gave a tour of the boat to local journalists, without telling Katherine. The next morning, she read an article in the *Buenos Aires Herald* under the headline, 'The Riddle of the Pacific: What Does Easter Island Mean? Scientific Expedition under Mr. Routledge to Attempt Solution'. Katherine's name was not mentioned once. They had agreed to co-lead the expedition, but Scoresby had presented it as his alone.

Scoresby Routledge with two men who boarded the *Mana* from a dugout canoe at India Reach, Patagonian Channels, December 1913.

If when they embarked on their voyage to one of the remotest islands in the world, Scoresby had indulged in dreams of grandeur – he had made himself 'Master' of the *Mana*, since he was not qualified to be captain – he soon learned that there was no place to hide from his mistakes on board. The yacht, their pride and joy, could so easily feel like a prison. When crossing the Atlantic and later the Pacific, they sailed for weeks at a time without glimpsing any trace of human life. In June, the boat was becalmed in the heat of the equator and no one could sleep. Restless, the crew roamed around with nowhere to go and nowhere to be alone. When the wind was against them, they would hardly make any progress for days; and even in the relative liveliness of port towns, they were often delayed for weeks waiting for the weather, or trying to repair the boat's engine or find new crew.

By August, five months into the voyage, with the boat in Buenos Aires, Frank Green described his existence as 'Floating Hell'. When the wind blew them back towards Argentina a few weeks later, Katherine remembered, 'One of the company declared that he had lost all sense of time and felt like a native or an animal: things just went on from day to day; there was neither before nor after, neither early nor late ...' By the New Year they were at Talcahuano in Chile, their last mainland port before crossing the Pacific. The boat's mild-mannered navigator, Ritchie, wrote to Crawford, 'Progress has been slower than a snail's funeral ... life on board is to me almost unbearable now ... I wish I had left at St. Vincent and come home with you, old card, and taken whatever consequences might have arisen.'

There were endless delays for maintenance work and provisioning. Then, within days of leaving the coast of South America in February 1914, sickness struck. Scoresby and the young geologist Frederick Corry both came down with a high fever. They were so unwell that the *Mana* had to turn back, and it fell to Katherine to care for the sick men, a job she did not relish. 'I was out certainly for fresh experiences,' she wrote afterwards, 'but not for the responsibility of nursing typhoid and dysentery at the same time in a small boat in mid-Pacific.' Back on the mainland, Corry was admitted to hospital in Valparaíso with typhoid and never rejoined the expedition, to Katherine's great disappointment. Scoresby was diagnosed with dysentery and recovered after a few days. There must have been times when she wondered whether they were mad to continue, but there was no going back.

At 5.30 a.m. on Sunday, 29 March 1914, in the *Mana*'s thirteenth month at sea and after twenty days sailing without a
glimpse of land, Gillam spotted Easter Island on the horizon.
The crew came on deck, stood together and 'gazed in almost
awed silence' as the ground ahead grew larger. 'The whole
looked an alarmingly big land in which to find hidden caves,'
Katherine wrote. In fact the island, at only sixty-four square
miles, was tiny. She and her companions would be staying
in a single village, surrounded by thousands of miles of sea.
The nearest inhabited land was Pitcairn Island – home to the
descendants of the Bounty mutineers – some thirteen hundred
miles away to the west. Mainland Chile lay 2,200 miles to the
east. Soon the 'alarmingly big' island would come to feel very
small indeed, and very remote.

7

Before There Is Bloodshed
Katherine Routledge on Easter Island, 1914

As the *Mana* dropped anchor in Cook's Bay, a group of rowing-boats filled with people came alongside to greet her. Islanders came down to the beach to watch, and according to Scoresby, 'pilfered every loose article on which they could lay their hands'. Before long, the visitors were greeted by Percy Edmunds, an Englishman who managed Mataveri, the farm that formed the island's entire economy, and a figure of authority on Easter Island.

Mataveri lay about two miles from the island's only village, Hanga Roa, and it became one of the Routledges' two base camps during their stay. As they ate dinner that first evening in a sparsely furnished room with open doors to the veranda, listening to the roar of the breakers and the drone of mosquitoes, Edmunds regaled them with dramatic stories of the island's past.

He told the Routledges of shipwrecks and uprisings. He told them that the farmhouse where they now sat had been built fifty years ago by a man who was later murdered by the islanders, and that one of his predecessors had been held in a state of siege for months, under armed guard, living in constant fear of attack from the locals. He spoke quietly and fluently, 'of events one hardly thought existed outside magazines and books of adventure', Katherine recalled, so that his listeners must have wondered what kind of story they themselves were about to take part in. Edmunds enjoyed sharing anecdotes with his new companions, but there was another side to this dinner-table history.

What Edmunds did not broach on that first evening, though Katherine and Scoresby would soon appreciate its significance, was the troubled history of Easter Island and the grievances brewing among the islanders themselves.

The people of Rapa Nui had suffered decades of misfortune and persecution. Since the earliest, albeit infrequent, contact with European sailors in the eighteenth century, disease had depleted the island's population. In the 1860s, Peruvian slave raiders had arrived and taken hundreds of captives back to Peru. The population may have reduced by as much as half, to around fifteen hundred, as a result of these incursions. A handful of islanders managed to return home from Peru, but they brought smallpox with them, which further ravaged the population. Meanwhile, Christian missionaries arrived and built a church, and by 1870 the entire community had been converted, nominally at least, to Roman Catholicism. An epidemic of tuberculosis broke out and killed yet more, so that by the late 1870s just 110 residents remained.

In 1888, the island was annexed to Chile, then leased to Williamson Balfour & Company, who ran it as a sheep farm under the control of a manager stationed at Mataveri. The company ordered their Rapanui workers to build stock pens and a nine-foot boundary wall, encircling Hanga Roa. The islanders were not allowed to leave the village without the manager's permission. They were effectively imprisoned labourers, and were paid very low wages in food and goods from the company's stores, rather than money. In the opinion of the management, they stole and lied and were not to be trusted. They had been 'gathered together', Katherine wrote, 'in order to secure the safety of the livestock, to which the rest of the island is devoted'.

The population had recovered a little, and there were two hundred and fifty residents when the Routledges arrived. They lived in huts, some made of stone, others of wood salvaged from shipwrecked cargo vessels, with floors of bare earth and no furniture; they had no school or medical care or sanitation. While listening to Percy Edmunds that evening, the Routledges may have been drawn into the romantic drama of their 'desert island', but they would soon witness the political fragility of this isolated community, caught in a cycle of debt enslavement, with no sovereignty and many hidden resentments.

During their first days and weeks on Easter Island, the crew of the *Mana* unloaded her tightly packed hold onto the beach, revealing a wealth of cargo. Countless sacks and crates of food; tools, utensils, camp furniture and scientific equipment; clothes, blankets and bedding; ropes, tents, saddles and tack, were all carried by the cartload either to one of the farm's wool sheds or to Mataveri itself for safekeeping. Almost immediately the stores were broken into at night and items were stolen. The Routledges were irate and told the villagers that the Chilean government would punish them, but in reality, with no police force and only Edmunds to maintain the status quo, there was little they could do except bear their losses and get on with their research.

Once they had organized their equipment and acquainted themselves with the island's geography, Katherine and Scoresby started mapping the great stone statues that littered the plains and exploring the coastal caves in search of *kohau rongorongo*, the inscribed wooden tablets that scholars thought might identify both the first settlers and the statues' makers. They travelled on horseback, stopping to sketch, measure, dig and take notes on local features, while Frank Green settled into his new role as expedition photographer. One of the village headmen, Juan Tepano, who had been enlisted to help them, became Katherine's closest collaborator on the island and acted as her 'escort' and mediator in her relations with the other villagers. Tepano, who had served in the Chilean military and was now employed by Edmunds as a foreman at Mataveri, was well placed to introduce Katherine to the history and culture of his people.

The research Katherine and Tepano undertook together was unprecedented in its scope. They documented and meas-ured dozens of archaeological features such as stone hearths, garden walls, house foundations and burial sites. They mapped the ancient quarries where the *moai* had been made, and they excavated a ruined ceremonial village called Orongo, hoping to find out more about past ritual practices. Scoresby often worked alone, looking for *kohau rongorongo* in the coastal caves, while Katherine and Tepano talked to the islanders about their religious beliefs and tried to work out their genealogies. Katherine wanted to discover whether they had any ancestral links to the land that might shed light on the meaning of the statues.

The Routledges' work would enrich scholarship, but it would also prove destructive. Visitors to Easter Island, whether scientists, sailors or traders, had always taken things away with them, and the Routledges were no different. They started removing small carved stone figures from the sites where they worked, along with spearheads and fish hooks, shells and beads and human bones, all of which they took back to their camp and packed up ready to take home. The villagers watched them work and bore witness to their treasure-hunting. There were now seven English people on the island, where previously Percy Edmunds had been the only one, and the *Mana*'s provisions represented a huge influx of wealth. In Hanga Roa discontent was stirring.

On 30 June, Edmunds was sitting on his veranda at Mataveri when he saw three villagers approaching in the distance. They were led by a small, elderly woman with expressive features called Angata, who held sway in Hanga Roa as a prophetess. Katherine remarked in her later book that Angata had 'a distinctly attractive and magnetic personality'. She walked up to Edmunds and announced that she had had a vision, a dream from God, that the island now belonged to the villagers, and God had commanded them to kill the farm's livestock and have a great feast.

Later that day, the two men who had accompanied Angata came back and handed Edmunds a written declaration that Angata had dictated to her son-in-law. It stated that Williamson Balfour & Company 'took this possession of ours [and] gave nothing for the earth, money or goods or anything'. They were asserting their God-given rights, the islanders declared. Later that day, eluding Edmunds, they raided the farm, taking more than ten cattle and slaughtering them, and that night they lit fires in the village and feasted.

Angata at Hanga Roa, Easter Island, August 1914.

After Angata's declaration the night raids escalated. Over the next few weeks, animals were regularly stolen and slaughtered, storehouses were broken into, and the women even said that Angata's vision gave them licence to take Katherine's clothes. Edmunds was facing a massive rebellion. There were only half a dozen islanders whose loyalty he could rely on; all the others were against him. He believed the rebels had a rifle, cartridges and some pistols; and, feeling the weight of his responsibility for Williamson Balfour's property, he wanted to give a show of force to bolster his authority. He talked it through with the expedition members at the farmhouse, but Scoresby warned Edmunds not to take action unless he was 'prepared to shoot say 10 men', for anything less than that would only serve to incite more violence. The ensuing scandal would be ruinous, Scoresby argued, the legal repercussions grave, and any amount of financial loss was preferable to conflict.

Edmunds reluctantly acquiesced, but the men took up arms and stood guard at Mataveri nevertheless. Katherine, who had been camping in the grounds nearby, moved back into the house for safety. She wrote in her diary: 'Most distressed as particularly wanted to establish friendly relations with ks [the 'Kanakas', islanders] in view of research.' Instead of getting to know the villagers, she was staying up late at night trying to persuade her comrades not to shoot them.

By mid-July more than a hundred animals had been stolen and killed, and Edmunds, although 'very nice' to the *Mana* crew, declared that he would shoot to kill the thieves whether the expedition members were with him or not. 'Dreadful so restless,' Katherine wrote hastily in her diary. 'It feels for the first time really lonely not only have we no help but no means of knowing if help is coming.' Their whole project was in jeopardy because they could not conduct geographical surveys or interviews with local people under armed guard. Though they refused to have anything to do with Edmunds' plan to kill any thieves, they were increasingly worried about a potential escalation of violence.

All their hopes now rested on the arrival of the Chilean navy. Two weeks earlier a passing ship had left them newspapers reporting that a naval training vessel, the *General Baquedano*, was on its way to Easter Island, but they had no idea whether the *Baquedano* was really coming or when it might appear. Day after day, the tension mounted. With Edmunds insisting on the need to take an aggressive stance, Scoresby went down to the village and offered to give the villagers two bullocks each week until the Chilean ship arrived, warning them that otherwise people would lose their lives in the raids. His audience simply 'laughed the suggestion out of court', declaring that the animals were theirs anyway, given to them by God, and they offered to pay Scoresby twenty bullocks instead.

When Scoresby returned to the farm that day having failed to reach a compromise, Katherine decided to try her hand at negotiation. 'This is a matter requiring tact,' she told him, 'and is therefore a woman's job; I will go and see the old lady.' It is unlikely that anyone had ever described Katherine as tactful, nevertheless she went down to the village to find Angata with Henry MacLean, a young Chilean who had joined the *Mana* at Juan Fernández as an interpreter.

For the short time that Katherine and Angata sat together outside one of the houses in Hanga Roa, joints of meat hanging from the trees and animal skins pegged out to dry around them, they took responsibility for every islander's fate. They shared an immediate mutual respect. Katherine gave Angata a knitted coat; and Angata called her guest 'Caterina'. They held hands, and talked of their love of God, but as soon as Katherine begged for the raids to stop, Angata's 'face hardened and her eyes took the look of a fanatic'. When Katherine insisted that God would not wish men to be shot, Angata replied that God would never let *her* men be killed. Their discussion quickly became futile, but they each promised to pray for the other, and Angata declared that if she ever had any chickens or potatoes, Caterina would be the first to receive some. 'We parted the best of friends but having accomplished nothing,' Mrs Routledge wrote.

The tension continued to mount, and Katherine could not sleep. Under pressure from Edmunds, Scoresby instructed the other expedition members to give him armed assistance, but only if Edmunds' personal safety was threatened. A couple of days later Katherine and Scoresby decided to move to the far side of the island for safety with 'the redoubtable Bailey', the *Mana*'s cook, as their guard, while the other expedition members stayed with Edmunds at the farm. Katherine took to carrying a rifle, and she checked the range of each of her guns, firing them against the stone cairns around their camp. A week later, when a group of twenty horsemen appeared on the horizon, she and Scoresby feared the worst and ran back to the house for their weapons, but their visitors were only bringing gifts: the promised chickens and potatoes from Angata. The Routledges accepted the offering reluctantly and sent Angata food in return, to 'discharge the obligation as far as possible', but Angata continued to send them requests 'for anything she happened to want' from their camp (including material for a flag for the 'new Republic' she intended to establish). With each of Angata's demands the pressure on the visitors increased. What would happen if they refused?

Scoresby believed that Edmunds was pushing the situation to the point of catastrophe, and Katherine filled her diary with 'much anxious thought'. 'We will probably shoot a boy in a raid ... the place will be in a blaze,' she wrote. They worried that if Edmunds embarked on some strategy that he could not see through, it would be far worse than doing nothing: then not only their work, but their lives too, would be at risk. 'We can only hope and pray and watch daily for [the ship's] coming, trusting it may be before there is bloodshed,' Katherine wrote. Then, on 5 August, Frank Green sent the Routledges a message from Mataveri to say that he could not visit the new camp as their lives were in danger. Shortly afterwards a note came from Edmunds saying that he could not leave the farm as the villagers were talking of coming up to the house and threatening to kill him if he resisted.

That night, the Routledges decided to return to Mataveri next day, knowing that the situation had reached its climax. They 'talked themselves silly' into the evening, and Katherine listed every aspect of the situation in her diary, point by point. Before going to bed they checked all their arms and ammunition. Next morning, she wrote, 'Of course if it were a stage play, the locals would start storming the place and then there would be cries of "the *Baquedano* is here" CURTAIN, but there alas! it is not.' Barely had she put down her pen when she heard the shouts of a horseman approaching: 'Ship! Ship!' The *Baquedano* had arrived. As they sat debating with each other late the night before, she had been lying at anchor in Hanga Roa. 'I almost broke down with the pure joy and relief. I had hardly known till then <u>how</u> great the strain had been.' Four of the men leading the raids had already been placed in irons.

The arrival of the *Baquedano* restored the balance of power and brought peace, but tensions remained. Katherine and Scoresby felt the ship's Chilean captain was too lenient. He had soon released three of his four prisoners and, to the villagers' delight, he proceeded to unload his cargo of charity clothing on the beach and distribute items among them. As far as the captain was concerned, the islanders had 'behaved very well not to have murdered Mr Edmunds'. He went on to warn the Routledges that he could not guarantee their safety after his ship had left and offered them a berth back to Chile, given that there was likely to be 'more feeling against foreigners'.

Scoresby and Katherine now felt bitterly let down by the Chileans and frustrated by the islanders. They wrote a four-page account of their position, which detailed the villagers' laziness, dishonesty, thievery and violence, claimed that the *Baquedano* crew had failed to deal with the situation, and warned of consequences 'of a most serious character'. But the captain had interviewed a number of local men during his investigation, and they had told him that they were underpaid and cruelly treated by Williamson Balfour & Company. He knew that peace was more important than punishment in this particular case, and he had chosen to be lenient. His diplomacy did not sit well with the Routledges, whose injured pride, financial losses and very real fears had left them instinctively expecting a more forceful response when it came to 'the natives'.

The Routledges were not ones to question their colonial status or the cultural hierarchies that ordered their world, but in more peaceful times Katherine could perceive the limits of her privileged perspective, even if she could not fully articulate them. In *The Mystery of Easter Island* she qualified her descriptions of the 'Kanakas' (itself a pejorative term for the Rapanui people that she used habitually) as though she sensed the inadequacy of her worldview but could not see past it:

> Their general morality, using the word in its limited sense, is, in common with that of all Polynesians, of a particularly low order ... [but Europeans] have seldom done anything to show that that of their own lands is in any way higher; a fact which should be remembered when complaint is made that Kanakas 'have no respect for white men' ... their lies are 'astonishingly fluent'; but lack of truthfulness is scarcely confined to Kanakas.

On considering the islanders' predicament further, she concluded: 'The marvel is not that the Kanakas are troublesome, but that they are as good as they are.' Years later, she could sympathize with their situation, but in the heated aftermath of Angata's rebellion she had expected them to be punished.

During the more peaceful months that followed the uprising, as Katherine's survey work on the island progressed, she could not help wishing that the islanders would be *better behaved*. She came to think of her Rapanui workers as 'my grown-up children' and was constantly frustrated by their indifference to her concerns. She marvelled at their lack of interest in working for her, and she grumbled at the high wages and 'any quantity of mutton' they demanded in exchange for their labour. Her employees (including her 'maid servant') always returned to Hanga Roa, on the other side of the island, at the weekends, and she never knew whether they would come back on Monday. Why were they not grateful for the honest work she was offering them? Their attitude was an inconvenience.

Katherine did not acknowledge that her own presence on the island might have been a catalyst for Angata's power play, but there were clear links between the uprising and the expedition's arrival. It was no coincidence that the men who were interrogated by the *Baquedano*'s captain singled out Juan Tepano as a focus for their grievances. Tepano had quickly become Katherine's closest colleague, and he was also one of the few Rapanui men to have penetrated the Williamson Balfour administration. His unique position gave him power, but it opened him up to criticism for enjoying his privileges without enough regard for the plight of his fellow islanders.

In the wake of the *Baquedano*'s departure that August, Tepano and Katherine spent more time together, away from the village, conducting their research into the island's history and topography with a small group of local men to help them. Over the next year they covered the whole island, measuring and describing hundreds of statues, interviewing village elders about their past and conducting amateur excavations. Tepano added comments and drawings to Katherine's notes and corrected some of the terms she used. Gradually Scoresby left them to it, while he entertained himself writing 'elaborate essays on the subject of stone chisels', a topic he found 'sufficiently absorbing' but which left Katherine 'somewhat cold'. Alternatively, he could be found paddling along the shoreline looking for lava tube caves and making detailed notes about the pebbles he found on the beach.

Juan Tepano standing with fallen *moai* at Ahu Tongariki, a large stone platform on the south coast of Easter Island, July 1914. The identity of the other man is unknown.

Katherine was the only member of her team to stay on the island throughout the expedition. Ritchie and MacLean left and returned to Chile on the *Baquedano*, while the *Mana* regularly sailed back to the mainland for supplies and mail deliveries, taking different members of the crew each time. In early December 1914, Scoresby and Frank Green went to Chile on the *Mana*. Scoresby caught dysentery again while in Valparaíso and did not return to the island for more than three months. Katherine stayed to interview the elderly villagers about their lives before Christianity, and despite Scoresby's long absence she wrote that 'every day was prized [on] which the yacht delayed her return, and there was little opportunity for feeling lonely'.

By March, however, people began to ask her why she was 'not becoming very anxious' about the *Mana* and what might have become of it. In her book Katherine wrote, dispassionately, that 'the futility of worrying was obvious' on such a remote island – although apparently it was not obvious to everyone else. On the day Scoresby arrived back from Chile, on 15 March 1915, she noted the arrival of the *Mana* in her diary, but she did not mention her husband.

Katherine relished the simplicity of the island, and the freedom it instilled in her marriage. She had 'dreams of beauty' at night, and dreaded 'leaving this stillness for the bustle of life'. 'I simply daren't think of it,' she wrote to friends, but that summer, as war tightened its grip on Europe, Katherine and Scoresby prepared to return home. She would have stayed longer if she could, for the sake of her research, but the crew's contracts were due to expire in the spring and they had to get back. On 18 August they watched Easter Island disappear over the horizon for the last time, as they sailed west for Pitcairn.

Their route took them to Tahiti, where on 16 September they anchored in the town of Papeete on the north shore. Here they picked up a year's worth of letters and newspapers that were waiting for them in two large sacks. In amongst Katherine's letters were several from her brother Wilson, written in April and May, telling her that their mother had died of heart failure on 13 April and that their family home, Woodside, had been sold. Katherine had sensed it at the time, writing 'Believe K. Pease is gone' in her journal in May, but hearing the news in this way forever tainted her memory of Tahiti.

Katherine had fought with her mother often, and so many of her decisions – to go to university, to move to London, to travel, to marry Scoresby – had been acts of defiance, but grief left her 'lonely and in sorrow'. She had said goodbye to Easter Island, 'very sad to know how improbable it is we shall ever see it again', and now continuing on home would bring its own irreparable loss. She needed to see Wilson, and for the sake of expediency she left the *Mana* in San Francisco and continued overland to New York, making arrangements for Wilson and his wife Joan to meet her on her arrival in England, while Scoresby and Gillam brought the boat back through the Panama Canal.

Katherine landed in Liverpool, alone, on 6 February 1916. The next day she took the train to Bournemouth, where Wilson was waiting for her at the station. At first he did not recognize the 'very round and short lady' on the platform, dressed in black and surrounded by baskets, parcels and canvas sacks. They stayed in a hotel with tiny bedrooms, up on the cliffs, looking across the bay to Swanage. 'Poor Katherine,' Wilson wrote, 'was always very near to tears.' Katherine cried. She was morbid and self-obsessed; she was obstinate, judgemental and superior. After a few days together, Wilson could not help thinking that she rather enjoyed her sadness and 'finds luxury in self pity'.

The Pease family at Woodside, Darlington, August 1912. Wilson stands at the far left; Katherine sits on the left of her mother, Kate Pease, who is in the centre. Wilson's wife, Joan, stands at the back right. Katherine's other brother, John, stands to the far right, and her niece, Evelyn, sits at her feet. This photograph was taken during Katherine's last visit home before her Easter Island expedition, and it would be the last time she saw her mother.

In one of her more commanding moods, Katherine gave Wilson and Joan a lecture about Easter Island over dinner, complete with maps and sketches. She told them about the uprising, and about German ships that had visited the island during the war. She was so rude about the crew of the *Mana*, and so 'furious' at Percy Edmunds because he lived with a local girl, that Wilson began to feel quite sorry for them all. Meanwhile, she quarrelled with the 'nice proprietor' of the hotel where they were staying, and when they talked about friends and family she was quick to criticize her relatives. She was incensed to learn that nine months after her mother's death some family members were already out of mourning, and when she told them that she had received no letters of sympathy from her friends, she burst into tears.

After a few days listening to Katherine, Wilson simply felt sad for his insufferable sister. He skilfully dissected her personality in his diary – and without mercy – but in the end he wished she could find more 'love, joy, peace'. 'She is ... so sure she knows what is just and her right,' Wilson wrote, 'and so determined that it is her duty to put the world right, and yet so morbidly anxious to be loved and liked that she must live on the rack.' It was, he thought, an awfully sad homecoming for her.

8

A Woman Has No Stuff in Her

Oxford at War, 1914–1918

The War was well into its second year when Katherine arrived home in early 1916. She thought the conflict 'most interesting' but she did no war work. Occasionally newspaper reports left her anxious. In June, she turned up on Wilson and Joan's doorstep in a 'state of nerves', having heard of heavy British losses at sea and speculation about an imminent invasion, and it took Joan some time to calm her down. On other occasions Wilson was astonished by her lack of empathy for those who had lost loved ones and accused her of 'brazen callousness' in his diary. Katherine declared that she was glad to be living through it and seemed to treat the war as another intellectual interest rather than as a personal ordeal.

In the spring of 1917, she visited Somerville to give a lecture about Easter Island and found Oxford transformed. The college had been turned into a military hospital and its members were living in temporary accommodation in the town centre. There were soldiers everywhere and very few students anywhere. Most young men at the university had joined the military. Just fifteen per cent of the undergraduate population remained: at Trinity College there were only fourteen undergraduates left, seven at Exeter College, and ten at Oriel. Many of the university's employees – tutors, domestic staff and administrators – had taken leave to join the war effort. The university grounds were filled with military tents and equipment, and residents woke every morning to the sound of 'incessant drilling and bugling' from the Parks, where recruits and cadets were training. There were battalion headquarters at Exeter College and Brasenose, recruiting offices opened at Balliol and on the High Street, and the town hall and University Examination Schools were being used as hospitals.

In the city's shops, schools, banks and businesses, women were employed in greater numbers than ever before. At one boys' school in Cowley, the last male teacher left in January 1916 and the head reported that 'the entire assistant staff now consists of lady teachers'. Female ticket inspectors were working on the railways, and 'girl conductors' on the buses. As manufacturers in east Oxford took on munitions contracts for the government, more women were seen smoking in the streets while walking to work and during their lunch breaks. Across the city, they were running canteens and clubs for soldiers, organizing fundraising and savings campaigns, digging new allotments in town and opening war kitchens for refugees and the poor.

Oxford was a colder, darker and less exuberant place to live, with growing restrictions on fuel and food, but it was a place increasingly, and very successfully, run by women.

*

Maria Czaplicka was one of them. Her Siberian expedition team had dispersed in 1916: Henry Hall moved to the United States to start work at the Philadelphia University Museum, and Czaplicka returned to Oxford in the autumn as a lecturer. She too was part of the strange new landscape of war, since her job was created when Leonard Buxton, a demonstrator in physical anthropology, left to fight in France. Thanks to Robert Marett who lobbied to hire her, and Emily Penrose who organized the funding yet again through the Mary Ewart Trust, Czaplicka became the first full-time female lecturer employed by the University of Oxford. It was a remarkable achievement. She taught ethnology (Europe and Asia) at the University Museum twice a week, to students enrolled on the anthropology diploma course.

For fifty years since its opening in 1860, the University Museum had been home to scientific teaching and research at Oxford. Built in generous parkland to the northeast of the city centre, the neo-Gothic cathedral to science housed departments such as mineralogy, zoology, chemistry and geology, and the collections of objects upon which they were based.

A galleried central courtyard with a pitched glass and iron-work ceiling displayed the best of these collections, from moths and minerals to stuffed birds and skeletons. Over the years, as demands for more laboratory space increased, buildings had been added on three sides. To the north was the Clarendon physics laboratory, the comparative anatomy department and the physiology laboratories; to the south lay the chemistry department and the Radcliffe Science Library. On the east side, one of the earliest additions to the museum was the ethnology department, otherwise known as the Pitt Rivers Museum, which opened in 1884 to house the extraordinary archaeological and ethnographic collections given to the university by General Augustus Henry Lane-Fox Pitt Rivers.

According to the terms of the general's gift in 1883, Oxford University had established a new readership in anthropology and appointed Edward Burnett Tylor, one of the most famous anthropologists of his day, to the position. Tylor, by then in his sixties, lectured to all interested students at the University Museum. John Myres remembered that the audience was small and Tylor's wife sat in the front row, 'watchful for confusion among the specimens'. 'Oh, Edward dear,' she would say, 'last time, you said that one was Neolithic.' When Tylor retired three years later Robert Marett succeeded him as Reader in Anthropology. Henry Balfour and Arthur Thomson gave demonstrations in amongst the display cases, and generations of diploma students attended lectures, inspected artefacts, measured bones, and sat their examinations at the University Museum.

Czaplicka may have been the first female lecturer at the museum, but she was certainly not the first woman to work there. Scientists at Oxford tended to be more liberal than their colleagues in the older humanities subjects, and as many as thirty women are recorded as having worked at the museum as researchers and cataloguers before the war.

Among them was Mary Porter, who had no formal education but considerable expertise in mineralogy. As a teenager she had been a regular visitor to the museum to study the ancient marble collections, and the Professor of Mineralogy, Henry Miers, had taken her under his wing and given her work as a cataloguer. She went on to work in London, the United States and Germany, to write books and publish papers, and in 1916, aged thirty, she returned to Oxford to work with Miers and study for her BSc.

Igerna and Hertha Sollas did research for their father, William Sollas, Professor of Geology. They worked for him without pay, even though Igerna had studied zoology at Cambridge and had previously held a teaching and research post at Newnham. Florence Buchanan had been research assistant to the Professor of Medicine John Burdon-Sanderson until his retirement in 1904, publishing research on electrical activity in muscles and heart-rate data. She continued working in the physiology laboratories at the museum after Burdon-Sanderson retired, and published her research sporadically during the war despite her failing eyesight.

Balfour was assisted by an ever shifting group of student volunteers, among them Barbara Freire-Marreco, who had catalogued a collection of amulets and 'magic-appliances' for him in 1909–10. In 1913 he employed a paid cataloguer called Winifred Blackman, and she worked for him throughout the war. Blackman, then a diploma student in her forties, was fascinated by Egyptian culture. Her younger brother Aylward Manley Blackman was a Fellow of Egyptology at Worcester College, and Winifred came up to Oxford in 1912 on her brother's recommendation. She started volunteering at the Pitt Rivers Museum the following summer. Then, when her father, a vicar, died suddenly a few months later, she appealed to Balfour and Marett for paid work to help support her bereaved family. Balfour already employed an assistant, George Kettle, but he was able to secure £20 from the University Museum's budget and took Blackman on as well.

She went on to launch a career as an anthropologist in her own right, but not before she had spent years devoted to the routine work of maintaining the collections at the Pitt Rivers. She attended lectures and tutorials alongside her job, and in the summer of 1915 she was awarded her diploma. She wrote her first article, on Egyptian ceremonial uses of fire, in 1916, all the while keeping the card catalogue up to date with new accessions. Towards the end of the war she also started work for

The first Oxford anthropology diploma students with Henry Balfour at the Pitt Rivers Museum, 1908. Left to right: Francis Knowles, Henry Balfour, Barbara Freire-Marreco, and J. Arthur Harley.

Marett as librarian, cataloguing books belonging to the School of Anthropology. Although Blackman had no formal schooling, she displayed, according to Marett, 'extreme accuracy and grasp of fact', and 'proved as energetic and capable as any assistant that I ever had'.

The museum was a place where a few select women infiltrated the overwhelmingly masculine culture at Oxford and successfully contributed to the academic life of the university. It was a hub for scientific research, but it also housed thousands of precious artefacts that needed constant care. The collections had to be cleaned, labelled, arranged for display, measured and drawn, fetched and carried, catalogued, wrapped and carefully stored away. These daily tasks fostered a collaborative atmosphere among the museum's academics, and demanded a more overtly domestic set of skills from them. Perhaps this is why women gained a foothold there in greater numbers than elsewhere in the university. Their contributions were often undervalued and overlooked, but nonetheless women worked there, against the odds, investigating, publishing and occasionally teaching, alongside their male superiors.

When Oxford opened its medical exams to women for the first time in 1917, after nearly three decades of lobbying by its more progressive professors, a second young woman joined Czaplicka on the museum's teaching staff. Alice Chance was a humorous, slightly frightening doctor from Dublin (one male student later confessed, 'I avoided Alice in the anatomy school because her wit was capable of destroying me'). The redoubtable Chance taught human anatomy to female students in a small attic room in the museum, and after the war she convinced the delegates – the museum's management committee – that she was capable of teaching mixed groups, which she proceeded to do with conviction. On one occasion, she concluded her questioning of an undergraduate on the subject of the female pelvis by saying, 'Mr Smith, your ignorance does you great credit.' Arthur Thomson had insisted on a separate dissecting room for female medical students, so a new annex was built for them to work in. Maria Czaplicka may well have shared this teaching space and the attic room with Alice Chance during the war.

Space was limited because, like many other university buildings, the museum had been commandeered by the War Office. Its lecture theatres were regularly filled with cadets and officers in training, and teaching rooms were used for instructing members of the Royal Flying Corps, who had also put up sheds in the grounds to house their engines and instruments. The geological and mineralogical bays of the central court were used by the RFC 'for the erection of aeroplanes', and when a blow-lamp exploded in their 'welding shop' there were concerns about the risk of fire. Some departments closed down temporarily while their rooms were occupied by the RFC: bookcases, collections and furniture were moved out, while new latrines and telephone lines were installed for military use. Meanwhile, dons gave special lectures to wounded soldiers, and one room was set aside for local women, Boy Scouts and Girl Guides to make, pack and dispatch clothing to men on the front lines.

Maria Czaplicka considered suspending her academic career to devote herself entirely to the war. She even thought about serving at the front lines in Europe, but when she was offered the Oxford lectureship she instead found time to work for the War Trade Intelligence Department alongside her job. Established by an Oxford historian, H.W.C. Davis, who recruited several Oxford women to his team, the WTID also employed Barbara Freire-Marreco, who recalled that Czaplicka undertook 'a considerable burden of confidential work for the Historical Section of the Foreign Office'.

It is likely that she wrote, for example, the booklet on Eastern Siberia published by the Foreign Office in preparation for the peace negotiations in 1919. She also spoke publicly in support of Polish nationalism, lecturing on 'The Future and Present of Poland' to the Women's Freedom League, and on Poland at Victoria Hall in Sheffield, the proceeds of which went to Polish refugees in Russia. She lectured on Polish history and nationalism at the Ashburton Club in London, at the London School of Economics and in Oxford, drawing attention to her country's sacrifices during the war and urging her listeners to support its freedoms when the conflict was over. 'In all her history, Poland never suffered such wounds and sorrows,' she told her audiences.

Maria had seen the effects of the war in Poland at first hand. On her way home from Siberia in August 1915 she had spent a few days in Warsaw visiting her family. She was there just 'a few hours' before the German occupation and witnessed the evacuation of the city. 'I never knew Warsaw to be so quiet,' she told a reporter, 'though to some of us it seemed horrible as well.' Everyone feared what would happen when the Germans arrived. Many residents had decided to stay, believing that the enemy would seize everything they owned if they left. There was hardly any food in the city, and people thought the Germans would let them starve. Warsaw had been under threat for more than six months, its inhabitants living with the sounds of battle and the sight of wounded soldiers being taken to hospital. Since May, enemy planes had dropped bombs almost daily, killing and wounding civilians. Nonetheless, the Poles had remained optimistic right up until the end of July. Then, ominously, the wounded were evacuated from the hospitals and the Red Cross relocated its headquarters to the east. Government offices closed, and finally the Russian troops retreated: German shells were still exploding outside the city, but now there was no reply from the Russian artillery.

As the city awaited its fate, Czaplicka spent a few days with her mother thanks to a special visitor's permit, but she soon had to rejoin Henry Hall in St Petersburg and travel back to England. As a last act of defiance Warsaw's railway stations had been blown up, and she managed to get out only with the help of an American journalist, Stanley Washburn, who was reporting on the Russian army for *The Times*. Washburn had been in Warsaw for eight months. He owned a motorcar that he kept on the outskirts of the city, and he drove Czaplicka to a point further along the railway line where she could board her train.

How hard it must have been, on the brink of enemy occupation, for her to leave her loved ones. None of Czaplicka's correspondence with her family survives. Her father, who had been a stationmaster, had died before she moved to England and is not mentioned in any of her letters. She had four siblings including a brother, Stanislaw, who was a doctor, and a sister called Eugenia. In a letter to a Polish friend, Maria referred to her mother's ambivalence about her chosen career, saying that although she loved her mother very much it would not affect her plans for the future. The family was not wealthy, but she and her mother sent each other money when they could. When Czaplicka had first heard news of the war while she was in Siberia, her thoughts had been with her mother in Warsaw; she found the anxiety of being unable to contact her while in the tundra 'almost unbearable'. According to a later newspaper report, she had relatives, including her sister, serving on the Russian front lines. Little wonder she told an English reporter in 1916 that 'as long as the war lasts I have no heart for leisure'.

Despite the uncertainties that the war brought with it, the years Czaplicka spent working at the University Museum were among the most fulfilling of her life. She moved into rooms at Lady Margaret Hall, a women's college with lawns leading down to the River Cherwell north of the city, just across the Parks from the Museum; here she was welcomed as an honorary member of the senior common room and joined a close-knit group of seven female tutors. They dined and worked together and met informally each week – for cocoa and cake in front of the fire in winter and with doors open to the gardens during summer – in an atmosphere of 'complete friendliness and fellowship'.

Maria's colleagues affectionately called her 'Chip', and Helena Deneke, the German tutor, remembered her as 'slight and graceful, golden-haired, not beautiful, but vivid and affectionate and passionately devoted to her country', dancing and whistling to mazurka tunes and getting drawn into fiery principled debates with her peers around the hearth as the evenings drew in. Unbeknown to Czaplicka, the cost of her room and board at LMH was met privately by the college principal, Henrietta Jex-Blake.

The tutors at LMH shared additional wartime duties, like patrolling the buildings to check for chinks of light from windows or doors, and marshalling students in the basement during the occasional air-raid warning. They collected ration-book coupons for the cook every week, and distributed the correct coal allowance into each person's scuttle when the shortages hit. As the German U-boats tightened their grip on British merchant shipping, produce like butter, fish and fresh meat became scarce, and the cook took to serving soup made from left-over bones on Thursdays. Potatoes were eaten at every meal 'except afternoon tea'. There was great excitement when the college acquired a large allotment for growing vegetables nearby in north Oxford, and soon afterwards a buck rabbit and two does took up residence in a hutch in the gardens, to 'help feed the students in Michaelmas term'.

Cultivating the land had become an act of defiance. New allotments were created across the city, and the tutors at Lady Margaret Hall dug theirs with such zeal that the college gardener scratched his head solemnly and admitted, 'I'll think twice before I say again a woman has no stuff in her.' Britain was desperately short of agricultural labour, particularly at harvest time, and by 1917 the Women's Land Army had recruited a quarter of a million women to work on farms.

Maria spent the summer of 1916 working on a farm in Gloucestershire with 'a party of Oxford women', and relished it. In her native Poland, women and men worked the land together and she saw no reason why she should not spend a few weeks each year working outdoors. 'I do not believe that Englishwomen realise how youth-preserving and health-giving work on the land really is or they would respond to the demand for women agricultural labourers more freely,' she told a newspaper reporter. Helena Deneke remembered volunteering with other women from LMH at Rock Farm in Winchcombe, Gloucestershire, where they were asked to clean out a stable 'a foot or so deep in hardened muck' while the regular farmhands, pipe in mouth, hung over the fences to assess their performance.

Perhaps the physical labour also helped Maria to adapt to life in lecture halls and college rooms after so many months in the great expanse of the Siberian plains. She confided to friends that she was struggling to write up her fieldwork and adjust to the demands of academic life. Among those who would help her find her way back into academia was a young woman from London, Beatrice Blackwood.

Czaplicka and Blackwood had first met at Somerville in 1912, when Blackwood was twenty-two and in her final year studying English. Blackwood had been captain of the Boat Club. She was intelligent and single-minded, although some tutors said she lacked flair in her academic work. She achieved a second-class in her examinations that summer and returned home to Cricklewood, northwest London, to live with her widowed mother and younger brother and sister. Three years later, she met Czaplicka again at the home of a mutual friend, and when Czaplicka admitted that she was trying to write a book about her Siberian research, Blackwood offered to help.

During the winter of 1915 and the following summer, they met in London to organize Maria's field notes and discuss ideas about Siberian culture. Their friendship grew, and over the next four years they planned their lives together. When Maria was offered her lectureship at Oxford in 1916 she persuaded Beatrice to come with her. Beatrice was 'more than willing', because she had become interested in anthropology and wanted to take the Oxford diploma herself. She was one of Czaplicka's first students, and some of her lecture notes survive, diligently recording the names of Siberian tribes, their languages, their marriage customs, the types of tent they used, the myths they told and the clothes they wore. All this must have already been quite familiar to Blackwood, who continued her private 'Ethnological work for Miss Czaplicka' alongside her studies.

Blackwood enrolled at Somerville again to study for her diploma, but Somerville was no longer in north Oxford. In 1915 the War Department had taken over its site, and Vera Brittain had declared, 'It is really splendid – much better as a Hospital than as a College.' The students were moved into buildings long vacated by serving undergraduates at Oriel College on the High Street and various houses nearby.

Somerville College, requisitioned by the War Office as 3rd Southern General Hospital during the First World War, April 1915.

Brittain thought the move to Oriel showed 'the immense progress in the way in which women students are regarded', but the accommodation was not luxurious. They ate in a small, dark oak-panelled dining-room, where the windows had never been made to open before. The bathrooms were in the basement, which doubled as an air-raid shelter on the few occasions that

Zeppelins flew overhead. The workrooms were badly lit, the chairs were hard and the green-baize tables unaccommodating, but Somervillians were now just a few metres from the Bodleian Library and living in the heart of Oxford for the first time. It was considered radical to house female students in the city centre, and on their first evening at Oriel Miss Penrose addressed them after dinner in the hall: 'She intimated that people were vaguely expecting us to do something unsuitable – she wasn't quite sure what, but anyhow she was sure we wouldn't do it,' wrote a contributor to the Somerville Students' Association magazine. With members scattered in lodgings along the High Street and street lighting increasingly limited, simply getting to and from the dining-hall in the evening was deemed to be a dangerous occupation.

Navigating Oxford's dark streets for dinner would not have troubled Beatrice Blackwood in the least. She was unflappable, and she was discovering a new side to herself now she was back at university. She had studied English literature as an undergraduate and was fluent in German; now, the wide-ranging diploma course introduced her to scientific subjects such as human anatomy and human evolution.

She became fascinated by archaeology and started going on excavations during her holidays. She was small in stature and liked to be the first to explore difficult or narrow caves, 'to make sure that it would be all right for the men to follow', she joked. She grew close to Professor Thomson, and in late 1917 started working for him at the museum in her spare time, typing and cataloguing. By the end of the war she was receiving a regular wage from Thomson for research assistance, while continuing her anthropology studies. She got a distinction in her diploma the next year, and began studying for a Bachelor of Science.

In the autumn of 1920 Thomson gave her a full-time job as a departmental demonstrator, and she began teaching diploma students herself, just as Czaplicka had taught her a few years earlier and as Barbara Freire-Marreco had taught Czaplicka before the war.

The war was a time of opportunity for Maria Czaplicka, Beatrice Blackwood and Winifred Blackman as they entered mainstream academic life for the first time. Across the university, the war necessitated a new, if temporary, status for women. By 1917 only a tiny fraction of the male student population remained in the city, mostly foreign students and those who were not eligible to serve. Women became more economically important, both within the university as fee-paying students and as tutors and administrators, and across the city as a whole. At the museum, both Thomson's and Balfour's male assistants left to serve in the military. Balfour reported his work as 'severely hampered' when George Kettle joined a labour battalion in 1918. The pressures of war were felt at every level and led many men to reassess the value of their female staff.

Czaplicka, Blackman and Blackwood were given their chances by a small group of Oxford dons who were bold enough to believe that women could contribute to their profession – if not always on equal terms with men, then at least on their own terms. The University Museum, in turn, provided a relatively democratic space where a few women already worked as volunteers and assistants and where it was more acceptable to employ them for academic work. Invaded by the Royal Flying Corps and maintained by a depleted staff, the museum still provided some sense of order in the chaos. Women were exhorted to stay in Oxford and continue their studies; and most did, rising to

meet the routines of University life in the absence of so many
of its men. The war brought anxieties but also opportunities. In
grief there could be new beginnings. No one understood this
better than Henry Balfour's assistant at the Pitt Rivers Museum,
Winifred Blackman.

9

Lifted Above Myself

Winifred Blackman Moves to Oxford, 1913

Winifred Blackman received the telegram at her lodgings in St John Street during the early afternoon of Sunday, 26 October 1913: she was to come home immediately, her father's heart had failed and he was dying. She took the train from Oxford to Cambridge and then on to Norwich, travelling alone for more than four hours. 'I shall <u>never</u> forget that awful journey home,' she wrote, but when she arrived at the vicarage in the nearby village of Old Catton that evening, it was too late. The Reverend James Henry Blackman had died just before five o'clock. Winifred went upstairs to sit with him in the bedroom, where he lay in 'beauty and absolute peace'. She was surprised by her own serenity. She felt 'no darkness of farewell' and she did not cry at all, because, she wrote to her brother later, she was keeping herself strong for the family. The Revd Blackman's death had left a void, one that would have to be filled.

In the weeks that followed, Winifred took responsibility for family decisions alongside her mother. Her younger brother Aylward, who was now officially head of the family, was away in Cairo working on an archaeological excavation. Although the Blackman women sought Aylward's approval by letter, there was simply too much to do to wait for his replies, so they had to carry on without him. For Winnie, this meant she felt a sense of empowerment within the pain of her grief. 'I feel so lifted above myself I never could have believed I could have kept up so, I feel as if his spirit rested on me,' she wrote to Aylward.

By the Tuesday, just two days after her traumatic journey home, Winifred was full of plans. There was good reason for her efficiency. The Revd Blackman had left his wife, three daughters and two sons in debt, with only his life insurance and Aylward's modest academic salary to live on. They would have to give up their house, St Paul's Vicarage, by the end of November. As well as arranging a funeral, the Blackmans needed to find somewhere to live.

Winifred had a bold, but sensible, suggestion: they should all move to Oxford. Aylward already lived and worked there during term time, where he was Laycock Fellow in Egyptology at Worcester College, and Winifred had been living there for the past year too, studying for her anthropology diploma. Her mother and sisters, Elsie and Flora, had visited and were familiar with the city. What is more, she was waiting to hear about the possible paid job at the Pitt Rivers Museum where she had been volunteering over the summer, and if she was earning a salary, as she hoped, then she and Aylward could take a house and 'keep it going' between them.

Winifred intended to help Aylward fill his father's shoes, and the thought that she might take some financial responsibility for her loved ones buoyed her in her grief. A few days later she received an encouraging letter from Marett about the job, and her dreams of starting afresh in Oxford looked increasingly likely to materialize: she would look for a house for them herself when she went back there after the funeral.

To Winifred, her father's funeral was 'like the triumphal progress of a hero'. James Blackman was a good-hearted, if beleaguered, parish vicar who struggled to make ends meet, but to his children he was a 'dear saint', noble, faithful and gallant, and an enduring example to them all. The letters of condolence that arrived from parishioners, the wreaths and crosses that decorated the church – which were, without exception, from 'those who loved and revered him, none as a mere compliment' – and the pews that filled with mourners, 'all coming without being asked', confirmed the justness of their adoration. The Blackmans wanted to be, above all, a well-regarded family, and to see their neighbours' admiration on public display gave them strength.

At home in the evenings, the Blackman women talked of Oxford. They were sure they could afford to rent somewhere quite central, although it might be small. Houses were always coming available, Winnie said. They would need enough space for Aylward to take private pupils at home to supplement his income, and Mother must have a garden. They would have to sell some of their furniture. The house must be built on gravel, not clay, and the water and drainage would need to be carefully checked. Winnie felt sure Aylward would agree to their plans, but such was the scheming at home that on 2 November Mrs Blackman thought to reassure Aylward, hundreds of miles away in a tent in the Egyptian desert – and to remind herself, perhaps – that 'of course the house will be yours as well as ours'.

The women had yet to hear anything from Aylward and they

awaited his verdict eagerly. Letters took more than a week to reach Egypt, and their plans blossomed, faded then blossomed again, in the intervening days as they wrote repeatedly to update him and seek his opinion. Aylward, whose words were destined to be at least a fortnight out of date, vainly urged 'the girls' not to worry, and told them to refer financial matters to him and their younger brother Barham, pointing out, 'I am the responsible person now.' He was concerned that they might be troubled by creditors, who must, he insisted, be told to wait until his return, when he would settle with them 'eventually'.

Winifred, though, took no heed of Aylward's efforts to establish a pecking order, and instead wrote to all the tradesmen who were owed money herself. She was not about to let her younger brother assume control of the purse strings without her input. 'We must discuss money matters,' she told him flatly. 'We must both feel free to say exactly what we think to each other, I shall never repeat anything you say to me to anyone, and you will, I know, do the same for me.' She proceeded to detail the family's financial situation and informed Aylward that, despite having some bills to pay, they did not need his money at present. In practice, Aylward held a limited sway over his mother and elder sisters.

When it came to their new house in Oxford, Winnie insisted on being responsible for the rent, reassuring Aylward that she would never tell anyone, because it could not be known that he was living in a house kept by his sister. She told him that the house would be taken in their mother's name, out of deference to Mrs Blackman, so that she would not feel dependent on her children. Aylward had different ideas and told his mother that the house 'had better be taken in my name I think', allowing him to some extent to 'stand in dear Father's place'. But he did not put up much of a fight. Besides, his greatest fear was that people should find out that it was in fact his sister who was paying the rent. 'It would let both me and Mother down frightfully. If it is anybody's place it is mine. I cannot appear to live on Winnie, in her house, as a sort of hanger-on.'

So Winifred's contributions went unmentioned, as did their mother's decision to take the house in her name, and Aylward's economic and emotional dependence on his family was safely concealed. He later wrote to Winnie, his tone both deferential and patronizing, 'dear girl do whatever you think right in the matter'.

There was no need to negotiate when it came to the city of Oxford. Aylward was delighted by the proposal, and – like Winifred – he felt the added substance of his new responsibilities, assuring his mother that it would be an honour and a privilege to work for his family now. In fact, his first thought, before he even knew whether his ailing father had died, had been Winifred's future. 'I must do all I can to keep Winnie at Oxford!' he wrote to his mother. 'It is so important.'

Since arriving in Oxford as a diploma student, Winifred had been happier than ever before. At first, not knowing how long she could afford to stay, she had lived in lodgings rather than in college to save money. Her letters home were upbeat and full of news: 'How I do love my life here, I shall break my heart when I have to leave. It just suits me, it gives one so many chances of learning.' Henry Balfour and his wife were unendingly kind to her and invited her to their house for Sunday lunches, while Robert Marett, who had shown little interest in her initially, was 'amiability itself' during her second term. In her letters she recorded a whirlwind of lunches, lectures, books and concerts.

Blackman, who had just turned forty, was living her own life for the first time – and she loved it.

Winifred's path to Oxford had not been simple. She was the eldest of five children. Aylward, who was eleven years younger than her, and Barham, fifteen years younger, had been educated privately, at St Paul's School in London. Aylward won a scholarship to Oxford, and Barham trained at Guy's Hospital to become a doctor. Winifred, Elsie and Flora had no formal education and lived at home with their parents, where they embroidered cushions for church fundraising bazaars, went to tea with friends, and attended the occasional dance, lecture or concert together. Winifred wanted more, and her brother's interests showed her the way.

Aylward had started collecting Egyptian curiosities and books

The Blackman family *c.*1890. From left to right, the Reverend James Henry Blackman, Elsie, Aylward, Anne Mary Blackman, Barham, Flora, and Winifred.

about ancient Egypt as a teenager, despite his parents' financial difficulties. Winifred, then in her late twenties, spent her days dressmaking to help pay the household bills and was saving up for a new coat and skirt for herself (as 'it would be more useful than a dress'), while Elsie and Flora were living with their uncle to reduce the family's expenditure. Meanwhile Aylward, still at school, bought himself an Egyptian sarcophagus, complete with an ancient mummy inside, which was delivered to the Blackman home one day to Winifred's delight and their maid's horror. He must have acquired it at an auction house; perhaps it had previously been in a private collection. There was a brisk trade in Egyptian antiquities through British sales rooms at the time, but mostly smaller items like alabaster jars, bronze statuettes or amulets. A sarcophagus was a bold purchase by any measure. When Winifred drew back the wrappings to reveal the mummy's exposed skull within, Alice the maid had exclaimed, 'Why, it's laughing, Miss!'

Aylward was sensitive to his older sisters and conscious of the difference between his opportunities and their lives at home. When he wrote to them describing his celebrations on receiving a First in Oriental Studies from Oxford in 1906, he apologized in the midst of his joy: 'I only hope the description of everything doesn't jar upon you . . . I shall be intolerable soon and shall need to be squashed by Winnie.' Later that same year, in Egypt for the first time on an excavation, he wrote to her: 'How I should love to have you with me! Can't you raise £50?!!!' Instead, Winnie stayed at home and filled a scrapbook with postcards from every town and ancient site her brother visited.

Aylward introduced Winifred to his Oxford tutor, Francis Llewellyn Griffith, Reader in Egyptology. Known to his friends as Frank, Griffith was a brilliant, gentle, energetic and slightly absent-minded academic. He was a widower in his forties, and he lived with his sister Agnes and his father-in-law at Riversvale Hall, a large Victorian house set in its own grounds near Ashton-under-Lyne. Winifred visited them there in early 1906, and went on long tramps through the Lancashire countryside, relishing the freedom from home. Over the next few years she read avidly about Egypt and bought all the books Aylward suggested: E.W. Lane's *An Account of the Manners and Customs of Modern Egyptians*, William Robertson Smith's *Religion of the Semites*, and E.B. Tylor's classic work in anthropology, *Primitive Culture*. She wanted to learn Arabic but could not find anyone to teach her at home, so Aylward suggested getting Wilmour's *Modern Egyptian Arabic Grammar* and starting by herself, promising to teach her when he returned.

By now, her heart was set on studying anthropology at Oxford, and she was reading standard texts in preparation: Tylor's *Researches into the Early History of Mankind and the Development of Civilization*, William H. Prescott's *Conquest of Mexico* and *Conquest of Peru*, and James Cook's *Voyages*. Unlike her sisters, who expressed only a polite curiosity about Egypt, Winifred longed to share Aylward's world. 'How I envy you!' she wrote while he was there excavating, but she wistfully accepted that his life had been choreographed differently from the start.

Then, in the autumn of 1910, when her opportunity finally came to join him in Haifa along with Frank Griffith and his new wife Nora, for some reason at the last minute, she did not go. Perhaps she was suffering from one of her 'attacks', because Aylward wrote to ask how she was and insisted on her seeing the doctor (albeit an additional expense) at the first sign of illness. There was another side to Winnie, when she became unwell and retreated to her room for days: the side that had led Aylward to caution his mother that April, 'Don't let her despair about Egypt', and on another occasion to ask in exasperation, 'What is the matter with her?' Whatever the matter, there was 'great grief' at Haifa that autumn when Winifred did not join them.

Two years later, her father scraped together enough money for her to start her diploma in Oxford – 'I hope I may be able to let Win have her wish,' he had written to his third daughter Flora in June 1912. 'It will be such a pleasure to me if I can.' And Win relished her new independence, writing letters to her sisters full of news, just like Aylward had always written to her. But the Blackmans barely had enough money for a second year, and Winifred worried that she would have to give Oxford up. Her only, slim, hope was to find paid work.

Despite her grief at the death of her father in October 1913, Winifred almost immediately sensed a new beginning. The opportunity to work for Balfour at the Pitt Rivers meant she could look towards the future with some confidence. She told Aylward about her job with businesslike efficiency, saying that she did not yet know how much she would be paid, but Balfour had guaranteed a long-term position and had promised to find funding from the university to improve her salary in time.

In November, she started looking for a suitable home. It had to be cheap but respectable, with a study for Aylward and a room for Winnie to work in. They took a house in north Oxford with six bedrooms and a room on the ground floor for Aylward to teach his students. It was more expensive than they had hoped, so to make ends meet they took live-in pupils: arrangements that had to be carefully presented to their friends. Mrs Blackman wrote to her son, 'We shall never wish our house to be looked upon as a lodging house – far from it – It would let us down in every way.' And nobody mentioned that Winifred supported her family financially. Respectability demanded that women like Winnie work hard to hide the fact that they had to work at all.

On 18 December 1913, Mrs Blackman, Elsie and Flora joined her in Oxford, and they set about moving into their new house and decorating it. Winifred arranged for two of her colleagues from the Pitt Rivers Museum, Balfour's assistant George Kettle and a technician called Henry Walters, to come and help them, pulling out the old carpets, putting up shelves and hanging pictures, and Mrs Blackman called in the museum's gardener to discuss the arrangement of the flowerbeds. They repapered the walls and installed their furniture from the vicarage in Old Catton, including a black cabinet that they put in the hall to display 'all the Egyptian things'. The house was sunny, and the air was a good deal fresher than in the city, according to their mother. She was delighted by the new motor buses that went past the door and took them into the town centre in just ten minutes.

They spent Christmas 'in a great muddle', but by the New Year the house was starting to feel like home. In early January, Winnie took the motor bus to her job at the museum, leaving home at 9.30 in the morning and returning between 6 and 7 p.m. Elsie hoped 'that going backwards and forwards won't be too much for her'. She need not have worried, Winifred was to work at the museum for the next seven years.

Several thousand catalogue cards in Winifred's hand survive as a visible legacy of her time there, each describing a single arte-fact, its provenance, donor and year of accession. Henry Balfour acknowledged Miss Blackman's work in his annual reports, as week by week, month by month, she dealt with objects from all over the world: musical instruments, fire sticks, charms and amulets, rosaries, bowls and plates, toys, lamps, spoons, spears, baskets, mirrors, combs, currency, human crania, and a large number of the museum's library books. She must have got to know the collections almost as well as Balfour himself, although neither would have admitted it.

And every year, Aylward departed on his next field trip to Egypt, where he excavated the tombs she had only read about in books, and worked with the scholars who had written the books she read, while she busied herself back at home with the museum's collections to help pay the rent, wondering whether her chance to see Egypt would ever come.

10

A Different Woman

Winifred Blackman in Egypt, 1920

'Well, here we are, most comfortable and in a perfect whirl of delight,' Winifred wrote to her sister Elsie on Christmas Day 1920. 'No pen can describe and no brush can depict the glories of this most wonderful place.' She was in Venice. It was the first time she had travelled abroad, and she was on her way to Egypt. She was forty-eight years old, she was in raptures, and she filled her letters with the thrills of tourist travel. The hotel was comfortable, the Italians were charming, and the staff gave such 'willing attention'. She was with Aylward and a group of his students, on their way to the archaeological excavation he ran at Meir on the west bank of the Nile.

After a few days sightseeing, they sailed from Venice en route for Alexandria. Winifred sat in a deck-chair all day, every day, looking out to sea and watching porpoises. On board ship she ate five-course meals with plenty of fresh fruit, felt rested, and had stopped taking the usual 'salts' that she believed kept her well.

After fifteen years studying Egypt and longing to go there, she was on her way at last. Her only worry was that her luggage had gone missing and she had no change of clothes.

Cairo felt like a 'fairyland', she wrote in her letters, and when they arrived at Meir she found it 'perfectly heavenly'. A desert site beyond the edge of the cultivated Nile valley, Meir is an ancient cemetery with a series of tombs cut into a high rocky outcrop in the sands. The burial sites, dating from between 2300 and 1800 BC, are decorated with murals and carved reliefs. Aylward Blackman was the first scholar to study them; he would go on to publish several volumes describing the most elaborate of the tombs.

On arrival Winifred was assigned a tomb and she set about drawing its ornate interior. She instantly fell in love with the desert and the winter warmth. She took to riding a donkey for the first time with relish and believed it was good for her health. After a few months she had lost weight, and told her family that she was 'almost slender again'. Everything was 'better and more exciting than my wildest hopes'. Most of all she loved the Egyptians.

Aylward had established relationships with a handful of Egyptian men who worked on his excavations and became his personal servants. It was usual for archaeologists in Egypt to retain their workmen on a small salary throughout the year, even though they only excavated during the cooler winter months. Aylward's staff greeted Winifred with delight and curiosity, looking after her with a care and deference she had never experienced before. She was flattered when they welcomed her with the gift of a locally made amber rosary and a shawl.

One man, in particular, became her close companion. Hideyb Abd el-Shafy was about thirty years old and lived with his wife and two children in the village of El Lahun, 150 miles north of Meir. They owned a small piece of land and a single buffalo to provide their milk, but they were poor and Hideyb had left his home to work for Aylward during the excavation season. 'He has a most charming face,' Winifred wrote. 'Very good looking, tall and slender, and holds himself beautifully.'

Winifred and Hideyb could hardly communicate at first, since he spoke little English and she was struggling to learn Arabic. Nevertheless, he quickly understood that Miss Blackman's real interest was not Egypt's ancient history but the contemporary customs of his people. He began to take her to local ceremonies in nearby villages. They stopped to watch a funeral procession one day, and he took her to see people making pottery and baskets so she could take photographs. He bought her ornaments and domestic utensils from markets to illustrate Egyptian life, saving her considerable expense because as an Englishwoman she could never have acquired things so cheaply. In the evenings, with Aylward acting as translator, Hideyb told Winifred about birth customs, medical practices and religious rites. After a few weeks she had given up drawing her tomb for Aylward and devoted herself to learning about Egyptian life from Hideyb instead.

He was supremely attentive, and Winifred felt he understood her personal needs better than anyone else. They quickly became inseparable. 'I could go all over Egypt alone, if I had Hideyb,' she said. He cooked for her, and stood behind her chair while she ate. He let her see only people that he considered 'good enough'. When she decided not to go with Aylward's party to meet people in a neighbouring village, preferring to rest at the camp, Hideyb stayed behind with her; and if she did not want to see the Egyptians who arrived to see her, he kept them away.

One day she fell from her donkey on the way home and Hideyb was 'off his donkey in a twinkling' to attend to her. Later he massaged her sore arm. 'I cannot think where he learnt it,' she wrote in a letter home, 'but he is a wonderful masseur.'

Winifred Blackman taking tea with local officials in Egypt. Hideyb Abd el-Shafy stands behind her.

With Hideyb's help, Winifred's confidence grew, and she began to see the academic potential of her situation. Her companion was 'a mine of information' and the perfect guide. Together, they could study the agricultural peasants of the Upper Nile Valley, the fellahin, in unprecedented detail. If she were to return to Egypt every year, as she hoped to, she could study one province at a time, recording the people's customs and beliefs. 'I can tell you,' she told Elsie, 'I have a perfectly unique opportunity in prospect here, the anthropological work to be done in this part of Egypt is enough to make me quite celebrated.' She was determined to become fluent in Arabic and to make her name as an anthropologist. She might even get a job in Egypt as a government anthropologist, or win a research grant to cover her expenses. She saw years of work ahead of her, if she could find the money to do it. 'I can never express all that this time has been to me,' she wrote to Elsie in April. 'It has opened out a new life for me and I feel a different woman.'

She would return to Egypt every winter for the next nineteen years, living for at least six months in a mud-brick house amongst the fellahin. The country would haunt her for the rest of her life.

In November 1921, Winifred Blackman travelled to Egypt for her second season, this time without Aylward. Her mother had given her the money. 'Thank you so much, darling mother,' she wrote from the boat to Cairo, 'for all you have done for me. I do hope and pray I may make a success of this trip.' She was going to live with Hideyb and his family in El Lahun.

The villages of Upper Egypt lay in 'the cultivation' of the Nile, bordering the wide expanse of the desert but protected from the sun by palm groves. The houses were made of mud bricks and plaster, some of the larger ones had two floors. On the flat roofs, hens pecked around between large circular granaries filled with grain, and cakes of cow and buffalo dung were stacked as fuel. Hawkers walked the village lanes below, selling vegetables, candles and cotton cloths. A few open-fronted shops housed tailors and coppersmiths. Fowl and goats wandered the streets; children played or sat on benches outside houses, while adults worked in the shade of the palm trees making pots and jars, baskets or bricks, to sell. In the fertile fields beyond the village they grew corn, and much of their time and effort went into irrigating their crops using waterwheels driven by an ox, a cow or a buffalo, and simple hoisting equipment to pull water out of the river in buckets, before feeding it through channels into the fields. They used oxen and donkeys to plough their land, sickles to cut the corn, and small grinding-stones to make flour.

Blackman was warmly welcomed at El Lahun, and people crowded around her in the streets. Hideyb and his wife Saida had gone to great trouble to make her comfortable. They had moved out of the upper rooms of their house and given her the entire top floor with a bedroom and sitting-room. The walls were freshly whitewashed, and Hideyb had built a toilet especially for her. He was so proud of it that he showed it to her twice, and his face lit up when she went in to use it for the first time.

Beyond the palm trees outside lay the open sands of the desert. She could watch people coming and going through the village from her bedroom window. A small open-air mosque lay just below the house, and she liked to hear the muezzin calling the villagers to prayer. Hideyb and Saida's two young children, Ali and Shama, were always running in to see her in her room. Winifred grew almost as fond of them and their mother as she was of Hideyb.

Hideyb accompanied her to the outlying villages, where she watched wedding ceremonies and funerals and talked to the inhabitants. By now she was planning 'a book of moderate size' about the fellahin, which would describe their lives from birth to death, their occupations and industries, their religious beliefs and superstitions.

Over the years, Blackman became famous amongst the fellahin. To the Egyptians she was a contradiction in terms: an Englishwoman who travelled alone and lived with them as their guest. Unlike other English visitors, Winifred did not impose herself: she was there to listen, observe and record what she saw. She was particularly interested in people's religious beliefs, quizzing them about spirit possession, sorcery, amulets and the evil eye. Ironically, as she toured the villages on her donkey she became known as a miraculous healer herself. She carried English medicines with her – simple tinctures, dressings and eye drops – which she dispensed to the villagers who gathered around her wherever she went. Children with sores on their skin, people whose eyes had been sealed shut by infection, and even burn victims came to her for help. The Egyptians had never known a foreigner attend to them in this way, and she soon had to insist on strict hours, between eight and nine o'clock in the morning, to try and control the demand for her treatments.

Winifred saw an important humanitarian role for herself in Egypt. She wanted to teach the women she met basic rules of sanitation and health care which she found terribly lacking. Hideyb, however, would not let her go near 'anyone who is very dirty', so she attended only to people who had minor ailments or eye infections.

As word spread about her healing powers, people travelled for miles to see her. She found herself greeted by crowds at every village. Many Egyptians had never seen an Englishwoman before. They talked of 'a very great one', and called her 'Sheikha Shifa' (Sheikha of Healing). There was even a rumour that she was the daughter of the king of England. She was equally renowned amongst government officials because she was a British woman in Egypt who felt more at home in the countryside than in the towns and cities. To the authorities she became identified with the wider region and was known simply as 'Miss Blackman of Fayum'.

Winifred Blackman with a group of Egyptians, date and location unknown.

Winifred revelled in her fame. Conscious of the money she had borrowed from her mother, she filled her letters home with news of the accolades she had received. Government officials told her they wished that all the English could be like her, and that her work was invaluable. 'I cannot tell you how humble all this makes me feel and how utterly unworthy I feel,' she wrote, but when she worried about money she comforted herself that she was doing good. In Egypt she was something she felt she could never be in England: she was recognized. She loved the attention. It convinced her that, one way or another, she must find the money to continue her work.

Winifred's love affair with Egypt was dependent on a steady cash flow, and she struggled to make ends meet. She won several small grants over the years – from Oxford University, from the British Association for the Advancement of Science and the Royal Society – but she could never plan beyond the next few months of her fieldwork and she regularly had to ask her mother or Aylward for cash, which upset her greatly. Financial concerns dominated her correspondence, and she was always anxious. She explained all her expenses in her letters home: she had to tip the errand boys, and the family who lent her a donkey, and the postman who took her mail; she paid Hideyb a weekly wage, covered his travel expenses as well as her own, and bought all their food. 'I cannot ever make you understand how awfully bad I feel at having to ask for money,' she wrote to Elsie, but she invariably needed more.

Aylward thought she should try harder to get a grant from the Egyptian government, telling her that she must push the officials she met to fund her work. She tried as best she could, but she told him that asking for money all the time was 'unpleasant' and 'undignified', and not as easy as he thought. English officials in Egypt were 'out for what they can get for themselves', and saw no reason to finance her private research agenda. She was always longing for news of the next grant and writing to her tutors to ask for their support. If only she had the money, she could do really good work, she assured them.

Winifred also felt increasingly responsible for Hideyb and his family, who struggled to make ends meet when she returned to England in the spring. Hideyb could not commit to another job because he had to leave himself free to work for her during half the year. She worried about his health and thought he did not eat enough. When she left Egypt, he told her, he was overcome with grief and anxiety. She longed for a research grant in part because then she could take full responsibility for him and pay him an annual retainer. In early 1922 she proposed bringing him back to England, so that he could work for her at home over the summer in Oxford.

The Blackmans now provided lodging and private tuition for around ten teenage boys in north Oxford. Some of their students lived in the family home at 24 Bardwell Road, and others had rooms a few doors away at number 17 where Winifred lived when she was in England. She suggested that Hideyb move

Hideyb aboard the *Malura* returning to Egypt after his visit to Oxford, January 1923.

into a small dressing-room at number 17, so that he could help her run the house and look after the boys. Aylward, who knew Hideyb well, agreed, and in May they travelled back to England together. There is no record of Hideyb's summer in Oxford, but Winifred's plan was that he should cook, and launder the boys' clothes. He was full of excitement at the prospect of working in England and said that he would become 'a great man in the eyes of all the villagers'. His chief concern was that she would meet an Englishman, get married, and never come out to Egypt again, so he told her that he would never let her drink tea alone with an unmarried man while he stayed in Oxford.

That year, Blackman won a grant from the Percy Sladen Memorial Trust, which specialized in supporting fieldwork abroad, but she still juggled smaller grants from Oxford, the Royal Society and the British Association to meet her costs, and suffered periods of terrible anxiety. The Percy Sladen trustees gave her £200 annually for four years, but she needed more, and when an acquaintance in the Egyptian government gave her the opportunity to state her case in a letter to the king of Egypt, she explained that to do her work properly she ought to have £600 'and the use of a small *dahabiyeh* [Nile boat]'.

In private, Winifred criticized some of the people upon whom she depended for funding. In January 1920, Marett, Balfour and the Oxford Committee for Anthropology had awarded her the status of research student and given her £25 towards her first trip. Although a small amount of money, it gave her official recognition as a researcher and might open the door to more funding. They renewed their grant the following year, but in 1922 she started to feel that her tutors were not doing enough to help. She had left her job at the Pitt Rivers Museum and given up her work for Marett as librarian at the

School of Anthropology so she would be 'quite free' for Egypt. 'I have done enough, I think, for the School of Anthropology in Oxford,' she wrote to her sister. She felt underappreciated, and although Marett had thanked her for her work, 'the other "gent" [Balfour] has, I think, behaved very badly to me, and not even given me a decent testimonial'. She had written to them, but they had not replied. 'I am not going to trouble any more about these Oxford people. When I have made a name for myself by lecturing in London and elsewhere they will be ready to do anything for me.'

One moment she was defiant, the next despondent. She could never let her feelings be known because, however much she wished it were different, she relied on the goodwill of men like Marett and Balfour.

Despite the costs, Winifred's commitment to her adopted country never wavered. Egypt was politically volatile in the years after the First World War and anti-British feeling ran high. She had arrived only a year after the violent 1919 Egyptian Rebellion, which three years later led to independence from British rule. In March 1919, several British soldiers and officials had been killed in Deirut, not far from where she was based. Every few months there was news of another protest, a riot, or an attack on British residents. Blackman told her family about 'trouble' in the towns, but said that all the Egyptians she met were friendly and little interested in politics.

In December 1921 the British authorities in Cairo had imposed martial law, and there was another wave of violent protest. Although Blackman did not expect the discontent to reach the villages where she worked, Hideyb was charged with taking her to the town of Asyut at the first indication of anti-English feeling, where she could safely stay in the house of a government official. She went out into the countryside as usual that month, to show goodwill, and never experienced any hostility. On the contrary, she felt that she was improving the reputation of the English wherever she went, because everyone liked her so much. The 'exclusiveness' of the English in Egypt, she said, had been one of their biggest mistakes.

Then, in April 1923, Hideyb was murdered. He was killed by 'young roughs' in an apparently unprovoked attack at a railway station in the town of Beni Suef. The details are unclear. He lived for a few days after the attack and Winifred described him as being 'very seriously injured'. It is possible that he had suffered burns, because there was talk of keeping him out of the fierce summer sun 'for a very long time to come'. Winifred may have been with him when he died, for she said that he had no fear at the end and his only grief was leaving those he loved. She had talked to him about 'all the happiness he was going to' and assured him that his family was safe in her hands. And if Winifred promised to provide for Saida and the children, they certainly carried out their duties towards her in return: just days after Hideyb's death, she wrote that Saida was 'managing everything for me so I have no bother at all'.

It is possible that Hideyb's relationship with Blackman had led to his murder. In the preceding weeks she had been concerned that she would not have enough money to bring him back to England with her again over the summer. 'I quite think we should hear he had been killed if I left him behind,' she wrote to Elsie. Perhaps people were jealous of his influence over her: she would work only with Hideyb and refused the attention of other men who tried to serve as her guide. Beni Suef, where Hideyb had been attacked, had seen violent anti-English protests since the 1919 uprising. Many believed that the monarchy was still in the service of British colonial interests despite Egyptian independence having been nominally granted in 1922. The British military continued to occupy the country, and there was still widespread discontent.

Quite apart from ongoing political tensions, Upper Egypt was a dangerous place to live. The fellahin were known to be suspicious and hostile to outsiders and Blackman witnessed several fights between groups from different villages. She described several spontaneous armed encounters over the years, in which men threw stones and slashed each other with leather whips and spears, while she, ever eager to record the drama, 'dodged about trying to get a snapshot of the conflict'. When friends begged her to withdraw to safety, she declared herself 'far too interested to beat a retreat', and stayed to make notes and take more photographs instead.

Blood-feuds, or revenge killings, which had a long history in the region, were less common but more brutal. Winifred visited one place where two men had been strangled to death in revenge killings, and another where several men had been attacked and beaten to death while sleeping in their cornfields. Families could become locked in a murderous cycle of retribution. Once, one of her neighbours had killed another man 'in a terrible way', apparently for stealing some onions. The authorities struggled to find out exactly what had happened in cases like these, because witnesses feared reprisals if they testified, and many crimes went unpunished.

Winifred observed this brutality with a scientist's detachment. She believed that violence was inherent in the Egyptian psyche, even rooted in the harsh arid landscape itself; she saw it as part of their way of life. When a man caused chaos by lashing out with a whip at a village festival without warning, it was only then, according to her, that 'the fun began'.

The cold-blooded murder of her friend was another matter, of course. Her family was rocked by the news of Hideyb's death and wrote impassioned letters asking her to come home, but she refused and tried to reassure them, explaining that an armed guard would accompany her when necessary. 'It is not as if I am in any danger for I am not,' she wrote. She kept a revolver with her in any case.

Winifred's relationship with Hideyb had been intense. He had guided her through her first years in Egypt and through him she had developed her love for the country and its people. For a long time after his death, her life there continued in his shadow: 'Sometimes I cannot believe that he is not here in the flesh, his presence is so real to me,' she wrote to her mother in 1924. She returned to El Lahun that autumn and moved into her rooms in Hideyb's house as usual. Now, Saida cooked her meals and slept outside her door every night. Winifred continued her work, but soldiers accompanied her through some of the towns, and Russell Pasha, the Police Commandant, arranged for Hideyb's brother Umbarak, a police officer and ex-soldier, to serve as her personal attendant on three months' full pay. Umbarak was quiet, honest and reliable, and when he got to know her better he was 'always laughing and joking', which kept her 'lively'.

They talked about Hideyb often. Blackman felt his spirit was with her: he 'took all the sadness away', she said. One night, Saida saw him sitting on Winifred's bed, talking and laughing; other people saw him too and told her that he was delighted she had come back. He never appeared to her, but she continued to experience 'the most extraordinary feeling of his presence'. She visited his grave and left palm branches for him there. 'He said before he died that he should never leave me,' she wrote to her mother, 'and I believe that he never will.'

Even when the violence happening in Egypt affected Winifred directly and grieved her so deeply, it did nothing to sway her confidence in the country. She felt it was her vocation to be there and that she must continue to return every year, despite her constant anxieties about money and her ongoing indebtedness to her family. She belonged in Egypt, and being there brought her courage and fortitude to the fore. It was a far cry from sewing cushions for the church bazaar or attending lectures at the museum. Few of her colleagues in England had sidestepped stone missiles in the midst of a chaotic crowd of combatants in the hope of getting a good photograph. Here, Winnie was a different woman altogether. 'I feel as if I were living in a dream,' she had written to Elsie during her first Christmas there in 1920.

Unlike any other anthropologist working at the time, Winifred Blackman managed to live with the subjects of her study for twenty years. In research terms it was an astonishing achievement, and certainly there was 'no greater authority' on the fellahin of Upper Egypt. Her standing in Egypt was built on her identity as an English, female anthropologist: she became famous for her fierce independence, her unique interest in the villagers' way of life, and for her medicines and trade goods. The fact that she was an Englishwoman in Egypt gave her prestige. Back at home, she promoted her work only as much as was necessary to secure a return fare. She simply wanted to be 'Miss Blackman of Fayum'.

II

A Most Adventurous Young Lady
Barbara Freire-Marreco Is Married, 1920

Barbara Freire-Marreco was married on Wednesday 21 April 1920 at the little Church of All Saints in Woking, Surrey. A local newspaper noted that the bride's kindness, courtesy and good works had endeared her to a wide circle of friends, and the church was filled with well-wishers, but it was a quiet ceremony and there was no reception afterwards. Despite the characteristic modesty of the occasion, news of Freire-Marreco's marriage appeared in the gossip column of *Tatler* magazine, 'In Town and Out', thanks to her unusual career as an anthropologist. The piece did not mention her new husband, Robert Aitken, at all, and Freire-Marreco was described whimsically in the past tense, as though she was something of a curiosity: a distinguished 'lady anthropologist' who had, a few years ago, been a research fellow at Somerville College, Oxford. 'She was a most adventurous young lady,' the reporter declared: she had once lived in New Mexico with a tribe of Pueblo Indians; now she was getting married.

Contrary to popular expectation, Barbara Freire-Marreco was still a distinguished anthropologist after her marriage, but as Mrs Robert Aitken she had different priorities. She remained an active member of the Folklore Society and the Royal Anthropological Institute, but marriage would be a turning-point in her career. As Barbara Aitken she frequently published book reviews, as well as a few short cultural observations in academic journals and one longer article on Native American religion, but her academic ambitions faded. In 1923 she gave a course of lectures at University College London to fill in for a lecturer who was ill, and another in Oxford, but admitted that she 'hadn't much of an audience'. She occasionally corresponded with her colleagues in the United States and apologized to them for not writing up more of her research. Then in 1928 the Aitkens moved to Hampshire, which was a 'great regret' to Barbara's academic circle in London.

In truth, Barbara's career had been compromised by her family commitments long before she met Robert Aitken. Her earliest correspondence with her Oxford tutor John Myres shows that her academic life was very much a family affair from the start. Her parents, Walter and Gertrude Freire-Marreco, were always there in the background, 'pressing' her to act, 'desiring' her to pass on their appreciation to Myres, 'hoping' to meet him and his wife. In one letter, written in 1908, she told Myres that she could never consider teaching in a school because it would mean leaving home for too long, whereas university teaching was a possibility because it offered shorter, more acceptable, terms. When her mother was ill, Barbara stayed at home. 'Thank you for asking my plans,' she wrote in that same year. 'It is difficult to make any, because of my mother's health.' Mrs Freire-Marreco, sensing the narrative that was emerging in her daughter's letters to Professor Myres, issued an invitation from her sickbed, which Barbara relayed to him: 'My mother hopes to meet you and Mrs Myres before long, when she is less withdrawn from society – she begs me to make it clear that it is <u>not</u> mental!' It is not clear why Mrs Freire-Marreco withdrew from society as frequently as she did.

The Freire-Marrecos lived in a large red-brick house with rooms on three floors, called Potter's Croft, in the village of Horsell near Woking, which they shared with three servants: a cook, a parlourmaid and a housemaid. Barbara's younger brother Geoffrey had been educated at Charterhouse and now lived in London where he was a director at Barker & Company, a coachbuilders' firm that made the bodywork for Rolls Royce cars. Barbara continued to live at home throughout her thirties, and despite going up to Oxford during term time she often had to postpone her work when her parents needed her back at Potter's Croft. Until their deaths – her mother's in 1918, then her father's in 1929 – Barbara's academic potential was always weighed in the balance against her role as daughter of the house.

She turned down more than one job opportunity in the United States because of her duty to her parents. In 1911 Edgar Hewett, Freire-Marreco's mentor in New Mexico during her fieldwork, had suggested she come back later that year to lecture on social anthropology at the American School of Archaeology in Santa Fe. Her salary would cover her travel costs from England, he pointed out, and the job would enable her to continue her research in the pueblos. Replying to him from Woking that May, she explained: '[M]y family are not at all inclined to give me a definite answer about it yet,' and asked him to 'keep the offer open' if possible. She very much wanted to return, she went on, but she could not count on being able to. A few months later, she still harboured notions of travelling to America for a second winter field season, but her mother was 'little inclined' to let her go so soon.

Hewett visited Oxford in the spring of 1912 for a conference, and when he met with Freire-Marreco he tried a different approach. Knowing she could not commit to a permanent post, he offered her a three-month lectureship in Santa Fe for the summer of 1913, to work on Navajo material. She turned him down again, saying that she was not inclined to work on the Navajo since they had 'no obvious connection with my own subject'. Although the Navajo had a long history of contact and trade with pueblo people, their culture was distinct in almost every way: they spoke a different language, had different religious beliefs, their own political system, building traditions and worldview. Barbara preferred to expand on her experience in the pueblos, and she was intent on raising funds for a second research trip of her own instead.

Hewett did not give up. He offered to pay her $200 for a written report on her fieldwork; this she accepted, on the basis that the money would help finance another visit to America. With an additional grant from Somerville College, she returned to the United States in the autumn of 1912 to work with the Tewa living in Hano, Arizona. Most anthropologists did not have the money to mount a follow-up field trip, and it is testament to Barbara's academic success and her tenacity that she was able to go back to the USA.

The Hano Tewa had migrated to Arizona from the Rio Grande pueblos at the end of the seventeenth century and shared a history with the people she had met in the Rio Grande two years earlier. Some elements of their culture, like their language and clan system, were the same, but each had developed a distinct cultural identity. By studying the Hano, she wanted to broaden her understanding of pueblo governance across all Tewa-speaking communities.

The community she visited in Arizona lived in the high desert, atop a flat, windswept sandstone plateau known as First Mesa. Arid and uncompromising, with views to the distant horizon in every direction, it was a breathtaking and otherworldly place to stay. Hano was nearly 6,000 feet above sea level, and sheer cliffs dropped 600 feet from the houses on the Mesa to the ground below. Flat-roofed, stone and adobe dwellings crowned the cliffs, with almost no vegetation to soften their structure. Stone steps cut into the Mesa enabled people to scale the steepest parts of the village. Wooden ladders rested against the houses, linking the earthen streets to the flat rooftops above, and low, narrow doorways led to small, cool, dark rooms within, with stone floors and pine roof beams. At the time of Freire-Marreco's visit, the residents of Hano carried all their water, firewood and food along steep, narrow trails from the land below the Mesa up to the village each day. They grew maize, onions, watermelons, squash, chillies and beans in the sand dunes below. They hunted rabbits and the occasional antelope, kept sheep, and made pottery, jewellery and leather goods for trading.

Freire-Marreco's colleagues had told her that the Hano people were 'more susceptible to the wiles of the ethnologist than their Rio Grande kindred!', but when she arrived in November 1912 she found it hard to gain their trust. At first they claimed she was a witch and made her send away some of her belongings, like the maize and tobacco she had brought as gifts, which aroused their suspicions. After a few weeks she was left hoping that no one would get smallpox, because she knew that she would get the blame. She relied heavily for information on a man named Leslie Agayo and his family, who were members of the Corn clan, and she lived with Agayo as his guest. He was a slightly built, earnest young man in his mid-thirties who spoke English well. 'Gentle, serious and obliging', he took great care over the details of Freire-Marreco's work, answering her questions and helping her with translation.

Other people in the pueblo resented their close relationship. One individual in particular, who had been 'intolerably forward' and whom she had 'snubbed' early on, turned out to be the son of a local official. He continued to make trouble for her periodically. 'Things here very pleasant and interesting, but precarious,' she wrote to an American colleague. She knew that many people there wanted her to leave them in peace, but she was determined to stay.

Barbara withstood the criticism levelled at her and her hosts, and spent four months at Hano. Agayo and his family showed her how to weave and embroider clothes, blankets and dancers' costumes, which they traded with people in neighbouring pueblos. Embroidery was an exclusively male pursuit here, and Agayo was accomplished at needlework. She also worked with him on long lists of phonetics and vocabulary as she improved her understanding of the Tewa language and its local variations. She recorded kinship terms, took notes on public dances, and found out as much as she could about local politics and the clan system.

Her surviving letters from this trip do not record her emotions at being back in the United States. She expressed none of the elation she had during her first visit, although she must have felt similarly on her return. Instead, her letters to colleagues contain anecdotal observations of daily life. She mused on the economic value of woollen and cotton dresses in different villages, and shared her notes on the changing nature of trade in beads or pottery. In one letter she wrote down the words of a song she had heard, and sketched the geometric designs she saw used in weaving.

One evening in January 1913, writing to John Myres, she described the scene in the house where she was working at the time. The family was 'all frowsting indoors, all busy'. The stepfather, an elderly shepherd, was weaving woollen leggings from undyed black and white wool, sitting on a stool with a small loom resting on his knees. His wife was out at a relative's house making blue cornmeal wafers, which the women cooked on hot flat stones. One of her young sons was threading shell beads, another was boring turquoise beads, a third was embroidering a wedding dress. One of her daughters was pulping yucca roots to make a soap to wash the men's heads, another was drying newly ground cornmeal while distractedly combing her nephew's hair. Freire-Marreco was particularly taken with the techniques and designs the old man used in his weaving, and her letter gives a tender vignette of family life.

After Hano, she paid a brief visit to Fort McDowell Reservation and Santa Clara again, so that she could compare their kinship terms with those used at Hano. In Santa Clara she was happily reunited with friends, only to find herself caring for them when they caught pneumonia. 'If it were not for the pneumonia, I would have had the time of my life here at Santa Clara,' she wrote to one of her American colleagues, the ethnologist John Harrington, 'but I come from nursing so dreadfully sleepy and stupid!'

No male anthropologist would have been taken up with nursing duties on a short research visit from Britain, but the distractions Freire-Marreco faced did nothing to diminish her academic reputation. Towards the end of her trip Edgar Hewett made his most generous offer of employment yet. In May 1913, while she was staying in Santa Fe, he offered her a permanent position at the American School of Archaeology with a salary of $1500. It was his third attempt to hire her.

Freire-Marreco wanted a job, and everything she had done in her career demonstrated her determination. She had fought hard for her start in academia. When she failed to get a research fellowship at Somerville in 1906, she had studied for the diploma in anthropology instead, negotiating every term for renewed permission from her cautious parents and fitting the work in around her home commitments. She applied for the Somerville fellowship for a second time in 1909, this time successfully. The three-year fellowship was a rare opportunity. She was only the third recipient, and she remembered the exact moment she received the news of her appointment: 6.45 p.m. on Tuesday, 15 June. She seized her opportunities and conscientiously broadened her skills, taking on editorial work and teaching, and publishing her research in academic journals. She asked Somerville for permission to give lectures at the LSE and at Oxford because, she said, the experience was 'a great advantage to me professionally'. She hoped that the subject of anthropology would grow fast enough to provide 'subordinate teaching work for people like myself' in the future.

Her achievements were remarkable. Only one or two women had lectured at Oxford University before, and then exclusively to female students or as part of the university's extension programme (a forerunner to the Continuing Education Department which offered courses to adult learners in other towns). Female tutors taught solely at the women's colleges and did not lecture at the rest of the university until after the war, a decade later.

She had embarked on her career against immense odds, and she was succeeding.

Hewett's lectureship, with its generous salary, was far more than she had ever been offered, or was likely to be offered, in England. The opportunity to stay in Santa Fe, to work, to live for herself and continue the research she had started with the Tewa people she loved must have been tempting, but Freire-Marreco once more declined Hewett's offer. She said she was truly gratified and hoped that she might work for him one day. She was, however, 'obliged to put it quite out of mind for the present' because she had commitments in England, both pro-fessional and personal, which she could not break. This was not entirely true. She had no professional commitments in England in 1913. Her Oxford fellowship had finished. The previous year she had worked for Myres as an editorial assistant on some of his publishing projects, but she certainly did not have a job.

When she wrote to Myres, who had counselled her at every stage of her career, and told him about Hewett's job, she made no mention of other professional commitments: 'The School here offers a job at $1500, but I ought to be at home for some time now,' she wrote. It was home, not work, that called Barbara back to England. She was thirty-four years old and on the brink of a long-sought-after career, but her parents took precedence in her life, just as they always had.

That summer, after eight months in America, she moved back to Potter's Croft and started writing a long, rather dry report, co-authored with her American colleagues, about the various plants grown and used by the Tewa people. She was also writing a report on the Yavapai whom she had visited in Arizona, and an article on Tewa kinship terms. She had planned to make a third trip to the United States in 1915, but during the spring of 1914 her father fell sick with a 'dangerous illness'. She wrote to John Harrington, with a sense of resignation: 'Maybe my field-work chances are over for good – I wish I had made better use of them.' In July, she took Mr Freire-Marreco away for a change of air. Then Britain declared war on Germany.

Unlike her contemporaries at Oxford, for whom the conflict brought new academic opportunities, Barbara's war left her no time for her research. In 1915 Hewett still hoped to give her a job in Santa Fe, but now she asked him to wait until peacetime: 'I hope you will bear me in mind when the war is over. If I am free to leave home again, my chief wish will be to work in New Mexico.' For the moment, all her energies went into war work.

Within a few weeks of the outbreak of war, she had become secretary of the Woking War Emergency Committee, which was mobilizing local women to help the war effort. The committee arranged to launder the clothes of more than two thousand troops stationed nearby, issuing bundles of washing to 'a little army of women anxious to be thus employed'. Early in the year, it was overseeing the employment of more than seventy-five women each week, washing, mending and making soldiers' uniforms.

As committee secretary, Freire-Marreco also organized public meetings to recruit servicemen, collected donations of food and blankets to be sent to local barracks, and helped to manage a free medical service for the wives and dependants of soldiers and sailors. She established a system for logging requests for personal services, employment and financial assistance, so that all those in genuine need could be helped, as well as administering the donations people had made in support of refugees and the Soldiers and Sailors' Families' Association. At a public meeting in February to report progress, she stood up to thank the chairman of the committee, Mr A.H. Godfrey: he had given all those involved, she said, 'a new interest in Woking, and' – to cheers of 'Hear, hear' from the audience – 'had made many realize for the first time how worthwhile working for their town was'.

Barbara may well have developed a new respect for her hometown, but the job also allowed her to exercise her skills as a professional woman: after a year, she moved to London to join the editorial staff of the newly established War Trade Intelligence Department, attached to the Ministry of Blockade (part of the Foreign Office).

Hundreds of women were recruited to work in government departments during the war, but the vast majority were lower-grade typists and secretaries, and Freire-Marreco was one of only a handful of university-trained women employed by the Foreign Office. She was probably recruited for her language skills, translating Spanish newspapers and correspondence as part of a monumental bureaucratic effort to check the credibility of thousands of commercial firms, traders, cargoes and transactions suspected – however vaguely – of benefiting the enemy. The WTID was responsible for establishing hundreds of dossiers on neutral firms, creating a vast 'Traders' Index' that was constantly updated, and for providing reports, on request, to other governmental departments regarding any trader, company or shipment. The job was demanding. 'My work for the Military Intelligence Department was interesting, but very exhausting, and I did little else,' Freire-Marreco wrote to a colleague after the war.

Perhaps this is why, in the autumn of 1917, she left Westminster and moved to Oxford to take up a position more in line with her academic training. She became secretary at Barnett

House, a new institution affiliated to the university and situated in the centre of town, that promoted social work among Oxford's disadvantaged. The staff at Barnett House organized lectures and conferences, maintained a library on social and economic problems, ran training courses and undertook local surveys. In many ways it was an ideal post for Barbara, combining her administrative and academic skills, but she felt out of touch with the war effort and after six months her conscience would not let her continue.

Barbara Freire-Marreco at her desk in Barnett House, Oxford, 1918.

In March 1918 she wrote to the director of Barnett House, Sidney Ball, asking to be released from her contract early, 'for more immediate service to the war'. Tens of thousands of men had been killed that month as a result of Germany's Spring Offensive and these recent heavy losses had driven her to act. She did not say what she was planning, although she mentioned the need to replace men in the auxiliary services and in agriculture. In April she told Ball that she was going to

London for interviews and a medical examination. Perhaps she intended to join the Women's Land Army or Queen Mary's Auxiliary Army Corps, which had been recognized for its gallantry during the German Offensive. Her plans did not come to fruition, however. In June her mother died, and this seems to have set her on a different course. She most likely spent the final months of the war working in Westminster again, where she met Robert Aitken.

Aitken was a tall, thin Scottish mathematics teacher. He was aged thirty-six in 1918, three years younger than Barbara. He had started a doctorate in geography at Oxford in 1914, but left the following year to enlist in the army. He served for two years in France, had been wounded twice, and began work in the civil service after his discharge. Like Barbara he was a Spanish-speaker, and before the war he had run a mining-company school in Huelva in southwest Spain. They most likely met in London towards the end of the war when he was working in the Intelligence Department at the Foreign Office. Perhaps their meeting derailed Barbara's plans to embark on more active war work; certainly, when she married him two years later, in April 1920, it signalled an end to her days as a professional academic.

All through the war Barbara had hoped to return to the American Southwest. In the summer of 1919 Hewett's close colleague, John Harrington at the Bureau of American Ethnology in Washington, DC, had offered her a job, but she declined, saying that she could not leave England. This time her thoughts were with Robert as well as with her father. When she wrote to Harrington early the next year she told him, without elaboration, that she and Robert were engaged to be married that April. It

Barbara and Robert Aitken at Saint-Valery-sur-Somme, France, 1924.

was the last time she would be offered a job in the United States, and although she considered visiting to attend conferences, she never went back there again.

After their marriage, the Aitkens lived in a flat in Hampstead and Robert continued to work, unhappily, for the civil service.

He tried more than once to get an academic job, but was hampered by the fact that he had never completed his degree in Edinburgh and the war had interrupted his later studies at Oxford. Barbara was better qualified than her husband, but now her letters focused on his career rather than her own. When he applied for geography lectureships he asked Barbara's old tutor John Myres for references – his own Oxford tutor had died of heart failure during the war. He explained to Myres that their happiness now depended on his leaving the Foreign Office, despite the loss of income. 'You will no doubt think, to some extent rightly, that this is going to be rough luck on Barbara,' Robert wrote, but Barbara appended her own note, insisting it was what she wanted for them both and that '[t]he loss of income would <u>not</u> be an excessive price to pay for suitable work'. Robert felt he was working under 'S.S. conditions' at the Foreign Office, but he had little hope of winning an academic post without a degree or recent teaching experience.

In 1927 he had 'an infernal breakdown' and was unable to work. He resigned from his job the following year. The Aitkens decided to leave London, and moved to the village of Broughton in Hampshire; Barbara wrote to Myres to say how sorry she was to have to give up her involvement with the Folklore Society in London. They spent more and more time in Spain, because Robert was fascinated by Spanish agriculture and was researching the history of the Spanish plough. (Years later, an obituary writer recorded that Aitken's wife, an anthropologist, had worked closely with him, 'particularly in the reporting of ploughs'.) They were a happy, reserved and kindly couple who lived frugally, went to church, read together after dinner, and shared private jokes. When they married, Barbara wrote him love poems:

Kiss me when the spring begins and when the
     autumn closes;
Kiss me for the last white frost, and through dark rain.
Kiss me when the heather's red, and kiss me for the roses.
When you've kissed the seasons out, o kiss them
     round again!

Later in their marriage, she wrote poems about the American Southwest:

How many years?
Thirteen – no fourteen, fifteen long, full years.
A stranger I should come
To those dun roofs I once called 'home'
Better, perhaps, away.
And seldom now I wander, dreaming,
Past houses somehow dim, estranged in feeling,
And wake unsatisfied to English day.

O, just in last night's dream I walked alone,
Hurrying, till some harsh limit should expire,
Hunting through houses where I once had friends,
And found all young, all busy, all unknown:
But at the ditch, where the pueblo ends,
I found the house at last –
Kind clasping arms and voices of the past –
And thought, Here nothing's changed, but all stands fast.
And there sits Filomena by the fire,
And in one moment now she'll turn her head –
But Filomena's dead.

12

All Fire

Maria Czaplicka in Bristol, 1921

On the evening of Friday, 27 May 1921, Maria Czaplicka was alone in her room at the house in Bristol where she lodged when she swallowed five pills of mercuric chloride. It had been six years since her return from Siberia and she was working as a lecturer at Bristol University. She had been busy and seemed happy all week, teaching her students. She had been to a party given by the Geological Society and to an evening debate at the Clifton Ladies' Debating Society. She had joined an excursion to the Redcliffe Caves and stayed that night with the Wills family, members of the great tobacco manufacturing dynasty and major benefactors of the university. The Willses lived at Burwalls, a red-brick, mullion-windowed mansion with views over the Avon Gorge. Maria enjoyed the fine food and wine, the gardens rolling down to the water, the lavish guest quarters and the comforts of central heating, all a far cry from her own modest rooms in the centre of the city.

On the Friday, however, she did not go into work as expected. Her colleagues must have assumed she was unwell. Only later did they find out that she had received news that plunged her into a deep depression.

Maria had been organizing the paperwork for her naturalization as a British citizen, a condition of her application for an Albert Kahn Travelling Fellowship. These private fellowships were open to members of all British universities. Eileen Power, an historian at Girton College, Cambridge, had become the first woman to receive an Albert Kahn fellowship the previous year. Recipients were expected to travel so that 'by the study and comparison of national manners and customs and of the political, social, religious and economic institutions of other countries, such persons may become better qualified to take part in the instruction and education of their fellow-countrymen'. Eileen put it more succinctly when she said they 'gave you £1000 and sent you round the world with instructions to widen your narrow academic mind'.

Maria had pinned her hopes on winning one of these fellowships: it was her ticket back to Siberia. Her position at Bristol University was ending that summer, and she desperately wanted to travel again. The Albert Kahn appointment committee had given her to understand that they would extend the deadline to Tuesday, 31 May so that her application could be considered. Instead, either that Friday morning the 27th or the evening before, she heard that they had awarded the fellowship to somebody else.

Details of the inquest were not made public, but official reports stated that Maria died from heart failure. 'It seems particularly desirable,' the warden of the women's hall at Bristol wrote to Emily Penrose, 'that her acquaintances and the students should not know of the inquest ... In case the news can be kept from Oxford, you will, I know, use your discretion in keeping it quite private.' The mercuric chloride had taken effect ten to fifteen minutes after Maria took the tablets. Her gastrointestinal tract bore the brunt of the attack, becoming severely damaged and haemorrhaging, and causing her intense pain. Her kidneys began to fail, and the massive fluid loss sent her body into shock. By the time the doctors arrived she was bleeding from the mouth and in agony, but there was nothing they could do. They stayed with her until the end, at around midnight. Only when she slipped from consciousness did her body ease, and she seemed to regain awareness a few moments before she died. She was thirty-six years old.

Four days later, on the day Maria had expected to hear about her fellowship, a requiem mass was held at the Pro-Cathedral of the Holy Apostles in Bristol. It was well attended by students, university staff, the vice-chancellor and the Wills family. Henry Balfour attended on behalf of his Oxford colleagues, and the consul-general of Poland travelled from London to represent his country, but the church was filled with local mourners. Maria had lived in Bristol for less than a year, yet she seemed to have 'universally endeared herself to people here – both University and others'. Her life, to those listening to her eulogy at the cathedral, seemed like a remarkable success story, but to Maria it had at times felt like a battle.

On her return from the expedition in autumn 1915, the press had showered her with attention: 'Intrepid Lady Explorer' – '3,000 Miles by Sledge in Siberia' – 'First White Woman Seen by Natives' – 'Brains and Beauty at Oxford' – 'Oxford's Only Woman Lecturer', ran the headlines; and her book *My Siberian Year*, published the following year, had been critically acclaimed both in the press and in various academic journals. It sold well, and another book, *The Turks of Central Asia in History and at the Present Day*, followed in 1918. Her lectureship at Oxford and her job at Bristol were notable achievements, but Helena Deneke, her friend from Lady Margaret Hall, remembered that Chip 'did not settle down and would come back to us for visits. I did not realize how deep was her grief at leaving Oxford and had tried to brace her when she spoke of being inconsolable.'

In these moments, her successes felt precarious and second-rate. The jobs were temporary, and she still had not published the detailed academic account of her Siberian fieldwork that she had always promised and that she was meant to be writing with Henry Hall.

Hall was the ever present absence in Czaplicka's life. They had lived together in London's Torrington Square for five months when they got back from Siberia, in the same lodgings they had shared before their travels. But in February, after delaying his departure for many weeks, Hall left for Philadelphia to take up a position at the university museum there.

He had been offered the job as a way of paying off the debt he had accrued during the expedition. George B. Gordon, the curator of the Philadelphia University Museum, had paid for Hall's trip to Siberia in return for his collecting artefacts in the field, but Hall had proved an unreliable correspondent and had twice asked urgently for more money with little explanation. In April 1915 when he and Czaplicka were nearing the end of their time in Siberia, Gordon received a telegram from Hall asking for another $500 immediately. Hall wrote to him explaining that travel had been more expensive than he had anticipated and the war had increased prices further. He had been forced to draw on his own 'slender' resources, was financially 'crippled', and did not know how he would manage to get home with the artefacts he had collected without Gordon's aid.

Gordon sent the money, but a few months later when Hall was back in London he received another cable, 'accident money lost', asking for a further $250. This time, no letter of explanation followed, and eventually Gordon wrote in exasperation to Czaplicka asking her what had happened. It emerged that Hall had 'lost' his wallet, containing Gordon's money, on a crowded train to Stockholm. The most Hall would say, when he wrote two months later, was that there had been 'an accident not easily explainable in a letter'. He apologised for not writing sooner, blaming 'pressure of work and other anxieties'. He and Czaplicka both said the money had been lost, but Czaplicka also mentioned that she thought it must have been stolen.

Whatever the truth of the matter, with no money Hall was stuck in London with Gordon's artefacts, and the curator had little choice but to send more if he was ever to see his new Siberian material. In January, he informed Hall that he would send him another $250, and also that he would hire him at the museum for two months, at a salary of $100 a month, when he arrived in Philadelphia. The job must have been part of Gordon's plan to reclaim some of his investment in Hall, a man he had never met and who appeared to be rather unreliable.

Hall left England on 12 February 1916, after nearly two and a half years living and working with Czaplicka, and would spend the rest of his unremarkable career at the University of Pennsylvania Museum. The evidence is fragmentary, but it seems that the friends saw each other twice again. The first time was in the spring of 1918. Hall had joined the army and he was able to visit Oxford during a short stay in England while on his way to serve in France. He told Gordon that there was not a great deal of time to do any work during this visit to Oxford, and on his way home, a year later, he wanted to visit Czaplicka again, but there is no record of their having seen each other. Czaplicka's own future was uncertain in 1919.

Her lectureship at Oxford ended that summer, when Leonard Buxton returned from the war to resume his position as demonstrator in physical anthropology. The discrimination women like Czaplicka faced at the university crystallizes sharply when one reads Leonard Buxton's correspondence with John Myres and Arthur Thomson about job opportunities in 1919.

Buxton's position at Oxford was by no means guaranteed at the start of that year, and he was not yet thirty years old, but his tone is affable rather than deferential. He declares his 'profound ignorance' when it comes to anthropology, but points out that he must have a job 'which will at least earn bread and butter'. He meets with various academics to talk about his future: one hints at a fellowship for him down the line; another suggests he join an ethnography survey project. Buxton 'thinks things over'. In his letters to Myres, he 'makes suggestions' as to his future role at Oxford and outlines his own job description in detail. Then, having declared the outlook gloomy at first, Thomson offers Buxton the job. Eventually Buxton is 'inclined' to 'stick to Oxford' after considering his options.

Buxton's cavalier tone attests to the camaraderie he felt with his mentors as a young man. He may have been their junior, but he shared an understanding with them nonetheless. His female colleagues showed none of this casual assurance when corresponding with their tutors. As Thomson wrote to Buxton about his new job, he also informed Maria Czaplicka that her position as a lecturer at the museum was no longer tenable due to lack of funds. The Mary Ewart Trust had ceased financing teaching posts in favour of women's research now that the war was over. Czaplicka must look for work elsewhere.

She tried to find a job in America. In March that year she sat down, pen in hand, to appeal to Franz Boas, a professor at Columbia University and America's leading anthropologist: 'Here I am writing to you again,' she began. 'I would like to make a move now to the U.S.A., where, as I told you, I should like to live.' After eight years based in England, she admitted that moving to the States would require sacrifices. She would have to start all over again, building relationships within the academic community and establishing contacts with publishers; but, she concluded, 'I trust that I may not be quite unsuccessful in the U.S.A., whither personal matters call me.' She was willing, she said, to take a pay cut, as well as starting afresh profession-ally, in order to be in America.

A clutch of the highest-ranking British anthropologists – including Sir James Fraser and Alfred Haddon at Cambridge, Sir Arthur Keith at the Royal College of Surgeons, her three Oxford tutors, and the Regius Professor of Greek at Oxford, Sir Gilbert Murray – wrote references in support of her finding a job in the United States. There was talk of her writing up the results of the Jesup expedition to Siberia, which had taken place twenty years earlier under the leadership of Boas and the American Museum of Natural History in New York, and which had yet to be published. The *Sunday Herald* reported that 'Miss Czaplicka, the only woman lecturer at Oxford, is to go to the States in September, as she has an appointment at Columbia University in New York for a year', but there is no mention of this job anywhere else in Czaplicka's papers and she did not move to New York.

Instead, with no firm opportunities on the other side of the Atlantic she turned her attention to a second Siberian expedition, and in May Marett wrote to Henry Fairfield Osborn, president of the American Museum of Natural History, asking for help funding Czaplicka's next field trip which she was planning to undertake with Henry Hall again. Czaplicka and Hall, he wrote, meant to travel up the River Ob, to the east of the Yenisei, and to 'push right up through the tundra' to the source of the river, conducting a survey of the people and their culture as they went. Hall would find his own funding, Marett continued, but Czaplicka needed £1000: 'She is not well off herself, and her work for our school comes to an end soon.'

Marett signed off wistfully, 'She really is a rather wonderful person.' But Osborn declined his request, and there is no mention of the proposed expedition in Henry Hall's surviving papers.

Unemployed again, in the autumn of 1919 Maria decided to embark on a lecture tour of the States, to meet academics, publicize her work and, presumably, to see Hall. In January 1920 she was in Philadelphia, where Hall now lived, and gave a lecture at the University Museum where he was working. She stayed in the States for three months, touring East Coast cities, giving talks and delighting journalists everywhere she went. She was erudite and perfectly unassuming. The New York *Evening Sun* quipped: '. . . she has such a feminine charm of manner and such a whimsical sense of humor that when she begins to tell you a little of the many things she knows she is promptly forgiven for being so learned'. While a writer for *The World* magazine, expecting to meet someone more masculine, was surprised at how delicate and expressive she was: 'a young woman, laughing much, and never for an instant dull'.

The tour was a public success but a private disappointment. Maria was no further forward when it came to financing a second field trip to Siberia, and her relationship with Hall was, if not over, then just as hopeless as ever. Barbara Freire-Marreco remembered her friend's trip involving 'great fatigue and strain, with little profit except in making new friends for Poland and herself'. She had failed to secure research funding, employment, or a commitment from Hall.

It is hard not to perceive a shadow cast over Czaplicka in 1920. She began the year in America, but by April she was sailing back to England, tired and without work. She went home to Poland that summer, but Warsaw was in the midst of another devastating battle, this time with Soviet Russia. The Treaty of Versailles had established Polish independence in 1919, but a series of border conflicts followed. Czaplicka visited during the decisive Battle of Warsaw and even went to the Bolshevik front. A newspaper correspondent in Warsaw said that she 'pushed her way into the city at a time when everyone else who could had left it'. Again, her home city was lit up at night by the burning of nearby towns and shaken by the incessant firing of shells. Its government buildings had been evacuated and tens of thousands of residents had left, but Czaplicka 'knew no fear' and apparently stayed to see Poland's famous victory and the Red Army's retreat.

She returned to England in the autumn to take up the lectureship at Bristol University, which Arthur Thomson had helped her to get. This was an accomplishment in itself, but it was only for a year and she did not want to leave Oxford. From Bristol she again wrote to Franz Boas at Columbia University:

'I am beginning my life here, but all my heart is in a plan for another expedition to Asia, only I have no funds.'

Her friends were not unduly worried about her state of mind. At Bristol, she was 'always so cheerful and gay'. She talked about writing more books: one on the Cossacks, one on Poland, another on prehistoric art, as well as a collection of her 'ethnological essays' to be published by the Clarendon Press. In March she toured Scotland again, giving lectures in Dundee, Aberdeen and Edinburgh. She was organizing the new School of Anthropology at Bristol and she had impressed her superiors enough for them to arrange for her salary to be doubled. They planned to tell her about her pay rise at the end of May, but she killed herself just a few days before.

On the day she died, Maria was overdrawn by £110; she owed a further £50 to each of two friends; Miss Jennings, who had done some typing and proofreading for her, was owed £20; the lawyers who were dealing with her naturalization application had invoiced her for £30; and various other small accounts, with her doctor and with shops, were outstanding. Maria was due to receive £20 in salary from Bristol University, but until then she had just £3 7s 4d to her name. The strain of maintaining a career that she had left her family in Poland to pursue became too much for her on the evening of 27 May, and there was no one to reason her out of her despair. In a cruel twist of fate, although she may never have known it herself, the Albert Kahn Travelling Fellowship that she had placed all her hopes on getting had been awarded to Leonard Buxton, the man who had returned to his job at Oxford after the war at the same time that she was forced to give hers up.

Among the many friends distressed by Maria's death were her fellow anthropologists from Oxford, Beatrice Blackwood and Barbara Aitken. Years later, Beatrice recalled hearing the news: 'I was, of course, deeply grieved, but not greatly surprised as I knew from experience that she was a very temperamental person, and was apt to become depressed when things went wrong. If no one was at hand to help her through some difficult period, she would see no other way out.' Barbara too recognized the frailties of her 'special and most understanding friend'. Although Chip's death was a 'terrible surprise', she understood that for some time she had complained of feeling ill and exhausted.

In Oxford, Czaplicka had lived in a strong community of academic women that she had not been able to replicate at Bristol. One of her Bristol friends lamented the fact that there had been no room for her at Clifton Hill House, the women's hall at the university: 'I cannot help thinking that if she had been with us, when the news came, it would not have seemed such an overwhelming blow.' Rumour had it that she had not intended to kill herself, but if she had regrets they were too late. Her friends, among them Barbara Aitken, Emily Penrose, Helena Deneke and Robert Marett, met the costs of her funeral, and she was buried in Oxford, her adopted home, according to her expressed wishes.

Three weeks after her death, on 20 June 1921, Henry Hall married an artist called Frances Jones in Philadelphia. When had Hall met Jones? Had he told Czaplicka of their betrothal? Barbara Aitken wrote to him at the end of May to tell him of Maria's death. She had died of 'heart failure', Barbara said, and according to her will he was to receive all her papers relating to their work in Siberia. He replied saying that he would complete Maria's work and publish it, but he never did. Fourteen years later, in 1935, he claimed to be still working on the Siberian material, but he was fired by the Philadelphia University Museum that year as part of a cost-cutting exercise brought on by the Great Depression, and his half-hearted hopes of having the work published there evaporated.

Later enquiries by interested researchers were met with evasion. In the early 1940s, scholars wrote to ask whether he would deposit the material in an archive, to allow others to work on it, but Hall 'did not feel in a very amiable state of mind' and never replied. He resented the museum for dismissing him after twenty years of service, and began drinking excessively. His wife died in 1941, and Hall passed away three years later, having lost all interest in the world around him. When his papers were turned over to the museum, Czaplicka's Siberian notes were not among them.

From the start, Maria Czaplicka's expedition to Siberia was shaped by her friendship with Hall, and the last bittersweet threads of that friendship irrevocably diminished its legacy. No one knows what happened to her papers. A number of researchers have tried to piece together the story of her travels and the exact nature of her relationship with Hall, but there are still more questions than answers. Czaplicka, Marett wrote, 'struck fire out of whatever she touched, her nature being, as it were, itself all fire, a flame too intense for mortal body to support. Too late, her many friends realised that she was living on her organic capital.'

She had relied on other people to ground her at times of anxiety, but on 27 May 1921, in her rooms in Bristol, there was no one to help. She had friends in Oxford, in Poland, in Siberia, and in America, but that night in Bristol she was alone.

13

Did He Ever Darn His Stockings?

Beatrice Blackwood Visits Sydney, 1929

A year after Czaplicka's death, a book was published that would change British anthropology forever. *Argonauts of the Western Pacific* was written by Czaplicka's friend Bronislaw Malinowski, whom she had met as a student at the London School of Economics in 1910.

There are poignant parallels in the lives of Czaplicka and Malinowski. Both Polish, they arrived in England in the same year to study anthropology at the LSE, and both went on to spend the war working in the field. While Czaplicka was strapping herself into a sledge in the Arctic in late 1914, Malinowski was pitching his tent on a tropical island in the Pacific. After the war, as her research gradually faded from memory, Malinowski not only became synonymous with Pacific anthropology, he put Pacific anthropology at the very heart of the discipline.

Czaplicka had played a small part in helping Malinowski get to Melanesia. Like her, he had sought funding from various sources for his fieldwork, and Czaplicka pressed her mentor Robert Marett to help him. Marett needed a secretary for an academic conference that was convening in Australia that summer. After talking with Czaplicka, he agreed to give the job, which included travel expenses paid for by the Australian government, to Malinowski. A few weeks after Czaplicka left London for Russia, Malinowski embarked on his journey to the Antipodes.

Stranded by the war, he spent longer in Australia and Melanesia than he had originally planned. Over the course of more than five years he worked for three months on Mailu Island, off the south coast of New Guinea, then stayed for two longer periods, of eight months and ten months, in the Trobriand Islands to the east of the mainland. In the interim he lived in Australia, not returning to England until 1920. It was Malinowski's research in the Trobriand Islands that became the subject of his seminal *Argonauts of the Western Pacific*.

Malinowski's writing in *Argonauts* was vivid and convincing. 'Imagine yourself suddenly set down,' his book famously begins, 'surrounded by all your gear, alone on a tropical beach close to a native village, while the launch or dinghy which has brought you sails away out of sight.' He presented himself as a lone ethnographer embarking on a rite of passage. His skill lay not simply in his ideas, but in his ability to transport his reader to the Trobriand Islands, and into the very psyche of the Trobriand Islander. He emerged as the unacknowledged hero of his own narrative.

Apparently effortlessly, he transformed the haphazard and piecemeal experiences of a foreigner living for a few months in a strange place into nothing less than an act of academic divination. It was as though he knew the 'essential Trobriander' better than the Trobriander knew him- or herself. His book combined fieldwork data, information about his research process and theoretical argument, creating a story that was seductive and an image of Trobriand society that was irresistibly coherent. It was, at the time, an unmatched achievement, and by the late 1920s *Argonauts* had set a new standard for ethnographic writing.

Malinowski was adept at self-promotion, but he was by no means the first to work alone for a long period of time in the Pacific. Several other young anthropologists had undertaken fieldwork on nearby islands. Gerald Wheeler, a brilliant linguist who had trained at the LSE, worked for ten months in the western Solomon Islands in 1908–9. A New Zealander named Diamond Jenness, who had graduated with an anthropology diploma from Oxford, had spent nine months working in the D'Entrecasteaux Islands, just south of the Trobriands, in 1910. Gunnar Landtman, a Finnish philosopher and anthropologist, had worked for two years, from 1910 to 1912, on Kiwai Island off the south coast of New Guinea, and Arthur Hocart, another Oxford graduate, had spent four years living in Fiji and travelling to islands further east in the Pacific, including Samoa and Tonga.

These men, however, did not publish their research until the late 1920s, after Malinowski's book came out (Landtman lost his field notes in a shipwreck on the way home and had to hire a diver to recover the trunk that contained them). More importantly, they did not share Malinowski's analytical prowess.

Malinowksi's work was part of broader shifts in the anthropological mission. By 1920 there was a concerted move towards research that focused on a single location, rather than collaborative expeditions covering larger regions. A.C. Haddon promoted the 'intensive study of a limited area', and his colleague at Cambridge, W.H.R. Rivers, advocated longer solitary periods of time in the field. Ethnographers, Rivers argued, should learn to speak the vernacular, witness local ceremonies for themselves, and pay special attention to volunteered information rather than relying too much on formal questioning. It was important not to rush in with a preconceived agenda. Rivers prioritized 'sociological' study over and above archaeology, museum collecting, and taking measurements of people's bodies, which was a common way of trying to document racial differences at the time. Anthropologists all travelled with calipers and measuring sticks at the ready to chart people's body types and head shapes, but this work, Rivers pointed out, risked undermining the rapport between the inquirer and their subject. Anthropologists should be less obtrusive and more attentive.

These ideas about field methods were new. Fieldwork was, by its very nature, a multifaceted and unpredictable art, and the urge to gather as much information as possible about other cultures before they were lost to the inevitable 'march of progress' meant that parameters remained broad. Human culture was infinitely various, but the resources available for studying it were slim. For the sake of expediency anthropologists invariably relied on paid informants, as Barbara Freire-Marreco had in New Mexico and Arizona, and often travelled across wide areas with a team of experts, as Maria Czaplicka had chosen to do. Katherine Routledge was by no means unusual in focusing on archaeology as well as ethnography in the field, and all anthropologists came home weighed down with collections of artefacts – including the inevitable clutch of human bones dug up from local grave sites – to stock the shelves of museums back home.

Even fieldwork itself was not compulsory, though it was increasingly popular. It still had the air of an undertaking that was valued for the fact that it happened at all. Some anthropologists spent their careers working in museums or universities, analysing the wealth of data other people had brought back from abroad.

In the interwar years, Malinowski changed all this. If anthropology was already charting its course as a professional field-based study when he worked in the Trobriand Islands, back at the London School of Economics during the 1920s he set out to determine its coordinates more precisely. He insisted that anthropological knowledge had to be generated in the field, not in museums or from books or from other people's reports. He argued that anthropologists must live with the people they studied, in a single community, so they could learn the language and understand the culture by participating in it for a long time, rather than simply visiting for a few weeks before moving on. He self-consciously promoted this form of research as the *only* way to glean useful information about other cultures.

He also insisted that all cultural practices, rituals and beliefs, however strange and irrational they seemed, were actually useful to the people involved. 'Primitive' people were not blindly following protocol or acting unthinkingly or according to instinct, as previous theorists had often assumed. Rather, humans, the world over, were essentially pragmatic. This 'functionalism' seemed 'brilliantly new', and his students joined in a kind of intellectual game of finding the hidden purpose in mysterious foreign customs.

Gifted, prolific, and determined to establish himself as the leader of British anthropology, Malinowski became Reader in the subject at the LSE in 1924 and Professor three years later. He established the University of London as an important centre for anthropology in Europe, and it quickly eclipsed Oxbridge as the place for students to train. He held his pupils in thrall. They felt they were 'striding along intellectual frontiers' with him, and his seminars were legendary. He had a razor-sharp mind and a quick wit, and he encouraged his students to voice their opinions while also questioning his own, creating an atmosphere that was both egalitarian and exacting.

Malinowski's influence was reaching its height just as Maria Czaplicka's friend and protégée, Beatrice Blackwood, set out for the Pacific. In August 1929 she arrived in Australia on her way to Melanesia, where she was planning to spend ten months doing research in the Solomon Islands. 'Sydney is <u>not</u> a place to enter by train,' she recorded bluntly in her diary on 9 August. It was wet and misty when she arrived, and she thought the local restaurants expensive and ordinary. She had a week ahead of her to see the sights, buy supplies for her trip and meet other academics.

The next day, she met fellow Englishwoman Camilla Wedgwood, a friendly, conscientious and dowdy young lecturer in anthropology at the University of Sydney. Wedgwood, who spoke in a clear, clipped, aristocratic voice, had studied at Cambridge under Haddon. Blackwood had never met her before, but they occupied overlapping academic worlds and knew many of the same people. Wedgwood took great care of Blackwood during her stay, taking her out to lunch and dinner and on the ferry to visit the zoo, advising her on local shops and introducing her to all the other anthropologists who were in town that week.

Sydney, it turned out, was humming with brilliant young anthropologists. Raymond Firth, Margaret Mead and Reo Fortune were all in town, and had all recently returned from

Beatrice Blackwood taking a photograph in Yoho National Park, Canada, 1925.

research projects in the Pacific. Firth, a slightly dazed twenty-eight-year-old New Zealander, was the most gracious. He had arrived in Sydney just a few days earlier, having spent fifteen months living on a tiny volcanic island in the Solomons called

Tikopia, and he was suffering from culture shock. He felt afraid of the traffic and the crowds in the city and found the people he met boring and trivial in the wake of island life, but Blackwood thought him charming and he took her shopping and out to dinner. He had just published a book, *Primitive Economics of the New Zealand Maori*, based on his PhD thesis, and Blackwood 'treated herself' to a copy from a Sydney bookshop out of admiration for him.

She also had tea with Margaret Mead, whom she found arrogant and patronizing. Mead was twenty-seven years old, a passionate, assertive American, on her way home from eight months working in Manus, the largest of the Admiralty Islands, off the north coast of New Guinea. She had previously worked on the island of Ta'ū in Samoa. Her first book, *Coming of Age in Samoa*, had been published in the United States while she was away in Manus, and she was hardly aware of the publicity it had generated, which would propel her to the forefront of American life when she got home. Mead shared her ideas about fieldwork with Blackwood in no uncertain terms, and Beatrice later wrote that she 'made me feel very small in Sydney'. Mead's husband Reo Fortune, a New Zealander like Firth, could be just as argumentative as his wife, but Blackwood did nothing more than note the presence of 'Dr Fortune' in her diary.

Watching over the activities of these young academics was Alfred Reginald Radcliffe-Brown – 'R.B.' – the Professor of Anthropology at Sydney University. He was a sophisticated and aloof Englishman, trained at Cambridge, who knew his own mind and liked the sound of his own voice. Now in his late forties, he had spent two years researching in the Andaman Islands in the Bay of Bengal, and his book *The Andaman Islanders*, published in 1922 (the same year as Malinowski's *Argonauts*), had helped to establish his foremost position within the discipline. Unlike Malinowski, though, R.B. expected silent reverence from his students and did not take kindly to being questioned, but his eloquent style and impressive intellect kept them loyal despite an absence of warmth for him personally. Blackwood met with him for 'morning tea' in his office and found him pleasant. He gave her various letters of introduction for her arrival in New Guinea.

Everyone was cordial, but nonetheless Beatrice was an outlier in this group. At forty, she was significantly older than everyone except Radcliffe-Brown, and she came from a different academic background. The traditions of Oxford anthropology, with its broad, museum-based curriculum, seemed archaic to Radcliffe-Brown, Firth, Wedgwood, Mead and Fortune. Its 'triumvirate' of tutors – Marett, Thomson and Balfour – were nearing retirement (Marett and Balfour were in their sixties, Thomson seventy-one), and their philosophy had become outdated. None of them were 'real' anthropologists in the modern sense because they had not done fieldwork. Robert Marett was a classicist by training, Arthur Thomson an anatomist, and Henry Balfour was a museum curator. They were increasingly seen as desk-bound, armchair anthropologists in the Victorian tradition, and easily characterized as more concerned with texts, bones and artefacts than with the social organization of real living people out in the world around them.

The young people Blackwood met in Australia, by contrast, believed in the new philosophical approach to anthropological research. They had almost all attended Malinowski's seminars at the London School of Economics, where they had been encouraged to make a self-conscious move away from the traditions held dear by Oxford's dons. Malinowski loomed large for

Blackwood in 1929. Everyone she met in Sydney talked about *Argonauts of the Western Pacific*, but she had not brought a copy with her. She tried to buy it, but she could not find it on sale anywhere in the city. She wrote to Arthur Thomson asking him to send her a copy but it did not arrive until March 1930 when she was deep into her fieldwork. She had read *Argonauts*, but she now regretted not bringing it with her to keep her 'up to the mark'.

Blackwood had a lot of experience, but in present company it was experience that almost counted against her. She had spent the last two years cataloguing around two thousand human skulls at the Oxford University Museum, exactly the kind of work that her peers in Australia heartily scorned. They had little time for museum collections and thought them at best a diversion, and at worst a distraction. Blackwood *had* worked in the field – she toured North America in the mid-1920s

Beatrice Blackwood with a friend and guide, Mrs Peters, in the United States of America, 1927.

collecting anthropological data – but it was not the 'right' kind of anthropological data. While there, she had worked primarily as a physical anthropologist, visiting institutions such as schools, Native American reservations and hospitals, where she measured people's bodies to chart their racial differences. She covered thousands of miles and visited places for only a week or two at a time.

To her peers in Sydney this was outmoded, even irrelevant, smash-and-grab style research, more concerned with comparative statistics than with a nuanced appreciation of people's everyday habits and beliefs. They dismissed it as being from a different disciplinary era. In short, Beatrice Blackwood had yet to prove her mettle as an anthropologist in the Malinowskian mould. When it came to anthropology like theirs she was a complete novice, and she knew it.

As she set sail from Sydney for New Guinea, armed with a bunch of sweet peas given to her on the quayside by Camilla Wedgwood, Blackwood was plunged into self-doubt; and there was plenty of time during the nine-day journey for her to contrast her own shortcomings with everyone else's achievements. She was travelling on the SS *Montoro*, a small cargo boat loaded with supplies for the islands, and there were only a few other passengers on board. She was sharing a cabin with a young mother and her four-month-old baby, and a missionary nurse who worked in New Britain, an island to the east of mainland New Guinea: 'You can just about swing a kitten … if you're careful and don't have too long a string,' she joked in a letter to Arthur Thomson back in Oxford.

The nurse told her that she should buy a full medical kit with surgical needles, syringes, lancets and wire for stitching, because the New Guineans would rely upon her for medical help. Beatrice immediately berated herself for not having any medical or midwifery training: 'I suppose I ought to have thought of it but I didn't anticipate having to do surgery!' This, on top of all the research advice she had received in Sydney, left her feeling overwhelmed. 'Talking with this girl and with Margaret Mead has left me terribly depressed about my fitness to cope with this job. I've bitten off more than I can chew this time and no mistake.'

Everyone had told her that the unremitting heat and humidity in the tropics, coupled with isolation from peers, left one 'slack' and made it easy to miss important details. She started to doubt both her practical skills and her academic potential, wishing, again, that she had packed a copy of Malinowski's *Argonauts* to help her prepare for what lay ahead.

It is little wonder that she was nervous. She later quipped that her instructions on leaving Britain had amounted to little more than 'Find an island somewhere in the Pacific with the least possible amount of contact with white people, and go and live in it.' Her remit was broad. She had been funded by the Committee for Research on the Problems of Sex, based in Washington, DC (the same body that would later fund Alfred C. Kinsey's famous research into sexual behaviour in the United States). She was charged with studying marriage, sexual practice, pregnancy, childbirth and adolescence in the Bismarck Archipelago, but exactly which island she should focus on, and how she should go about gathering information once she arrived, was not specified. It was left to her to identify a suitably remote community where she could safely work, and then find something astute to write about it.

On her way to New Guinea and throughout her time there, Blackwood felt great pressure to come up with something meaningful to say about her research. Anthropology, after Malinowski, was presented as a scientific exercise, but it was essentially an interpretative subject. It required an ability to see through everyday activities and reveal their deeper meaning: this was the 'ethnographer's magic', a kind of academic insight that could seem hopelessly elusive when your greatest challenge was to follow basic conversations in an unfamiliar language.

She had Malinowski's most recent book with her – *The Sexual Life of Savages in North-Western Melanesia* – but every time she read it she lost all her confidence. It seemed as though he had said all there was to say about Melanesian society and she felt 'overshadowed by him all the time'. To prove herself she needed to find a new perspective, or aspects he had not covered in his books, but she thought he had discussed everything. What is more, he had discussed everything brilliantly. '[H]e seems to have a broad grasp of fundamental principles which I lack, and can theorise about things which to me remain facts.' In these circumstances, working alone in a strange culture, for a relatively short time, Blackwood wondered whether she would ever discover some magic of her own in New Guinea.

She arrived in Rabaul, then the capital of the Mandated Territory of New Guinea, on 26 August 1929. The island had first been divided by colonial powers when the Dutch formally annexed the western half, now known as Western New Guinea, in 1828. The eastern half was further divided in 1884, when Germany established a protectorate in the north and Britain did the same in the south. British New Guinea then became Papua, a Territory of Australia, in 1906, and German New Guinea became the Mandated Territory of New Guinea, also under Australian administration, in 1920.

Rabaul was a pretty, small but rapidly developing, outpost town with around fifteen hundred non-native residents. Set into a curved bay below a volcano, the wharves and warehouses bustled with trading companies who serviced the needs of Australian government administrators, plantation owners, and miners who came to the Territory in search of gold. In town, roads crossed the main street at right-angles and were lined with flowering trees: Blackwood listed African tulips, mangoes and 'all sorts of palms, pawpaw and betel nut' in her diary. She was surprised at the number of motorcars, and bicycles ridden by New Guineans in lap-laps (loincloths made from European cloth). Rabaul boasted a post office, two banks, two big stores, a cinema, a dispensary, various watering holes and hotels, as well as government offices, a botanic garden, tennis courts and a sports ground, although there would be no electricity until 1932.

She stayed in Rabaul for a few days, seeing the sights and 'talking shop' with the government anthropologist stationed there, Ernest W.P. Chinnery. Chinnery was an Australian administrator who had been a patrol officer in Papua before the war. War service had led him to England, where he went on to study for the diploma in anthropology at Cambridge under Haddon, who became his friend and mentor. In 1920, Chinnery and his English wife Sarah moved back to Papua, and in 1924 'Chin' became government anthropologist in the Mandated Territory of New Guinea, stationed in Rabaul. The Chinnerys had four small daughters and lived in a bungalow on Malaguna Road, which ran parallel to the bay, with a beautiful garden overlooking the harbour. Chinnery's duties included training district officers and cadets in anthropological matters, and surveying different tribal groups across the Territory. He would ultimately decide where Blackwood worked.

Chinnery met her boat at the wharf and drove her to her hotel in his car. He was a generous host, but he was reluctant to give her permission to work anywhere too isolated. She had hoped to go to the Tanga and Feni Islands on the north coast of New Ireland. She also talked to Chinnery about the isolated Mortlock Islands, but he decided she should go to Buka, in the Solomon Islands, instead. Chinnery placed all the anthropologists who visited New Guinea, assigning villages to Mead, Fortune, Blackwood and, later, Wedgwood. His priority was Blackwood's safety, which meant that she could not go anywhere too remote. A boat sailed between Rabaul and Buka every six weeks, which made it a good location from Chinnery's point of view.

At first she was disappointed not to be going further afield, but she soon entered into the spirit of the adventure, learning pidgin and finding out what she could about local culture from people she met in Rabaul. She had some time to fill – the next boat to Buka was not due to depart for almost a month. When she learned that another anthropologist, Hortense Powdermaker, was working in neighbouring New Ireland where boats travelled more frequently, she decided to make a surprise visit.

Powdermaker was a single-minded, straight-talking American in her early thirties, who had met Malinowski as a graduate student at the London School of Economics and been persuaded by him to study for a doctoral degree. She had, by her own admission, stuck with anthropology simply because she had liked the people she met in London and could not think of anything she would rather be doing instead. For the past four months she had been living in Lesu, a village of 230 residents on the east coast of New Ireland. It was breathtakingly beautiful, with long, gleaming white coral beaches bordering thick tropical vegetation, which concealed the settlement of sago-leaf huts. There was only one road, and Lesu was a ninety-mile drive from the wharf. When Beatrice Blackwood appeared, Powdermaker was astonished – and delighted – at the arrival of another female anthropologist. Blackwood stayed with her for ten days.

Powdermaker talked herself hoarse for the first few days, she was so glad to have someone to share in her work. She helped Blackwood learn pidgin and gave her practical tips about village life, including how to make bread with coconut yeast and how to develop photographs in the dark late at night. In the evenings they walked among the fireflies and sat on Powdermaker's veranda listening to the villagers tell stories around a hurricane lamp.

Now that Beatrice could finally be part of village life, her confidence returned. Reading books had made her anxious, but in Lesu she began to enjoy herself. She was full of admiration for Hortense, and wrote to Thomson, 'I wish I may be as successful. I'm eager to get to work at my own little bit but as I have to wait for transport anyway I'm lucky to have this chance of seeing it done and of getting away into the bush.' They swam in the sea before breakfast, walked around the village together, and Beatrice started to learn about local family politics and the influence of the Methodist and Catholic missions on religious practice in Lesu. There were tombstones in the cemetery, and the villagers were already practising their dances for Christmas, but despite the infiltration of Christian traditions Blackwood filled her diary with the detail of an unfamiliar culture. Everything was new and of note, from the layout of Powdermaker's two-room hut and the design of the hollow log drums people played when they danced, to the pigs and dogs running loose around the village. She watched as her new friend offered sticks of tobacco in return for telling stories, and sat with elderly men and women to work out their genealogies. She began to feel that she could do this job, after all.

Malinowski had established fieldwork as an academic rite of passage for young anthropologists, and working in his shadow, Blackwood and Powdermaker were among the first professionals to see their own fieldwork as a form of initiation. There is not the same self-consciousness in the travels of Barbara Freire-Marreco, Katherine Routledge, Maria Czaplicka or Winifred Blackman. Of course, their work changed them and had the potential to secure their academic reputations, but the effects were cumulative and the framework for success was still in flux. Fieldwork did not have to be solitary, stationary or prolonged. They could choose to travel with colleagues, move around from place to place, or visit a community for just a few months at a time. The parameters were fluid and the kind of knowledge that was generated in the field varied from person to person.

By the late 1920s, fieldwork had become more clearly defined; it had the power to transform you from a student into a prophet, someone who had been to other worlds and come back with visionary insights into the human condition. It was something you did on your own, in a far away place, for at least a year. It was lonely, haphazard and fleeting, but in the right hands it could make you immortal. To pull it off required both intellect and courage, but also considerable creative skill, because fieldwork could only be deemed successful once it had been convincingly transformed into a book. The achievement lay not simply in grasping the nuances of a foreign society in a relatively short space of time, but in writing something coherent and revelatory about it afterwards.

Powdermaker remembered feeling envious of her fellow

students at the LSE who had done fieldwork and already had 'a people' of their own whom they could talk about with authority. It was an initiation rite that gave power and a voice to those who had successfully completed it.

Now that fieldwork had assumed this status in the discipline, Blackwood felt huge pressure to succeed in Melanesia, and often doubted herself. 'Did he ever darn his stockings?' she once asked in good-humoured exasperation while pondering Malinowski's masterpiece. Needles and thread did not make it into academic monographs, and neither did feelings of depression and inadequacy, or government officials and missionaries, or the myriad ways in which anthropologists, and the people they studied, depended on the colonial infrastructure. There was no truly untouched community where an anthropologist could safely work, nor was there a completely coherent, self-contained story to be told that revealed the timeless essence of a society. Malinowski was a master storyteller. He was a conjurer and a theoretician, and every anthropologist's career now relied on these skills.

The idea of writing any book at all after only a few months in the field understandably filled Beatrice Blackwood with horror – '[i]n about twenty years' time I might be capable of doing so . . .' – but her sojourn with Powdermaker and 'seeing it done' had restored her confidence, and by the time she set sail for her 'own little bit' of Melanesia on 21 September 1929, she was full of romantic optimism. From the boat she wrote with good humour to Thomson: 'I get dumped at Buka Passage on Wednesday evening or Thursday morning with all my gear, and I expect I shall recall Malinowski's description in the "Argonauts" of his feelings in like case.'

14

I Shall Wish I Could Go Back Again

Beatrice Blackwood in the
Solomon Islands, 1929

Beatrice Blackwood felt as though she was on a film set when she landed on Petats, her tropical island in the Pacific, on 30 September 1929. The sea was smooth and very blue, and home to flying fish that came close in to shore. The land was flat and well wooded, with sandy shell beaches and huts made from mangrove poles and palm leaves.

The locals wore lap-laps and went bare-chested, and their children played in canoes and dipped coconut husks in the water; they crowded around her and shrieked in delight when she gave out balloons, which they had never seen before. She walked around the village, talking to people as best she could with only a few words of their language, and watched the women making baskets and the men fishing and mending boats. She began exchanging sticks of tobacco and metal knives for stone axes and shell money, which she planned to take back home to Henry Balfour at the Pitt Rivers Museum. At night the only sounds were of frogs croaking and grasshoppers chirping.

Petats is one of a string of coral islets fringing the west coast of Buka, one of the most northerly islands of the Solomons. It is very small, covering an area of about fifty acres, but several hundred people lived there at the time of Blackwood's stay. They relied on canoes, and traded fish caught in the lagoons for taro, a root vegetable grown by their neighbours on larger islands. There were no other colonial residents on the island, and for the first few days Blackwood was delighted to be working there and eager to make a good impression on the villagers. In a matter of weeks, however, the idyllic scenery had lost its lustre and her mood had soured.

The warning signs were there from the start. There was an active Methodist mission stationed across the lagoon, two coconut plantations on nearby islands owned by 'white folk', and two nurses, Sister Vivian and Sister Elizabeth, who visited Petats regularly. Mr Cropp, the missionary, claimed that he did not interfere in the lives of the locals, but the longer Blackwood stayed, the more she realized that hardly any traditional ceremonies had survived – because, as the villagers explained to her in pidgin, 'Mission e capsize altogether fashion belong before.' The people she met went to church every evening and twice on Sundays. They no longer practised their old rituals associated with launching canoes, or killing pigs, or celebrating puberty rites. When they danced, they no longer dressed up, and all their marriage customs had been modified. They seemed ashamed of their own culture. At first Blackwood hoped the older residents would at least describe their earlier traditions for her, but they were reluctant to talk in case she told the mission people.

Within a few weeks she was so concerned about the impact of the mission that she was wondering whether she should move elsewhere, and after two months at Petats she was raging with frustration and resentment. Chinnery, the government anthropologist, had fobbed her off on a 'soft, safe place', she realized now. In November she visited another village, Kieta, on the other side of neighbouring Bougainville Island, trekking into the hills to meet the people who lived there. This left her resenting Petats even more. '[Kieta] is the sort of place I ought to be living in, not with this hymn-singing, tale-hearing mission-ridden bunch, who are ashamed of their own culture and tell you they know better now when you try and find out anything,' she fumed.

The problem was that she had limited time. She had already spent two months in Petats and was due to begin her journey home in July the following year. If she moved to a different village now she would have to start all over again, meeting new people and learning a new language, and she did not want to 'make a mess of both jobs' by not giving enough time to either. For more than a month she was paralysed by indecision. One day she would resolve to stay 'and make the best of a bad job', the next she was determined to find somewhere else. 'I realise more and more painfully what a fatal mistake I made in settling here,' she wrote to Arthur Thomson. It was the last straw when, in December, the mission announced they were going to open a new school in Petats. Two weeks later, with enough provisions packed for a month, Blackwood left and travelled north to the village of Kurtachi, which would become her primary field site.

Kurtachi was on the north coast of Bougainville and its position, on top of a cliff with a sheer drop down to a small beach below, meant it was not easily accessible by water and relatively iso-lated. The village headman was conservative, so more of their traditional customs had survived. There were a few isolated copra plantations on Bougainville, but none nearby, and the only other colonial resident was the district officer who lived ninety miles away at the other end of the island, and rarely visited.

Kurtachi was one of a string of villages on the cliff edge bordered by thick jungle behind. Beyond, the government road ran around the north shore. All the villages lay between the road and the sea.

Some of the huts sat on top of the cliff, and others, where there was enough flat land, were on the shore below. Notched logs, set into the steepest parts of the cliff, acted as steps. The huts were arranged in one or two closely set lines, with a clear space left in between for dances. They were made from thatched sago-palm leaves, which arched on either side almost to the ground. Single-file tracks led through the bush – an 'almost impenetrable tangle of large trees, small trees, shrubs, and rank undergrowth, well garnished with thorny creepers and hanging vines' – from village to village, and out to the taro gardens that were the villagers' main source of livelihood. The men had to dig new gardens after every taro crop so as to allow the soil to lie fallow for several years, and much of their time was taken up clearing the forest for cultivation. The women planted and tended the crops, which included coconut, banana, breadfruit, canarium nuts and almonds as well as taro, and the men caught fish from their canoes.

The jungle was 'all too green' according to Blackwood and not particularly colourful, but a few bright red and blue parrots and 'dazzling white' cockatoos flew about. There were opossums, and flying foxes that kept her awake by barking all night. Frogs and grasshoppers joined in the nightly chorus, and pigs and dogs wandered freely around the village. Inside the huts, there was no furniture other than beds made from wooden planks set on logs. Cooking pots and coconut shells, used to store water, lay on the bare earth floors, and valuable possessions like knives and medicine bundles were stowed in the roof rafters.

One hundred and thirty six people lived on Kurtachi when Blackwood worked there, although there were almost always visitors from other villages staying. There was a local Catholic mission teacher too, but Blackwood thought him 'harmless' since, although some people went to mass every day, they were largely indifferent to his teaching. They lived a life 'full of small but absorbing interests', and despite having to work hard at times to subsist off the land, they were left plenty of leisure time to 'lounge about the place' and gossip. She found everyone friendly and keen to talk to her about their way of life.

After her first week, Blackwood declared that she had learned nearly as much in a few days at Kurtachi as she had during her entire three months at Petats, and a few weeks later she went back up the coast to get the rest of her belongings. It took her two days to hike back, with a band of carriers. 'Everything I have here has been carried on the heads of women chiefly – but the biggest on a pole between two men – up five miles of overgrown forest track very far from level.' Against all of Chinnery's advice, she had moved further out of reach of colonial society.

She was cross with Chinnery for, in effect, belittling her and her work by sending her to Petats, but he had acted as the colonial community expected him to, for Blackwood was up against deep-seated fears surrounding women working alone in New Guinea.

*

The few white women who lived in the Territory had almost all arrived as the wives of government officials, businessmen or missionaries. Their role was to support their husbands and adhere to the particular social codes of colonial society, which were formal and traditional. They lived in a sharply segregated society. In Rabaul there was a large population of Asians, who had emigrated under the Germans and lived exclusively in the district known as Chinatown. They carried out much of the town's construction work, owned 'trade stores' and provided services for the 'Europeans' (a term used colloquially to describe both Australian and European residents). New Guineans occupied the lowest rung of society, working as indentured servants in houses and hotels, and as labourers on the wharf, on plantations and in the mines.

When Blackwood arrived in Rabaul she encountered the rituals of racial segregation in the colonial outpost town for the first time: '[T]he little boys are called "monkeys", the men are all "boys",' she explained in her diary, and noted that she was always attended by 'boys', who served her meals, carried her luggage, and waited outside her hotel room until dark in case she needed anything.

New Guineans were treated as innately inferior. They were believed to be simple-minded at best and brutish at worst. Their village life seemed lazy, their material culture undeveloped, their religious beliefs were classed as pagan, and they were usually assumed to be untrustworthy and immoral. Many Europeans believed that New Guinean men were subject to animal-like sexual urges and posed a particular threat to white women. One or two minor, isolated, and non-sexual incidents had been ambiguously reported in the local newspapers over the years, which had incited public concern. In 1926, the governor of neighbouring Papua, Hubert Murray, had introduced the White Women's Protection Ordinance, which made the rape of a European woman by a Papuan man a crime punishable by death. But far from making colonial residents in Papua feel more secure, it provoked a kind of hysteria, despite no actual reports of sexual assaults by local men.

There was a belief that women had to take some responsibility for mitigating the situation, since New Guinean men could hardly help their base instincts. Colonial residents frowned upon 'the younger generation of white women' who were thought to be too familiar with their servants. Expatriate women were expected to conduct themselves 'carefully' and ensure they had a positive influence on their staff at all times. There were two popular, and completely unproven, lines of argument. The first was that women might provoke attacks through imprudent behaviour; and the second was that traditional relationships between employers and employees, which were well established on the plantations, had been eroded by the growth of urban life and recent arrivals to New Guinea were not as strict in performing their superior role when it came to the locals. In these circumstances, professional single women were viewed with particular suspicion. Indeed, some people thought they were asking for trouble. Anthropologists like Blackwood, who actively shunned the colonial community to live on their own in remote villages, had practically taken leave of their senses.

Female anthropologists were certainly a headache for Ernest Chinnery, who had to find suitable field sites where they could work safely. A few weeks before Blackwood arrived at Rabaul, he had written to a colleague in England: '. . . if any more lady anthropologists are thinking of coming out here you had better suggest that they bring a husband with them. I know of no place where a woman can work without fear of molestation from the natives.' Blackwood was only the second unmarried female anthropologist, after Hortense Powdermaker, to arrive in the Territory, but Chinnery found his responsibilities towards them a burden, nevertheless.

He had sent Hortense Powdermaker to Lesu because it meant that he could keep an eye on her during his regular patrols through the area, and he and another male anthropologist working nearby, Gregory Bateson (later to become a leading academic in America), had stayed with her for the first two weeks until she was settled. Powdermaker had wanted to work amongst the Mafulu in the mountains of central New Guinea, but Chinnery had written to her in Sydney advising her – 'which meant commanding' – not to go there as it would be difficult to transport her and her luggage through the bush. Later, she learned that the government had feared for her safety in such an isolated place, and was anxious about its responsibility for her as the first woman to work there. She felt she had no choice but to accept Chinnery's decision to send her to Lesu. Although at times she 'yearned romantically for an "untouched" people' and thought of moving to a more remote island, she came to realize that the influence of colonial society in Lesu was relatively superficial and her research was worthwhile.

On the boat from Sydney to Rabaul, Powdermaker had spent much of her time trying to 'escape from the women's neverending tales about the danger of being raped by native men'. None of her fellow passengers had any interest in Melanesian culture, and she had dismissed their concerns as ignorant chatter. Nevertheless, she did not object when Chinnery handpicked two servants from Rabaul to travel with her and attend her while she lived in Lesu, and when he visited her she enjoyed his company. About once a month she walked three and a half miles to have tea with Mrs Gosse, the wife of a plantation owner, to talk about clothes and enjoy inconsequential gossip, and when she was invited to a party by the district officer she was thrilled at the chance to escape her daily routine and put on an evening dress. She never felt in danger, and she could have worked in a more remote location, but she certainly did not mind the encroachment of colonial life.

When Camilla Wedgwood was preparing to do fieldwork in Melanesia in 1932, Chinnery discussed her field site with everyone but Wedgwood herself. He ruled out various options because, as he reported to Haddon, 'the white women didn't like the idea of Camilla being alone in the villages'. It seemed that the whole community had a say in where she should work. A plantation owner eventually suggested Manam Island, and later, while on a visit to Sydney, Chinnery 'yarned' about it with Raymond Firth, and the two of them agreed that Manam would be the best option. The question of where to place female anthropologists was clearly a popular topic for discussion, but when the researcher in question arrived in town she was presented with Chinnery's decision as a fait accompli.

There is no record of any female anthropologist in Melanesia being sexually threatened. The expatriate community's concerns were born of prejudice and paranoia, but Wedgwood and Powdermaker dutifully accepted Chinnery's instructions. Wedgwood considered him a 'great friend', and Powdermaker reconciled herself to her work in Lesu. Beatrice Blackwood, on the other hand, had deeply resented Chinnery's decision to send her to Petats and defied his orders. She had little time for any 'Europeans' in New Guinea.

Blackwood's letters are littered with disparaging remarks about the expatriate community. 'I do most heartily wish I need not see another white person till it's time to go home,' she wrote. 'The missionaries and the planters and the Government officials are all at each other's throats and I have to keep on good terms with all of them! Damn them all!' She avoided them as much as possible, and did not go down to meet the boats when they arrived bringing mail and supplies to the island. When, on rare occasions, someone visited her, she felt imposed upon and intensely irritated. She did not miss the comforts of Rabaul, insisting: '[T]here is not a single white person in the whole Mandated Territory with whom I have any desire to exchange a single word.' She thought that most of them were ignorant, small-minded, or common 'scoundrels' in any case and she simply wanted to be left alone with her 'natives'.

The clothes she wore signalled her status as an outsider. Expatriate women in New Guinea wore formal dress and put on their hats and gloves for tea, but Blackwood wore loose cotton shirts and breeches, which were more practical for her work. After nine months in the field, her clothes were wearing thin so she decided to convert one of her skirts into working breeches, but sewing was not her strong point. 'I regret my misspent youth,' she wrote to Thomson, 'when I ran away and hid, in order to read *Robinson Crusoe* or *The Swiss Family Robinson*, instead of attending the dressmaking lessons my mother was so anxious to give me.' She considered wearing a lap-lap but, she explained to Thomson, it took a lifetime to learn how to keep one on, and the locals expected her to dress differently from them in any case. Beatrice Blackwood certainly did not look like other European women, and at first the native police laughed at her 'rough, useful clothes', but they soon came to admire her for her resourcefulness and knowledge. She looked unconventional, one patrol officer remembered, but she 'didn't seem to care about it'.

Blackwood may have made up her own rules as far as dress was concerned, but when it came to her research she tried to follow the example of Bronislaw Malinowski as closely as possible. In Sydney, with Raymond Firth's help, she had written up a 'Plan of Fieldwork' – 'after Malinowski' – which included the kind of information she should record. She was to make a plan of the village and of a typical house, draw a map of the island, keep a list of all the payments and exchanges she made with the locals, and record as much genealogical information as possible. She was to write a daily diary, keep tabular information on local events, and take as many photographs as possible.

Beatrice Blackwood was a conscientious fieldworker who enjoyed her daily routine. The villagers were friendly and pleased that a European wanted to understand their culture. Each morning she breakfasted, then walked around the village, saying hello to people on their verandas. They invariably invited her to join a fishing or a hunting trip, or she would go with the women to work in their taro gardens.

Their way of life was traditional, but Kurtachi was far from untouched by international trade: European goods were being used in remote villages like this by the 1920s. The villagers had steel knives and hatchets. The people she met showed great disdain for the older generations who used stone knives – everyone thought they were mad for not using metal. There were still some old stone axes, but they were now used to sharpen knives, or as weights, or hammers for cracking nuts, or else they were just left lying about. Blackwood picked up disused stone tools from the ground, paid for them with sticks of tobacco, and packed them up for Balfour in Oxford. Similarly, bows and arrows were scarce, and few people knew how to make them any more. Lap-laps had almost entirely replaced grass skirts, and only a few older men in the remote mountain regions still wore the traditional skirts. She came across some mass-produced bottles, boxes and bowls in the village, a couple of hurricane lamps without any paraffin, and a few of the houses had doors with metal hinges. On the other hand, only one or two men shaved with metal razors, most of them still used shell razors instead.

Blackwood employed a 'cook-boy' from Petats. She may not have had much in common with other Europeans living in New Guinea, but she needed a servant. All anthropologists working in Melanesia had servants. Powdermaker employed a married couple to run her house in Lesu, and Margaret Mead – or rather, Mrs Fortune and her husband – working on Manus Island had been supported by a houseboy, a head cook (sixteen years old), a deputy head cook (thirteen), a 'kitchen knave' (twelve), two smaller boys who helped out, two sixteen-year-old girls who did their laundry, and a woman helper and informant called Main. After a few weeks on Manus, Mead reported in good humour, '[T]he child household was in good running order. No one had more than a minimum of work to do, everyone was gay and happy, serious about their tasks, running away to run canoe races while I slept in the early afternoon.'

In Kurtachi, there was enough work to keep Blackwood's cook, Ross, busy during the mornings and evenings, while he had the afternoons to himself. He collected rainwater from the tank at the side of the house, chopped wood for the stove – made from two paraffin tins with the tops cut off – did

Blackwood's laundry and ironing, heated water for her daily bath in a galvanized-iron bucket, cooked her meals and washed the dishes. If it had been particularly wet for a few days, he took out all her belongings and spread them in the sun to dry. Anything made of leather had to be rubbed with Vaseline because the tropical humidity turned everything mouldy.

She may have seemed eccentric to some expatriates, but Blackwood was in no danger of 'going native'. She could not stomach the boiled taro that everyone ate, 'surely the starchiest stuff in the world', and declared that if she ate as the locals did 'it would soon reduce me to a state of inefficiency'. Ross baked her bread using coconut yeast, and she ate bacon and eggs with toast and marmalade for breakfast, washed down with a cup of coffee. In the evenings she dined on fish soup, pigeon soup if Ross had shot a bird, or cheese and eggs, with beans and tomatoes from her garden. She had brought tea and biscuits with her, and seeds from England for sowing, but she usually ate the local vegetables, 'most of which taste like spinach'.

Soon the thrill of adventure gave way to the familiarity of daily tasks and she settled into a routine. She worked in the gardens or went fishing on the reef with the women. She typed up notes outside her hut, tended to the villagers' minor wounds and illnesses, sat on 'various verandahs' listening to the day's gossip, and joined in opossum hunts and excursions.

Back at home, friends worried about her safety. In Oxford, Arthur Thomson feared she might be in danger or unable to cope. His letters do not survive, but Blackwood's replies were dismissive of his concerns. In one, she told him not to worry about sharks; in another she explained that she did not want a companion because they would probably quarrel and she could look after herself. 'Your constant references to the dangers and discomforts I am supposed to be experiencing embarrass me greatly. Fain would I have a few of either if by so doing I could enhance the value of my work.'

Blackwood was fearless. In July, she convinced some of the Kurtachi men to accompany her to villages on the west coast of the island that were deemed 'uncontrolled', or outside the government's administrative area. Chinnery would never have allowed it. There were regular reports of fighting between groups living in these regions and it was considered dangerous for a visitor to venture into areas where there was no patrol or good relations between administrators and the villagers. Her local friends only agreed to take her because she was a woman and would not be considered a threat or suspected of being a government representative – making this 'the first time in my life that my sex has been anything but a disadvantage to me'. She visited several villages where the inhabitants had never seen a white person before, but she never recorded any animosity from them. She never had any reason to doubt that she was perfectly safe. She did suffer from anxieties, but none were about practical matters, only about her academic work.

While she was in the Solomon Islands Blackwood repeatedly read Malinowski's books, and Margaret Mead's *Coming of Age in Samoa*, to remind her of 'points I might be missing'. Whenever she did so, she was plunged into depression. She felt the need to find a new aspect to life in the Pacific, something novel and revelatory about their society, but she could not think of anything. Malinowski seemed to have already said everything there was to say about Melanesian culture. She lamented more than once that whereas he had had three years in the field, she had had less than one; and that while he was a master theoretician and 'a perfect genius at languages', she had – she said, with characteristic humility – 'some facility for picking up enough of the language to carry on a casual conversation'. In her darkest moments she felt that her time was running out before it had even begun, and all she could do was what Mead, Malinowski and Powdermaker had done before her.

Her emotions constantly shifted, however, and at other times she was upbeat. The longer she spent in Melanesia, the more she saw through the bluster of the other anthropologists she had met in Sydney on the way out. Margaret Mead bore the brunt of her wrath. 'Personally I disliked the woman intensely,' she wrote to Thomson. 'For one thing – a person who spends six months in a place (during one month of which I afterwards discovered she lived with a white woman nursing a sprained ankle) – and then says she speaks the language perfectly and knows all about the natives – always makes my hair stand on end.'

Beatrice Blackwood sensed the element of artifice in the anthropological endeavour, which required you to craft something consistent and eternal out of an experience that was brief, unpredictable and incomplete. She was haunted by the things she might be able to say, if only she could see them clearly enough.

In April, she learned that an initiation ceremony – involving sacred *upi*, a kind of hat worn by adolescent boys – that she had been hoping to see would not take place until July, when she was due to return to England. She was disappointed, especially as she suspected it might be the last such ceremony ever performed, since no new *upi* were to be given out and the younger generation were now against wearing them. She wrote to Oxford and managed to extend her stay for an extra three months, but the villagers were evasive whenever she asked about it. In August she resorted to 'bribing and threatening' in an effort to get them to stage it before her departure. Someone told her that the chief responsible for scheduling the ceremony lived in a remote village in the mountains and was determined not to hold it until she had left. In the end, she delayed her leaving for as long as possible, but to no avail. 'If these blighters would only get on with that ceremony I wouldn't mind – but they are just fooling around,' she wrote in exasperation.

Blackwood never did see the *upi* ceremony, but she left Bougainville in October 1930 feeling philosophical nonetheless. She felt that she had done her best – as well as anyone could do under the circumstances. She knew she had only scratched the surface, but she also knew that she had gathered valuable anthropological information. Now all she needed to do was turn it into a good book.

She travelled home via Australia, New Zealand, Hawaii and America, meeting colleagues and museum curators at every stop, but all the socializing made her homesick. 'I just want to have tea and cherry cake with you beside a cosy fire in the Department and talk shop,' she wrote to Thomson. 'And you will ask me lots of questions I can't answer and I shall wish I could go back again and find out.'

15

Weighted Against Women

Katherine Routledge Is Taken
to Ticehurst House, 1929

In June 1928, as Beatrice Blackwood began to plan her trip to Melanesia, Katherine Routledge was inviting the press into her home. Twelve years had passed since her return from Easter Island. She had inherited considerable wealth after the death of her mother and was living in a large Regency house at Hyde Park Gardens in London, which she had filled with expensive furniture and art and fitted with a modern kitchen and bathrooms. It was in one of these bathrooms that she was 'camping out'. She had dismissed her servants, thrown out her husband Scoresby, cancelled all tradesmen's deliveries, locked the doors, and set up home in the bathroom. Here she had installed a table and chair, and a small stove for cooking. She slept in the bathtub.

Katherine was in the midst of a desperate battle for her independence. Scoresby had secured a series of High Court orders against her claiming she was no longer of sound mind: first to freeze her assets, then to give himself sole access to a portion of her money, and finally to take possession of her home. In desperation she barricaded herself in. 'I am taking this action as a protest on behalf of women,' she declared. 'The administration of the law today seems to me to be heavily weighted against women. If an attempt is made to force an entrance into my home I shall not resist, though I shall not admit them voluntarily.' Her marriage had fallen apart and now her freedom was under threat.

Katherine and Scoresby had arrived back from Easter Island in 1916 armed with field notes, maps and drawings, and set about presenting their findings to the waiting academic community. Katherine led the charge. She gave interviews, joined the Folklore Society, spoke at the annual meeting of the British Association for the Advancement of Science, and at the Royal Geographical Society, which had admitted female fellows for the first time only in 1913.

The secretary of the RGS had initially assumed that Scoresby would deliver the Routledges' paper. Scoresby was quick to put the matter right: 'I gather from my wife that I failed to make my wishes clear . . . Mrs Routledge will address the Society on the subject of Easter Island and not me.'

When the day came, Katherine impressed her audience. Sir Hercules Read, one of the most prominent archaeologists in the country, stood up to declare: 'If any excuse were wanted for admitting ladies to the Fellowship of this Society – I do not think that any excuse is wanted, for it has been demonstrated to-night that it was a very good move.' He had never heard a lecture at the Society given with such clearness, he said, one that took the entire audience on the journey as though they were living it themselves, and he marvelled at the 'extraordinary mass of evidence' the Routledges had accumulated on their expedition. The president of the RGS, Douglas Freshfield, thanked Katherine warmly. He had planned to say, having read her 'masterly' paper beforehand, 'I do not think we have ever had a lecture which has dealt with its subject in a more capable manner and one which has held more closely the attention of the audience,' but he thought better of it and crossed the sentence out in his notes, perhaps not wanting to appear too enamoured of a female speaker.

Katherine and Scoresby had set out to write the definitive history of Easter Island. Now that they were back after three years' absence, the academic community was awaiting their conclusions eagerly. Expectations were high. Katherine started writing *The Mystery of Easter Island* from their London home and Scoresby hired a team of assistants to help her: a secretary to take dictation and type up her field notes, a cartographer, a draftsman to turn sketches into diagrams, and an artist to make drawings of the island. Even with this team in place, it took Katherine three years to work through her notes and write the book, which, she assured her readers, was popular in tone and only preliminary, and was to be followed in due course by a more scientific report on the expedition's findings.

In academic circles there was an ongoing debate about the cultural history of Easter Island. The present islanders were of Polynesian descent, but most anthropologists thought an earlier group of Melanesians had colonized the island and erected the ancient *moai*. They accepted a clear division between Melanesian and Polynesian culture that is not recognized today, deeming Melanesian culture to be older and less advanced. This debate subsumed the Routledges' work, as their peers awaited the next piece in the puzzle and definitive answers to their questions: Where were the very first islanders from? Who made the great ancient statues? And what did the statues mean? But Katherine could not satisfy them. Despite all the information she had accrued, it was, she wrote in her book, 'a very complicated subject, with regard to which much work still remains to be done'.

Almost as soon as they arrived home, Katherine and Scoresby's colleagues had suggested they embark on another expedition to the Pacific to explore neighbouring islands to the west of Easter Island in the hope of finding cultural links that could illuminate its early history. Unlike most anthropologists – including Barbara Freire-Marreco, Maria Czaplicka, Winifred Blackman and Beatrice Blackwood – the Routledges had all the money they needed to travel again, and after her book was published, rather than write a more academic sequel as she had promised, Katherine turned her attention to the possibility of a second voyage, to clarify the results of the first.

The Gambier Islands lie about twelve hundred miles to the west of Easter Island. They are the first in a group, including the Marquesas and Austral Islands, that today make up French Polynesia. This was where the Routledges' interests now lay, and they took a more pragmatic attitude to their second Pacific expedition. They had sold the *Mana* in 1916, and instead of buying or building another boat, they chartered a yacht. This time they travelled as a private couple and made no attempt to assemble a scientific team: perhaps they had learned from painful past experiences, or perhaps it was because their interests had become more focused. They also spent less time researching beforehand, leaving in late 1920 with no firm plans and without knowing how long they would be away.

They spent the first few months of 1921 in Jamaica, and by midsummer they were sailing on to Tahiti and the Austral Islands, stopping along the way to find out about local stone-working in the hope of finding links to Easter Island's carving traditions. However, the historical evidence became more complex the further they explored, and Katherine found nothing that linked directly to Easter Island. By November they were in Mangareva, the largest inhabited island of the Gambier group, and here they settled for fourteen months. According to Katherine, it was 'much more comfortable and not nearly so thrilling as Easter Island'. She had long known of a local story that told of two brothers who made an early voyage from Mangareva to Easter Island, and she collected as much evidence as she could, writing down folktales and myths, surveying archaeological sites on Mangareva and neighbouring islands, and excavating a double burial that they came across. She was happy, living in a wooden beach hut with a metal roof, surrounded by palm trees, but there was neither the urgency nor the energy that had shaped her Easter Island work, and after a year they began to think of coming home.

It would have been easy for the Routledges to sail from Mangareva to Easter Island, but they never did. A New Zealander, John Macmillan Brown, was working there now, and Katherine worried that he might make discoveries she had missed. She told newspaper reporters and correspondents that she longed to visit again, but perhaps she knew that a second trip to the island could never match her memories of it. She referred to her work there as her 'love's labour lost'.

On their way back home, while they were in Tahiti in February 1923, Katherine picked up the mail that was waiting for her there and learned that her sister-in-law, Wilson's wife

Joan, had died four months earlier. It was unexpected, Joan had been only fifty-eight, and Katherine was heartbroken and distraught to think of her brother's sorrow, writing: '[Y]ou and she were "not two persons at all" ... you had every daily thought and interest in common and the separation must be grief inexpressible.' Then, just two weeks after she arrived back in England, Wilson died too. He was only fifty-five.

Each time Katherine went away, it seemed, she lost someone. Hearing of Joan's death must have brought back painful memories of her voyage home from Easter Island seven years earlier when, in the same town of Papeete in Tahiti, she had received letters from Wilson telling her of their mother's death. It was when they reunited in England a few months later that Wilson had found her 'always very near to tears', sanctimonious and self-absorbed. She was grieving for her mother 'who was no longer here to welcome our return', but she was also struggling with a kind of grief for her island life in the Pacific. Now, on her return from Mangareva, she had lost Wilson, who had been her closest friend.

Katherine was not easy to love. When she was growing up, her widowed mother had been unable to show her affection. Kate Pease had denied her children toys and read them essays with titles like 'Blessed Be Drudgery' and 'A Cup of Cold Water Has Some Good Things in It'. Once, when Wilson was in his mid-forties, he was helping his mother with the servants' wages one day when she suddenly jumped up out of her chair, threw her arms around his neck and exclaimed, 'I must give you a kiss, you dear boy!' Wilson was shocked. It was the first impulsive kiss she had ever given him.

Neither Wilson nor Katherine had lived up to their mother's expectations. Wilson never got a job and lacked ambition, and

Katherine was abrasive and uncompromising. She had – controversially – gone to university, married the wrong kind of man, and spent her money pursuing her own intellectual interests; she had caused her mother 'much unhappiness' as a result.

Cantankerous though she was, Katherine had highly developed 'family feelings', according to her other brother, John; Joan thought she was 'terribly insecure about her place in the family'. Katherine's vulnerabilities could surface as a form of aggression. She had raged when some of their relatives stopped wearing mourning after her mother's death, and she cried when none of her friends wrote her letters of sympathy, even though she had been abroad and inaccessible at the time. Katherine was caught in a cycle of desire and disavowal when it came to her family, eager to reach out but often incapable of doing so. When Wilson died, she lost the one ally whose loyalty she never doubted and whose phlegmatic temperament could be relied upon to neutralize her passions. Wilson was everything that Katherine was not: placid, amenable and surprisingly ordinary. She needed him.

Despite her grief, when she first arrived back from the Pacific she seemed full of bravado about her work, telling journalists about the exciting links they had discovered between Mangarevan culture and Easter Island, and at the end of 1924 she announced that she had 'just started seriously to work on my new book'. She presented her work at various learned societies and gave an illustrated lecture for the Royal Colonial Institute entitled 'Travels in the South Seas', to a large public audience. She and Scoresby attended academic meetings and regularly contributed to the discussions, sometimes together, sometimes alone.

Katherine was working hard, but it was taking its toll. In

the summer of that year, the Routledges placed a notice in *The Times* announcing that she was 'seriously ill from overwork' and could only respond to important correspondence. It was the first of several announcements on the newspaper's 'Court Circular' page regarding Katherine's absence from London, her ill-health and her inability to attend to letters. At home she ate little, slept little, and became rude and controlling. She and Scoresby lived increasingly separate lives. It was then that she bought the seventeen-room mansion at Hyde Park Gardens; Scoresby occupied a separate suite of rooms on the second floor for which he paid rent, 'as a lodger might'. He also spent time away from home, staying at his London club or at their cottage in Bursledon. Katherine spent her summers living in various hotels outside London.

By now the boundary between her imagination and her reality was losing focus, and she struggled to maintain her family relationships. She became interested in spiritualism and began attending seances, which Scoresby hated. Their relationship deteriorated to the extent that they saw each other only by appointment. In her increasing isolation, Katherine heard other people's voices. People from her past populated the house, telling her what to do. Her parents, grandparents, uncles and aunts, Wilson and Joan, all now dead, appeared to her as if they were real.

Wilson came after I was in bed and was very excited and delighted to hear you had written ... Joan tells me I am to write this ... Joan came after luncheon today and asked to have your letter read ... We were always so confident of your love dear Katherine she said ... Wilson is here now ... uncle and aunt Arthur [sic] told me to say ...

She told her niece, 'They see through my eyes so to speak – the pictures in my brain.' These visions were her comfort and her torment. Her journal was called 'Things Unknown told to me by The Spooks'.

As Katherine's interior world came to life, the real world left her feeling alone and on guard. She challenged Scoresby, opened his mail and went through his papers. She thought he was greedy and self-serving and resented the fact that he did not help her enough with the book she was writing. He had shown her, she said, 'a want of sympathy and assistance in her pursuits'.

In 1927 she threw him out of the house and changed the locks. Scoresby promptly put his things in storage and sent his wife the bill. The marriage was collapsing and the Routledges' lawyers tried to agree a judicial separation, but Katherine refused the terms. Tensions escalated. She gave Scoresby two weeks to remove his belongings from the house. He refused, and after the fortnight was up, he tried to retake possession. He arrived one day with a policeman and a private security guard from the Corps of Commissionaires, and they locked themselves inside his second-floor rooms. The commissionaire said he would stay indefinitely, but Katherine, not one to be intimidated, told him that if he decided to stay she would lock him in Scoresby's rooms from the outside. At first the commissionaire held his ground, but when she proceeded to padlock the door as she had promised, he quickly changed his mind and asked to be allowed to leave.

Alone in the house again, Katherine hired a locksmith, entered Scoresby's suite, packed up his books and other belongings, and sent them to various London warehouses for storage. Her husband then applied for a court order compelling her to give him access to the house and allowing him to keep his possessions there.

Scoresby's court order was refused, but while this case was proceeding Katherine was issued a separate court summons. This time it related to a £100 bill she had refused to pay for the storage of some of Scoresby's belongings. These were the things he had taken from the house of his own accord when they first separated, and Katherine saw no reason why she should pay his warehousing expenses. Nonetheless, the court issued a sequestration order on Scoresby's behalf. Katherine asked for an adjournment because she was not well enough to attend court, but in June 1928 she received a High Court order stating that under the Married Women's Property Act of 1882 all her property was to be placed in the hands of four male court representatives. These men had the power to enter her home at any time, and to collect and receive all rents and profits, all her goods, and her entire personal estate.

Never one to go quietly, Katherine settled in for the long haul. She refused to pay Scoresby's £100 bill on principle, since as far as she was concerned it was his debt and she was not liable for it. She dismissed her five servants because it would 'not have been fair' to involve them; then she boarded up the windows on the ground floor so that nobody could see in, and locked herself inside. She stopped answering the telephone, and only answered the door by appointment.

Then she called the press. She gave interviews, explained her predicament and showed journalists around the house. Having camped out in one of the bathrooms at first, after a while she took up residence in two rooms on the third floor instead. Days went by without the neighbours seeing her, although she sometimes slipped out secretly to buy food and other provisions, and even to eat at a nearby hotel. When the bank refused to cash her cheques, she sold her pearls to raise money. She started emptying the house of papers and other items, some of which she threw away, and some she took to Paddington Station for storage.

Katherine entranced the journalists who waited outside the house to report every development. When she spoke to them she did so lucidly. She knew that her actions seemed irrational, but she insisted that 'from my point of view the whole business is carefully reasoned out'. She felt that she was being treated unfairly, and had decided 'to take up this somewhat startling attitude' to draw attention to the situation. 'Much of the treatment which I have received in this matter is simply due to the fact that I am a woman,' she pointed out, and she promised to set up a society for the reform of the administration of the law. She received numerous letters of support and donations from women who were outraged by the court's actions, including two shillings and sixpence from a working-class woman in Nottinghamshire who promised to send her more when she could afford it.

For all Katherine's bravado, it must have been very lonely for her at 4 Hyde Park Gardens that summer. Apart from anything else, she was used to having a team of servants to provide for her, but now she had to do all the cooking, cleaning and shopping herself. Left alone in her large empty house with her research papers and her unfinished book, knowing that men might come knocking at her door at any moment, she was in a desperate situation. Her money had set the balance of her marriage from the start. It had given her power over Scoresby in their decision-making, so much so that her brother John thought she struggled after the separation because 'she has no one to manage now', and said that she could not be happy either with Scoresby or without him – no matter that Scoresby was busy taking his sister's inheritance away from her in a court of law. Now, Katherine could not even rely on her money. Her husband was intent on stripping her of her financial assets, and with them the independence she had been determined to retain her whole life.

At the end of June, she went to stay at a hotel in Dover. Perhaps she knew that Scoresby would arrive at Hyde Park Gardens a few days later with two sequestrators, a solicitor and his clerk, a male and a female bailiff, and a locksmith. They broke in and took a full inventory of the contents of the premises. Katherine told newspaper reporters she had been informed that unless she paid Scoresby's bill, an arrest warrant would be issued and she would be sent to Holloway Prison. She could not pay the bill, she said, because 'so far as I can see, I have no access to my property and securities', so she expected to go to prison. Furthermore, she intended to circulate a statement about her predicament to both Houses of Parliament. She visited London in August and found her house in 'a scandalous condition'. Eventually, the sequestrators took enough items to pay the warehousing debt, and Katherine moved back in.

She did not stay there for long. In January 1929, she started to nail handwritten notices to her front door. One was printed in the newspapers:

> She who lives in this house is the victim of a design formed
> in and through the Law Courts against her property ... For
> months she has been each day engaged in a struggle with
> Death, by poison (as is well known) and also, as she again has
> evidence, by violence ... She appeals for justice to God and
> to her fellow citizens.

A few weeks later eight men, including two locksmiths and two doctors, forced their way into 4 Hyde Park Gardens and took her to a waiting car. Reports differed in the detail as to what happened that afternoon: some journalists reported hearing shouts from inside the house and said that Katherine 'protested vigorously'; others said she opened the door and two nurses walked her to the car; one neighbour remembered her being carried out on a stretcher. There were plenty of stories published on the day she was taken away, but after that, the reporters fell silent. Katherine was committed to Ticehurst House Hospital in Sussex (now part of The Priory group), 'The Lunatic Asylum', as she referred to it in her letters. She was to stay there for the rest of her life.

Ticehurst House was 'the Mecca of private asylums', and only the wealthiest families could afford the fees. Scoresby paid more than a thousand pounds a year for his wife to have a large private sitting-room and bedroom. The institution was set in three hundred acres of private grounds, complete with pavilions, tennis courts, a small golf course, a cricket pitch and a bowling green, and 'an aviary for gold and silver pheasants'. One nurse was assigned to every patient, sometimes two, and patients were housed either in the main building or in smaller 'villas' in the grounds. Everyone had their own bedroom, and many also had their own sitting-room where they could eat in private. There were weekly dances, musical events and occasional lectures. Friends and relatives could visit and eat there free of charge, and some patients were granted permission to go for drives in one of the hospital's motorcars. They were allowed their own personal effects, and in the early months Katherine charged for the services of a draper, so perhaps she ordered clothes or curtains to try and make herself feel more at home. For all Ticehurst's comparative comforts, she was a prisoner nonetheless.

She had been admitted against her will, thanks to an urgency order obtained by her family's solicitors and signed by a doctor. It is hard to imagine the distress she must have felt at being imprisoned, not knowing whether she would ever get out. Although Ticehurst was relatively comfortable, it housed eighty-seven people who were extremely unwell. Some were suicidal and had to be watched twenty-four hours a day; others became restless, confused or violent. People banged their doors at night, tore the bedclothes, were aggressive and 'difficult to manage', or 'delusional'.

Katherine wrote angry and indignant letters to her family and friends asking for help, but only a few survive and the hospital staff may have destroyed the others. The doctors, who saw her every day and diagnosed 'systemized delusional insanity', declared her condition incurable. She had to wake at 7 a.m. and was locked in her room at 10 p.m. every night. When she was given 'parole' to pursue her own interests, like walking in the garden, she played truant and announced that she 'had done it on principle'.

Clinical records of the patients at Ticehurst are subject to a hundred-year closure rule, which means that Katherine's are not yet available to researchers. Nevertheless, there are a few poignant documents from her stay, like the letter written by Scoresby's solicitor addressed to the medical superintendent at Ticehurst, in which 'it is proposed to effect the removal of Mrs Routledge on Monday next' from her home in London. One imagines Katherine locked in her shabby mansion in Hyde Park Gardens, as yet unaware of her fate, while the doctor at Ticehurst opens the letter and reads about her case for the first time. Then there are financial records, which list her spending on postage and items from the hospital's newsagent, scant semblances of her previous life, bought to punctuate the routines of institutionalization.

Sometimes charges were made to Katherine's account for 'additional nursing' for many weeks at a time, which meant that she needed a night nurse. Why did she need a night nurse? Had she become sick, depressed or 'unmanageable'? Most heart-breaking of all is to find Mrs K.M. Routledge listed in the hospital's 'Register of Restraint and Seclusion' for 1929. She was secluded, for 'violence', in a room with the windows, shutters and doors locked, for a total of twelve hours during the week of 15 August that year, then for another twelve hours the following week, nine hours the week after that, and so on. Her name is written in the register again and again, week after week, every week, until the volume comes to an end, in mid-October.

There is no equivalent register available for 1930. These are all the fragmentary, distressing insights we have into Katherine's time at Ticehurst. She had disappeared from view into a closed, secret and sinister world. Her family beyond the hospital gates receded and she could not escape. She never managed to convince the authorities of her sanity. Instead, she lived in enforced exile at Ticehurst House for almost seven years. She died there on 13 December 1935 of a cerebral thrombosis, at the age of sixty-nine.

Rano Raraku is a wide grassy basin, formed from the crater of a volcano at the eastern end of Easter Island. On one side the ridge of the crater is high and gives way to sheer cliffs beyond, but to the north and west the land is gently sloping and open. The island here is densely covered with *moai* statues, because this is the ancient quarry where almost all of them were made before being transported to their distant coastal positions.

Carved out of the stone cliffs, and in every stage of manufacture, *moai* still litter the land: some stand half-buried in the ground, others remain part of the rock face.

In July 1914, Katherine had caught her breath when she came face to face with 'the mighty dead' at Rano Raraku. She described the place as having 'an indescribable sense of solemnity' and beauty, particularly at sunset when the stone figures darkened against the fiery western sky. Here, the ancestors held their secrets, and 'the whole air vibrates with a vast purpose and energy which has been and is no more'. Katherine believed that Rano Raraku was key to solving the mystery of how the *moai* came to watch over Easter Island.

She and Scoresby had set up camp at the foot of the cliff face, so they could survey and excavate the statues and try to understand how they had been made and transported. Katherine invited elderly people from the village of Hanga Roa to walk with her around the quarry and tell her what they knew about its past. When she asked how the *moai* had been moved and why some had been abandoned along the way or left unfinished, they each told her the same story. There was once an old woman, they said, who was cook to the 'image-makers' who carved the *moai*, and she moved the statues by supernatural power, 'ordering them about at her will'. One day she found that the sculptors had dined on a fine lobster in secret, and left none for her. She 'arose in her wrath' and told all the statues to fall down, bringing work at Rano Raraku to a standstill. This 'invented' story 'entirely satisfies the native mind', Katherine reported. Another person told her simply, '[T]hey walked, and some fell by the way.'

Of course, the statues could not walk, and the villagers' answers seemed irrelevant to the vexing question of how they were actually moved. It was a logistical conundrum. With no wood on the island to make rollers and no material for ropes, it was hard to see how men could have pushed, or pulled, the huge blocks of stone. Katherine wondered whether they had been raised up on banks of earth or dropped into ditches specially dug for the purpose, but the islanders seemed unable to shed any further light on the matter.

Today, a strong body of evidence suggests that Katherine should have taken the stories she heard at Rano Raraku more seriously. The islanders have always described the statues as 'walking'. For a long time after her visit, their explanations continued to be discounted and archaeologists explored other possibilities. The Norwegian ethnographer Thor Heyerdahl led an expedition in the 1950s that tried to move a medium-sized *moai* on a sledge made from a forked tree, but it took 180 islanders a lot of time and effort to drag the statue just a short distance. The locals had been sceptical, insisting that their ancestors had made the statues 'walk'. In the 1980s Heyerdahl and a Czech engineer named Pavel Pavel conducted the first experiments in 'walking' the statues in an upright position with a rhythmic pulling and twisting, a little like 'walking' a heavy refrigerator into position in a kitchen. They managed it, and Pavel came to believe that a small group working carefully together could walk a *moai* as much as six hundred feet a day. Since then, more experiments have shown that the statues can 'walk'.

The Easter Island statues are ingeniously designed with a centre of gravity that is relatively low and forward, at about a third their height, which makes them very stable when in motion. Their shape reduces the energy needed to make them rock and increases the amount they can safely be swung: a *moai* has to tilt to almost 60 degrees before it falls over. Katherine had faithfully recorded the clues to a theory that was beyond her imagining. She noted that some of the fallen statues lay face up, while others were face down. This simple fact is crucial to the theory of 'walking' them, for if they had been moved on sledges one would expect all of them to have been abandoned the same way up. Instead, their alignment correlates with whether they were travelling uphill at the time, when they usually fell on their backs, or downhill, when they tended to fall on their faces.

Katherine also observed, while sitting on a high rocky slope at Rano Raraku one day, that the statues were positioned in lines, or paths, through the landscape. In the low evening sun she could make out a track stretching out before her on the plain below, with statues lying every few hundred yards along it. She started to map these 'image roads' across the island. Her maps remained the primary documentation of the paths until the year 2000, when archaeologists started to analyse and measure them systematically, adding many more paths to those she had found. They became one of the key clues to understanding how the *moai* were moved: rather than being part of a general, multi-purpose transportation network, the paths begin at the quarry sites and end at the site of installation. They are all slightly different, which suggests that the statues were moved at different times by different groups of people.

Katherine worked conscientiously on Easter Island for sixteen months, producing the first comprehensive corpus of evidence about its history. Since then, Rapa Nui has become 'one of the most intensively studied specks of land anywhere in the world'. Aspects of her work have been validated, but inevitably much has been proved wrong as our understanding of the island's history develops. Katherine herself knew the limits of her knowledge and her humility as a researcher was one of her greatest strengths.

Once, when she was inspecting a statue positioned at the top of a sheer cliff, with a slope on the other side 'as steep as a house roof', her local guide turned to her and said, 'Do you mean to tell me that that was not done by *mana* [supernatural power]? But how could you do it any other way?' He was incredulous that her team was trying to work out how men could have moved the *moai* using nothing but ditches and ropes. She included his comment in her book as if to admit her own shortcomings. She never solved the mystery of Easter Island, but her even-handed assessment of the evidence does her great credit. She included observations that did not make sense, facts she did not understand, and testimony from the islanders that seemed misguided. With little training and no expert help she tried to be openminded, and gathered a great deal of information that is still of value today. The oral evidence she took from people living in Hanga Roa is particularly precious. She felt a strong sense of responsibility to her subjects. Writing down the testimony of people who remembered the Peruvian slave raids of the 1860s, she noted: 'Ten years ago more could have been done; ten years hence little or nothing will remain of this source of knowledge.'

Katherine came to believe that the current islanders were directly descended from the people who had made the *moai*. Despite scepticism from her colleagues, who believed that a separate, earlier group of Melanesians had erected them, she worked hard to prove her theory. She traced family lineages to specific plots of land to substantiate her theory that there was cultural continuity through to the present day, even though the islanders showed little interest in the statues themselves. Asking their opinion directly was, she wrote, as hopeless as trying to get an old woman selling bootlaces at Westminster to tell you the story of Oliver Cromwell. However, the islanders did tell her the names of individuals and clans who were associated with one or two of the *moai*. She also saw links between the design of the statues and smaller wooden figures that the villagers called 'wooden *moai*', as well as other ritual practices that existed in the nineteenth century.

Katherine's theory of cultural continuity has since been proved right. Evidence convincingly shows that Easter Island was only colonized once, from Polynesia, by between thirty and a hundred people in around AD 1200. These seafarers most likely travelled from Tahiti out into the vastness of the Pacific Ocean in double-hulled canoes, reaching the island and surviving there, against all the odds, for centuries.

Katherine's own expedition to the 'loneliest spot on the globe' had been expensive, inconclusive, and fraught with bitter disputes and physical hardship. The island, she found, was neither beautiful nor striking; on the contrary, it was bleak and unforgiving. The past penetrated the land, all-consuming and vague. Among the ancestors of Rano Raraku, she scrambled up the grassy slopes to sit atop the cliffs above the limitless ocean. '[E]verywhere is the wind of heaven,' she wrote of Easter Island, 'around and above all are boundless sea and sky, infinite space and a great silence.'

16

A Stone Age Culture

Beatrice Blackwood in New Guinea, 1936

In June 1936, almost six years after her first visit to New Guinea, Beatrice Blackwood was sitting in the government anthropologist Ernest Chinnery's office again, fighting her corner.

Her book *Both Sides of Buka Passage: An Ethnographic Study of Social, Sexual, and Economic Questions in the North-Western Solomon Islands* had been published the previous year. It was a thorough survey of the culture she had found in Kurtachi, covering marriage, pregnancy and childbirth, adolescence, technology and aesthetics; there was even a chapter on dreams. The book was comprehensive without being revolutionary. She had contributed to a growing corpus of anthropological data on Melanesian society, but she had always wanted to 'tackle another group on similar lines'. She felt sure that she could make a better job of it second time round, with all her experience to draw on.

Henry Balfour had given her the opportunity by organizing a

travel grant for her to collect objects for the Pitt Rivers Museum. She was in Rabaul again, and Chinnery was 'trying hard' to dissuade her from venturing into the interior of mainland New Guinea where the people were, he said, hostile and aggressive. He suggested as an alternative the island of New Britain which, he promised, was 'easy to get at, [had] easy people to get on with, interesting ceremonies and rich material culture'. This was an area suited to a lady anthropologist, unlike the New Guinea interior, which comprised small, inaccessible settlements scattered through mountainous jungle. The people who lived in the highlands were known to be unpredictable and prone to violence. To travel there, she would have to fly to the tiny airstrip at Bulolo in the newly opened gold-mining district, at considerable expense. Then she would have to hike through thick, steep bush, with a string of carriers and under armed guard. When she had found a suitable village, Chinnery assured her, she would find the people hard to deal with; they spoke 'an impossibly difficult language' and had a 'dull culture' that was hardly worth recording.

Despite Chinnery's best efforts, Blackwood refused to compromise. She was determined to get into the mountains. She wanted to go to Mount Hagen in the Waghi Valley, famously 'discovered' by an Australian, Mick Leahy, during an aerial reconnaissance trip over the New Guinea highlands just three years earlier. Leahy's exploration suggested that as many as two hundred thousand previously unknown people lived in the fertile valleys of Mount Hagen, and possibly thousands more. Given that the known indigenous population of the Mandated Territory of New Guinea was only four hundred thousand and the mountainous inland regions were thought to be inhospitable and uninhabited, this was an astonishing find. Chinnery and a group of government employees had surveyed these areas in 1934 for the first time, and the anthropological community in Britain eagerly received their published reports and photographs.

Chinnery had found settlements of round bamboo huts on grassy flats, and sophisticated patchworks of gardens edged by treacherous cane swamps. The people he met there stared at their visitors in disbelief, some laughing or crying, some trying to touch them, while others, silently dazed and awestruck, assumed they were ghosts. And some were indeed hostile, raising their spears, shouting and threatening the newcomers as they approached.

In Oxford at the Pitt Rivers, Balfour and Blackwood had followed the discovery of Mount Hagen. Balfour, the consummate museum curator, was fascinated by these people who still used stone tools and had never seen metal before. Chinnery's report stated that the government patrol could not persuade them to take steel tomahawks or steel knives in payment for food because they did not understand the value of metal. If Blackwood could reach these tribes, she could watch stone tools being made and send back unique collections for the museum, along with detailed information on an almost pristine pre-industrial society. She wanted to go, despite all the risks.

When she arrived in Sydney in 1936, she heard to her great disappointment that the Australian government had closed the Mount Hagen area to visitors because it was considered too dangerous. There was nothing she could do: she was too late. Since Leahy's reconnaissance trip in 1933 a number of armed affrays between gold prospectors and New Guineans had led to deaths on both sides. Now there was, at best, a state of 'armed truce'. Tensions were running high, both between neighbouring villages and between New Guineans and the colonial newcomers.

There were regular inter-village raids. Even natural deaths might be attributed to enemy sorcery by people in the mountains, and prompt violent retaliation.

Reo Fortune, whom Beatrice had met in Sydney seven years earlier (and who had since divorced Margaret Mead), had been given permission to work in the New Guinea highlands the previous year. He had been allowed into the eastern region near Mount Hagen, but only with an armed guard, and on condition that he slept at a native police post and not alone in a village. Although he lived largely at peace with the people there, on more than one occasion he had faced men with fully drawn bows and arrows, and he witnessed many fierce and fatal battles between neighbouring groups. After five months, the raiding and fighting became so intense that the government ordered Fortune to withdraw – less than halfway through his fieldwork. The police post where he was staying had been surrounded by warring villagers and he was in danger. His experiences took their toll on his physical and mental health, and his brother, Barter Fortune, felt that he never fully recovered from the episode.

In the year since Fortune's departure, the highlands had been declared 'uncontrolled' and closed to new non-administrative personnel, as the government worked to pacify the region. Under the circumstances, it is not surprising that Blackwood's application to work in Mount Hagen was turned down, but there was still a chance that she could live on the southeastern fringe of the highlands amongst the Anga tribes, who lived near the well-established government patrol post at Otibanda, on the edge of the uncontrolled area. Working with the Anga became Blackwood's new objective.

The Anga were also notoriously violent, and Chinnery no doubt told her about the men who had been killed or injured by

them in recent years. In 1931, the German prospector Helmuth
Baum had pushed deep into Anga territory with twenty carriers,
looking for gold. Baum had lived in New Guinea for years, and
was known as a peaceful man who took all knives and axes from
his men at night so that they could not provoke an attack from
the locals. In Anga country, though, his long-held policy failed,
and one night while asleep in his bunk he was clubbed to death
in an apparently unprovoked attack. The suspects were arrested
and several villages were decimated during the reprisals.

Within weeks, another group of prospectors had been
attacked. Mick Leahy was exploring Anga country with his
brother Pat when one day their camp was raided, just before
dawn. Mick was struck on the side of the head by a man with
a stone club, and Pat, who succeeded in drawing the attackers
off with his revolver, was hit by two arrows, one deep in his left
shoulder and the other in his arm. It took their group more than
a week to stumble back, weak, in pain and unable to sleep, to
the nearest coastal town, Salamaua, to see a doctor.

The Leahys recovered from their injuries, but the stories of
Anga ferocity did not end there. In 1933 a government patrol,
marching deep into the territory in search of a suitable location for a new airstrip to support the burgeoning gold-mining
industry, came across the bodies of two dead white men rotting
in the jungle. The murdered pair were prospectors who had
travelled without government permission or protection. Keith
McCarthy, the twenty-eight-year-old patrol officer who found
them, captured eight Anga men in retaliation and set off to
Salamaua with them as prisoners. The first part of the trek
passed without incident, but when they were only a couple of
days from the patrol station, they were attacked. In a hail of
arrows, McCarthy was struck in his stomach and thigh, and

several of his men were seriously wounded; one later died in hospital.

McCarthy, who became a lifelong member of the Australian colonial service in New Guinea, certainly thought the Anga unpredictable. Although most were friendly towards him and willing to trade, he never knew when, or why, they might attack. On his next patrol, under orders to burn off the bush and clear an area for a new landing strip, he came under fire and so retreated to set up camp. As his team erected their tents, McCarthy looked up to see a group of Anga men on the steep slope above, working to loosen a boulder to roll down on top of them. They quickly removed their equipment and supplies, and watched as the rock smashed through the spot where their tents would have been. Then, just as suddenly, the mood changed. 'Half an hour later, I'm damned if they didn't come down to the camp, all smiles, offering to sell us kau-kau [sweet potatoes].'

Almost everyone Blackwood met in those first few weeks in New Guinea told her to be wary of the Anga. They routinely raided neighbouring villages and lived, apparently, in an almost constant state of animosity. Chinnery spent more than a week trying to dissuade her from going into 'cannibal country', warning her that it would be difficult, dangerous and unproductive. Day after day, '[I] had all the disadvantages of working "on top" [in the mountains] pointed out to me with great emphasis.' It made no difference. Beatrice knew the risks, but she was adamant that she would stick to her plan. 'I suppose I am several different kinds of fool,' she wrote in her diary, 'but I still want to go "up on top".'

Her determination won out. Reluctantly, Chinnery agreed that she could be based in the village of Manki, a four-hour trek from the patrol post at Otibanda, on the edge of uncontrolled Anga territory. Otibanda had been opened in 1932 to protect gold miners working in the nearby creeks. There were about 250 miners in the area and 2,500 indentured labourers, who regularly traded with the Anga living in nearby villages like Manki.

Blackwood spent July 1936 travelling further inland. When she arrived at Manki in August after a series of frustrating delays, she was neither frightened nor elated: she was bitterly disappointed. She had walked for hours through the bush along with the assistant district officer and a train of carriers and policemen, but when she emerged into the grassy clearing at Manki she saw before her all the signs of government infiltration and the influence of missionaries.

The houses were built on wooden piles in a style used in heavily administered coastal villages (known, in pidgin, as 'fashion belong mission'). The villagers were wearing lap-laps and blankets made from trade cloth, not the knee-length grass skirts and bark-cloth capes the Anga traditionally wore, and were using metal tools. The village was clearly 'not at all "belong before"'. She had no doubt Chinnery had sent her to another place that had been irredeemably altered by colonial infrastructure, but there was nothing for it: she had to unpack her things in the government rest house and organize the building of her own hut in the village. She knew this was the best she could hope for under the circumstances.

Beatrice Blackwood's work would always be limited by an insurmountable and eternally frustrating problem: forbidden from living in the uncontrolled areas, beyond the reach of the government administration, she was forced to work with people whose culture had been affected by contact with colonial settlers and who had, she added, almost regretfully, 'ceased to fight'.

She did not blame anyone and she acknowledged that the assistant district officer, Ken Bridge, had made her presence in Manki possible thanks to the four years he had spent establishing a good relationship with the people there. It was only because of Bridge that the villagers accepted her at all, and they did so grudgingly. They remained reserved and suspicious throughout her nine months with them. Bridge considered Manki a risky enough proposition for her work, never mind more distant settlements. He remembered years later:

> Her only disagreement with me was when I took her to the supposedly, or at least, temporarily 'safe' village of Manki to begin her work – not that any of those villages could be termed 'safe'. Later on, and with great reluctance on my part, she wandered and camped in the Sibanda, Waiganda, and thence to the Upper Slate Creek villages – which were not at all 'safe' ... I always expected her to be killed by some marauders, but she got on excellently with all the villages she came in contact with.

Blackwood was not a loose canon, but she pushed her luck. Had Manki been more promising, she might not have been tempted to wander, but the people there were neither 'cooperative' nor, apparently, particularly interesting from an academic point of view.

The village consisted of two hamlets, each with ten huts, and a handful of huts further away in a forest clearing. She called it an 'artificial village' because the inhabitants had been induced to come together by the government and the nearby Lutheran mission, for their greater convenience. The mountain people traditionally preferred to live scattered through the forest over greater distances, in groups of just two or three houses, but this made it harder for the patrols to monitor them. The three local groups – the Manki, the Nauti and the Ekuti – were historically enemies, and although alliances constantly shifted and some were friendly at the time of Blackwood's stay, they continued to raid each other's villages.

Fear of government reprisals alone kept the people Blackwood met from open warfare. There were about 130 individuals in Manki, half of whom were children. They had moved there from two different areas and still spoke different dialects. Not everyone could understand each other, and Blackwood faced the prospect of learning not one difficult language but two. Still, she knew it was the 'artificial village' that made her work possible. She simply could not have studied a group of people dispersed over a great distance who were hostile to strangers.

Manki lay at an altitude of five thousand feet, on very steep ground. The terrain was rocky, with spurs, gullies and streams running down the mountain. The hillsides were heavily forested and the clearings were covered in coarse *kunai* grass, which grew several feet high and which the villagers kept down by burning. Single-file paths were cut through the bush from hamlet to hamlet, along their hunting tracks or to the villagers' gardens where they grew sweet potato, taro, yams, sugar cane and bananas.

At Manki, tomatoes, cabbage and maize had recently been introduced, but the villagers sold this produce to local miners because they did not care to eat it themselves. Blackwood had brought pea, runner bean, carrot, beetroot and lettuce seeds with her, and people promised to continue growing them after she left. The villagers cooked moss and ferns from the forest as vegetables, and used vines and other creepers to make string.

Meat was hard to come by. With bows and arrows and the help of a few dogs they hunted wallaby, opossums, tree-rats, and birds such as cassowaries and pigeons. Catching prey was not easy and they also ate lizards, snakes and grubs if they could find them. Sometimes they dammed a stream and shot fish, or pounded up poisonous roots to stun them. They had no pottery, and cooked their food in lengths of green bamboo or tree bark over the fire. Holes in the ground filled with hot stones sufficed as ovens.

Their huts were made from vertical wooden logs and thatched with grass, bamboo leaves, or pandanus leaves 'bearing an absurd resemblance to corrugated iron and nearly as efficient'. The floors, made of bark strips or split bamboo, were slightly raised off the ground. The people had few possessions. Although traditionally they had used stone and wood to make adzes, clubs, digging sticks and bows and arrows, now they had metal trade tools. Bamboo was used to make water containers, bow strings, knives, torches, pan-pipes and Jews' harps. They made string bags for carrying 'anything from babies to sweet potatoes'.

The Anga had the hallmarks of a 'primitive' people, but they were challenging subjects for an anthropologist. Personal names were secret and could not be used openly even among the villagers themselves, and as it was also taboo to speak the names of the dead it was virtually impossible for Blackwood to record genealogies, a task that was a basic requirement of anthropological research. Social groups were very fluid. There were no chiefs and no set political hierarchy. She found it hard to get to grips with how families were related to each other, whether they were organized into clans, or how people in one village were linked with those in another. This made it difficult to understand the basis upon which they traded with each other, or why they fought. So much of the culture depended on who was married to whom, or whether someone was an uncle or a cousin or a niece, that Blackwood could not fully comprehend what was going on around her.

She was not helped by the fact that the language, as Chinnery had warned her, was difficult to learn, and for a long time she had to rely on interpreters who could speak to her in pidgin. This distanced her from the community, and the younger people who spoke pidgin knew nothing of the secret rites and cultural histories that were so crucial to Blackwood's work. As the days and weeks went by, Chinnery's cautionary words rang loud and clear in her mind, fuelling her doubts. She accompanied villagers to their gardens every day, watched them making bows and arrows and net bags and building houses, but she could not access the deeper levels of their cultural life. There were, apparently, no ceremonies and no decorative arts – 'I have never seen a people so nearly lacking in the fine arts' – probably because they were 'so much taken up with the struggle for existence'. Living on poor ground and surrounded by hostile neighbours, the Anga's 'two main – and almost only – interests are food and fighting'. In October she concluded glumly that 'nothing especially interesting has happened during the three months I have been here'.

One of Blackwood's best assets during her visit was a tabby white kitten called Sally, which someone had given her while she was at the Upper Watut aerodrome on her way to Manki. The Anga had never seen a cat before, and Blackwood remembered that, 'some of the toughest old warriors would spend hours trailing bits of string for her to play with'. Sally not only helped to break through people's reserve, she was also a dear companion when Beatrice found her work frustrating. 'Sally the kitten,' she wrote in her diary, 'is the only satisfactory thing in this thoroughly unsatisfactory place.' In November she tried again to persuade Bridge to allow her to enter the uncontrolled area with a government patrol, but that same week fighting broke out again. The administration took prisoners, which led to more casualties, and her hopes of reaching the 'real' Anga were dashed. She had no choice but to stay at Manki.

Anga men with Blackwood's kitten Sally in New Guinea, 1936.

In her diaries, the villagers remain remarkably inscrutable. In early December, exasperated that she could not find out more about their origin myths, she wondered, 'Don't they know or won't they tell?' A missionary told her that it took four years to gain the confidence of the Anga, which must have been depressing when she had only nine months and was already halfway through her stay. Still, she was learning a little more about their medical remedies, myths and magic.

In mid-December she moved to another village, Andarora, where, she had been assured, the people had less contact with miners and government officials. Andarora comprised about twenty huts scattered through the forest, so that only two or three could be seen from any given point. They were built in a more traditional circular style, with a thatched roof that reached almost to the ground all round. This design obliged visitors to crawl underneath the roof, then make their way around below the eaves until they found the doorway, giving the occupants plenty of time to scrutinize their approaching guests. The Anga, Blackwood explained, 'trusts no one'. In Andarora, they used more stone tools, and she finally felt she was 'justified in coming inland, in spite of all the expenses and difficulties I might have avoided by settling on the coast'. This, she told Balfour, 'really is a Stone Age culture'.

Perhaps because of the relative isolation of Andarora, her presence caused tensions. The people there tolerated her, but barely. That same month she decided to attend a villager's funeral, but his family was angered by her presence and fights broke out. People were hurt, there were 'a few bruises and a little blood spilt', but nothing serious, and she was told this was 'quite common'. She was anxious to know how much her presence had affected the situation. Ten days later, the dead man's widow died too, then rumours began to spread that Blackwood had brought sickness and death with her. Some thought she was the 'spirit of dead people, bringing trouble'. A group of boys broke into her house, stole her trade knives and left it in a mess. A messenger boy who had delivered one of her letters to Bridge was beaten up because it was thought she was sending a request for prisoners to be taken. One of her informants, who had come with her from Manki, was receiving death threats, and for weeks the villagers kept asking her to leave. She refused. Meanwhile the boys who had robbed her went to Manki and started 'making trouble', forcing her to go back and check that her house and belongings there were safe.

During Blackwood's stay, three planned fights between neighbouring groups were called off because of her presence, and she heard about other fights, held in secret so she could not attend. The subtleties of Anga raiding and warfare before European contact in the 1930s are not clearly understood. Anga communities were impermanent, members of different groups frequently moving between settlements, and violence was central to their culture. Almost certainly, colonial contact had affected the way fighting played out in the mountains by the time Blackwood arrived. In the early days, when gold prospectors came across these people and often suffered the consequences, Anga aggression was the *only* aspect of their culture that outsiders experienced. They became known as violent, without anyone properly understanding the way violence was valued in their communities or how it shaped individuals' identities.

Beatrice learned that there were different kinds of fights, depending on whether the participants were from the same group or not. When people from within the same group fought, it might be because someone had taken another man's wife or laid claim to someone else's piece of land. Sometimes fights were spontaneous, at other times the injured party issued a formal challenge. She described these situations as 'more or less harmless'. They involved lots of yelling and letting arrows off into the air, but few serious injuries. Fights between groups could be more brutal. Raids might be planned to steal valuable trade goods like metal tools, or could result from arguments over hunting rights, or a theft, or disputes over women. Often groups raided each other in a cycle of revenge killings. The men returned from a successful raid walking through the forest singing, the women and children would wear ornaments and flowers and prepare celebratory feasts that lasted into the night.

Blackwood listened to stories about fights, but she never witnessed one. She heard that they were afraid to fight while she was there, presumably because they feared government reprisals. Once she went to a place where a fight was being planned, but the women called her off and the men dispersed before anything happened. The Anga were very suspicious and did not want her to see anything important in case she told the government and had it stopped.

Blackwood was businesslike, but the difficulties she had getting information and the fact that she was unwittingly causing strife for her informants took its toll. She found it hard to sleep and had nightmares, and she began to suffer from painful boils and illnesses. Nevertheless she stayed in Andarora for ten weeks until February 1937, when Assistant District Officer Bridge asked her to visit another village, Ekua, to collect information for him on the relationships between the inhabitants and the surrounding communities. It is likely that Bridge asked her to move because he thought it was too risky for her in Andarora. She certainly found Ekua disappointing – there were only five houses. In March, she wrote in her diary: '. . . but oh! how bored I am with this dud village! Walked to edge of Kimai and looked over the valley. Felt shut in and "stuck".'

Despite the hazards she faced and the fatigue, Beatrice Blackwood still wanted more: more time and more autonomy to understand the deeper significance of Anga culture. All her work there seemed to her slightly superficial, as though the 'real' story was just out of reach, but time was running out.

In the spring of 1937 she had to leave the Anga. Henry Balfour had asked her to collect items from other parts of the country too, before she left New Guinea in August. Assembling a museum collection required covering greater distances, to get a representative selection of objects from a range of different places. The Anga had little material culture, she had collected everything she could, and from Balfour's point of view there was no reason for her to stay longer. However, she did not want to leave. She worried that she did not have enough information to satisfy the social anthropologists back home who expected her to write a detailed monograph about the Anga. She felt she had hardly scratched the surface of the culture, but she had no choice. Balfour, she wrote to Chinnery, 'does not care about social anthropology'; he only wanted museum collections. She had to move on.

Back in the mining town of Salamaua that May, she heard there were plans to open a new government station in the uncontrolled Mount Hagen region. She radioed Balfour to ask for a six-month extension to her leave from Oxford in the hope she might, after all, get to go further into the highlands. Balfour duly arranged the extension, and she set about writing to everyone she could think of who could help her get to Hagen – government officials, missionaries, prospectors, anyone of influence who could support her application.

Her efforts were to no avail. A few weeks later, in June, news came that plans for the new government station had been 'indefinitely postponed' again and 'no women' would be given permission to go to Mount Hagen. Perhaps it had been

postponed because of her lobbying. Certainly, neither the colonial administration nor the Anga particularly wanted Blackwood
in their province. She told the government anthropologist in
neighbouring Papua, the Australian F.E. Williams, that she
'drove Chinnery nearly to cursing point with my rendering of
the importunate female! But the Administrator was adamant.'

So she went back to New Britain, and the capital Rabaul.
From there she travelled along the southwest coast to the
opposite end of the island, to collect artefacts from the Arawe
people. Balfour was particularly interested in the Arawe practice of head-binding, to elongate the skull. When Blackwood
visited, the head of almost every Arawe child, male or female,
had been bound tightly with strips of bark cloth immediately
after birth. The binding was replaced daily by the mother, and
the extent of the elongation was a matter of personal preference.
Some children still wore the binding after their first birthday
whereas others kept it on for only a few months. Many Arawe
had almost pointed heads. They did this purely for aesthetic
reasons because long heads were considered attractive to the
opposite sex, and they wore their hair short at the sides and long
on top to further accentuate the shape.

Scientists had debated the effects that head-binding might
have on a person's intellect, although by the time Blackwood
visited it was generally agreed that it caused no harm. Balfour
asked her to go there specifically for him, to acquire Arawe skulls
for a series of craniums he was arranging at the museum. She
was surprised at how willing the Arawe were to sell her human
skulls – they even dug them up from burial sites for her. Their
willingness may have been partly because their traditional
funerary rites, now frowned upon by the mission, had involved
exhuming the skulls of the dead at a later date for a second set

of rituals in any case. It also helped that they were due to pay government taxes soon and needed the income.

Blackwood fulfilled Balfour's requirements within two weeks, but her own ambitions were increasingly compromised. New Britain held little interest for her academically. Another anthropologist, John Alexander Todd, had recently visited, so she felt that her work there had been 'for the benefit of the Pitt Rivers Museum only'.

Thanks to her extension from Oxford, she had another six months' leave and could stay in New Guinea until early 1938, but after leaving the Anga she gradually descended into depression. She was plagued by indecision about where to go, and haunted by the disappointment of her curtailed research in the mountains. In September she went back to Rabaul to try to make up her mind about what to do next, and found the town in ruins. A sudden and powerful volcanic eruption three months earlier had destroyed it, leaving five hundred people dead and thousands more homeless. Her stay there was almost unbearable because of the heat, the destruction and the thick layers of pumice dust everywhere. She was, she wrote, 'reduced to the semblance of a bit of chewed string and did nothing that wasn't absolutely essential'.

When F.E. Williams offered to help her get permission to visit a different group of Anga in the mountains, she declined, in resignation that her work there was finished. The material culture of this group was much the same as that of the people she had already studied, and Balfour's instruction was that she get artefacts from different places. 'While I don't want to be a mere snapper up of museum specimens,' she wrote to Williams, 'I must think of that side of the question seeing that is what Balfour sent me out for to do.' She decided, instead, to go to

Madang, on the north coast of New Guinea, a place of little professional interest to her because it had already been widely reported on by anthropologists, but one that was rich in material culture.

Accordingly, she made preparations to study the Bosmun group of villages on Madang's Ramu River. She arrived in late October and settled herself at the vacant government administrative house. By this stage, she was exhausted and dispirited. She had never been convinced that Bosmun was the best place to spend her last few months, and within weeks she was blaming herself for not going further north to areas that would have been 'quite untapped'. When she learned from the local Catholic priest that another anthropologist was writing a book about Bosmun and that various Germans and Americans had studied the area, she was left further demoralized. 'Why the hell did I ever come here??' she wrote in her diary. Feeling that the whole trip and everything she might do in Bosmun was pointless, she began to procrastinate and long for home.

She watched the local women making pots and the men carving canoes, and bought tortoiseshell ornaments, bark cloth, axes and drums for Balfour, but the village was very hot and humid and full of mosquitoes, which made living conditions unbearable. She took to wrapping her legs in brown paper in a futile effort to stave off the insects. Unable to get up any enthusiasm for her work, with time running out, she did not know whether to stay or move somewhere else. In mid-November she decided to trek north to Awar, but regretted it even before she had left Bosmun. Once in Awar, she missed a boat that was going north, and when another was due to leave a few days later for New Britain she thought about getting on it but could not bring herself to do so. 'I lay low and let her go without me,' she wrote. 'Felt absolutely rotten – lay on couch and read various books and papers and kicked myself all to pieces for having left Bosmun.'

She hated herself for every decision, and stayed inside reading 'rubbish ... to try and forget what a mess I've made'. Depressed, unable to sleep, struggling to control her emotions, dithering and unable to work, obsessed with the opportunities she believed she had missed and feeling 'imprisoned', Blackwood's diary ends abruptly on 13 December 1937 while she is still in Awar, a few weeks before she began her journey back to Oxford.

Beatrice Blackwood arrived home early in 1938, after almost two years away, and brought with her more than two thousand artefacts. From the Anga she had acquired shell necklaces, bows, arrows and adzes, bark-cloth cloaks and string bags, and from elsewhere in New Guinea there were dance masks and headdresses, carved canoe paddles, shell ornaments and combs, drums and other musical instruments, pots, baskets, spears, daggers and hunting equipment. Each object had a story to tell about life in New Guinea in the 1930s, but few were as evocative as the reels of 16mm cine film she shot while she was there.

Cine cameras were very expensive and it is not clear where she acquired one or who paid for it. At the time, filming was not a usual part of anthropological research, and given the cost and the practical difficulties of transporting the equipment it was extremely rare for someone to take a cine camera into the field, but Blackwood did. She filmed the Anga making their stone tools and string bags, digging up sweet potatoes and dressing their hair and it is likely that Balfour encouraged her endeavours. Although her obligations to him had compromised her personal aspirations in New Guinea, without his emphasis on material culture she might never have decided to record her trip in this way. Today, three reels of 16mm film survive at the Pitt Rivers: two of the Anga, and one of the Arawe in New Britain.

Watching them today, silent black-and-white images of the people Blackwood met come to life on the screen. This form of time travel is arresting. Suddenly the viewer is there, in a mountain clearing, in another world. The scenes are only a few seconds long, immediate and fragmentary. Two men make fire using nothing but a piece of wood and a strip of bamboo. A girl sits and laces a string bag on her fingers. A group of women dig their gardens with long sticks. A man binds the point of an arrow to its haft. Performing for Blackwood almost ninety years ago, the participants are nameless now. As the frames flick by, each person stares at the camera with a profound intensity. The act of filming distracts them from the roles they are meant to be playing. They are curious, perplexed, wary, and sometimes amused by this strange show in which they must participate for a white woman and her box of metal and glass.

Held in their gaze for a brief moment, the viewer is Beatrice Blackwood: we watch them, they watch her. She is the camera's ghost, always present but never seen. Beatrice wanted to disappear behind the camera. She took hundreds of photographs in the field, but not a single one of her in New Guinea survives. Her films, astonishing as they were for the time, were not shown in public. She had made them as educational tools and she showed them to her students at Oxford, but she was not interested in sharing them more widely as a testament to her own achievements. She hated media attention. In 1953, Colin Simpson, a journalist who was writing a book about New Guinea, contacted her. He wanted to include a chapter on her research with the

Anga and asked for information and photographs of her. She replied with a firmness bordering on hostility: 'I must begin by saying that I intensely dislike any form of personal publicity other than the minimum necessary to authenticate my work.' There was no photograph of her available, she continued, and even if there were she would not give it to him. She saw no point in providing him with her own biographical information, since his book was about the Anga and not about her. This was typical of her no-nonsense attitude.

Blackwood may not have intended the films to be about her, but they survive as a testament to her groundbreaking work. She filmed daily activities in the village, tasks passed down for generations, but there was nothing routine about this situation. The camera changes everything. The villagers have never performed like this before. There Blackwood is, fiddling with the equipment, setting up the shot, directing the action, doubting her abilities and wondering at her opportunities: an extraordinary woman, the first and only anthropologist they had ever met.

17

A Life of Perfect Unselfishness

Winifred Blackman in North Wales, 1950

Most anthropologists worry that their research is too fleeting and fragmentary. Beatrice Blackwood despaired of writing anything about New Guinea after ten months there; Katherine Routledge, Barbara Freire-Marreco and Maria Czaplicka all intended to publish more about their fieldwork, but stalled because they hoped to go back and find out more first. It was obvious to the anthropologist, if not to everyone else, that a visitor to an alien culture could hardly become an expert after only a short time living there.

Yet these women knew that distance was part of the deal. Freire-Marreco bemoaned her limited time in New Mexico, but she also reminded herself of the risks that came with staying longer: 'Nothing less than a full year's work can be satisfactory among people so reserved as the Pueblo Indians – but my consolation is, that if I had known them for a year I could never have left them!' The observer needed critical perspective and that meant standing back, going home, and translating their experience for a different audience. 'Going native' was hardly scientific.

Winifred Blackman spent nineteen years working in Egypt. She told her colleagues that she could not afford to miss a single season there. To do so would be 'absolutely fatal', because she 'should never be able to pick it up again in the same way', but she published relatively little. For Winifred, sharing her research became the greatest challenge.

In 1927 one of Winifred and her brother Aylward's closest professional friends, T. Eric Peet, Professor of Egyptology at Liverpool University, was called upon to review her first book, *The Fellahin of Upper Egypt*, for the *Journal of Egyptian Archaeology*. He ended his review with an appeal that was unusual in its directness. No doubt, he wrote, Miss Blackman was possessed of a 'divine anxiety' to collect as much information as possible before it was lost forever, but unpublished research hidden in private notebooks was just as effectively lost as that which had never been gathered. The present book was a 'semi-popular volume', by the author's own admittance, and written in a simple style for the general reader. Peet was left hoping for more. Soon, it would be Blackman's duty 'to review her position' and decide, definitively, how she was going to divide her time between research and publication.

Colleagues at Oxford also criticized her reticence. Leonard Buxton, who had returned to work at the museum in 1919 after his war service, became Reader in Physical Anthropology in 1928. He had little time for Winifred Blackman. 'I gather that Miss Blackman's idea is to live in Egypt at someone else's expense in order that she may keep a large house in central Oxford, at her own charges, to use when she likes,' he wrote to John Myres. Buxton dismissed Blackman's methods as casual and her work on 'folklore' as inconsequential, and Myres could not help but agree that 'to sit in a suburb of Cairo is not quite what was contemplated' when the British Association for the Advancement of Science, of which he was president, had awarded her funding.

Henry Balfour, however, was more measured. He pointed out that Blackman had published a book and several academic papers, although he agreed that it would be prudent for Myres to ask her for a progress report before sending her another instalment of money. Without a corresponding list of publications, fieldwork lost its academic value: all anthropologists were expected to earn their keep, and there was some doubt as to whether Blackman was doing so.

In 1927 she had won some reprieve financially when a private collector in London, the pharmaceuticals magnate Henry Wellcome, granted her £250 a year in exchange for objects relating to the history of medicine – mostly Egyptian charms and remedies – for his Historical Medical Museum. For the next five years she built a life on Wellcome's modest grant, spending most of her time in Egypt and coming home only for the summer months. From her base in Cairo she rode out to nearby villages on a donkey or travelled by train, attending markets and looking for artefacts. She was writing two more books, one on Muslim sheikhs and Coptic saints and another on Egyptian magic and medicine. Collecting for Wellcome suited her, and there was the potential for long-term financial support if she could keep him interested.

In Cairo, she lived near the Rod El Farag market, one of the largest in the country, which drew traders from all over Egypt. People came to Blackman constantly to sell things.

'I literally had to push them away from my flat before I left,' she told Wellcome at the end of one season's work. At home, she employed a servant who cooked lamb cutlets and mashed potato for her lunch parties and waited on her guests. She had a little garden where she sat in the shade of the vines in the early summer heat. As she spent less time in the villages, her letters home were taken up with her domestic concerns rather more than with her intellectual projects.

Wellcome funded Blackman for only one season at a time, so she was constantly seeking his favour. She wrote him painfully repetitive letters full of anxious assurances, eager for his continued support. No other collector could do this work, she told him, and certainly not on the limited budget he provided; there was always so much more to collect and so many excellent specimens she had been forced to turn down because she did not have enough money; and even her Egyptian friends were astonished at her achievements. She alone could make him this unique collection, she pointed out, with characteristic persistence: 'If you did work as I am doing here yourself you would realize that it would be impossible to do more than I have done. It would simply be impossible to do more, and most people could not do as much as I have done.'

Then, towards the end of his life, Henry Wellcome's expansive attitude to collecting began to change. He had acquired an incomparably large collection housed in various warehouses and properties across London, many of which were stacked with so many boxes of objects that his staff could no longer access the various rooms to see them. In his late seventies, for the first time Wellcome began to think about organizing all the things he already owned instead of buying more. In 1932, the Wellcome Historical Medical Museum closed and his staff made arrangements for a new museum to take its place, focusing their efforts on cataloguing the tons – literally tons – of material kept in storage. That summer, Wellcome told Blackman he would not support her for another season.

Winifred, who was at home in England at the time, was shocked and begged him to reconsider. She regularly dealt with his deputy, the museum's curator L.W.G. Malcolm. She pointed out that she had told Malcolm she was keeping her house in Cairo from year to year, and Malcolm had replied that she was quite right to do so. Now, Blackman held him to his word, arguing that he had led her to believe that she should keep the house on, and neither he nor Wellcome had given her enough notice of their decision. She was paying rent, and since 'most of my possessions are in that house, including books and clothes', she could not afford to go back and get them without another grant. Having written to Malcolm, she then appealed directly to Wellcome, beseeching him for one final instalment so that she could retrieve her belongings. She met with Malcolm in London to argue her case, and in October, after two months of uncertainty, he informed her that Wellcome had agreed to a small allowance of £100 for one last collecting season.

Blackman set off for Egypt again in early 1933, but she did not give up her house and it would not be her final season. She was to live in Cairo until the outbreak of the Second World War, even though she could hardly afford it. Her family must have found the money, because there is no record of her receiving any further grants from the institutions that had supported her in the past. Neither the British Association nor the University of Oxford had funded her for years. In truth, her chances of getting professional funding now were slim. She was in her sixties, she had spent twelve seasons working in Egypt, and she had not published anything for six years.

Even Winifred's family had begun to doubt her commitment to finishing her next book. She and Aylward fought over it, so much so that she feared coming home. 'A. makes such a fuss and does go on at me so and I really cannot stand it,' she wrote to her sister Elsie. 'He does not understand my kind of work and what a long time it takes and I am not strong enough to stand a lot of shouting at me as to why I have not finished.' She went on to remind Elsie that she was a very hard-working woman who had devoted her life to her research and it was not the kind of work that could be done quickly. Perhaps she worried that Elsie's loyalty was waning too. Winifred announced that she would come home, but 'if there is a great fuss' she would pack her bags and depart for Egypt again straight away.

Winifred and Aylward Blackman with friends near Dairut, in Egypt in the 1920s.

It was often Winifred who made fusses and caused disagreements. There were times when she hardly spoke to her youngest brother Barham, who was a doctor and had married a woman of whom the family did not approve. Barham distanced himself from the others. In letters they mentioned his 'selfishness' and the fact that he forgot birthdays and did not keep in touch, but while Elsie and their younger sister Flora managed easier relationships with him despite the strains, Winifred did not. With Aylward too, who could be irritable and had a fierce temper, the other women defused the drama, but not Winnie. When Mrs Blackman lamented recent family arguments in a letter to Aylward, she added, 'not that Elsie or Flora or you or I ever had anything but peace and unity between us', which rather put Winnie and Barham in their place as the prickly ones.

Winifred could hold a grudge. If she felt that her siblings owed her letters she would refuse to write to them, unlike Elsie, who gently tried to smooth relations.

Elsie played a crucial role for Winifred. The sisters had been born just two years apart and were the eldest of the Blackman children. While Flora had married, they lived together with their mother and Aylward, attending church fetes and embroidery groups, singing around the piano, writing letters and playing cards in the evenings. Winifred was sociable and could be forthright, anxious and reactionary, while Elsie was steadier and more self-contained. One friend described her as 'always serene and always amused and full of humour no matter how great the stress', while another called her 'a perfect dear, so loveable and sweet'. Winifred's world had opened out when she was forty years old and she had started the anthropology diploma at Oxford, but Elsie had remained at home.

While Winifred was away in Egypt for eight or nine months of every year, Elsie ran the household. 'What a life of perfect unselfishness and devotion yours has been, I can only in mind [sic] approach you on my knees,' Winifred wrote to her sister. Her work depended, she knew, on Elsie's commitment to their mother; on Elsie 'being worked to death without servants' because money was so tight. Winifred worried about her, particularly in later years. Both sisters wished they could be more like the other. Winifred praised Elsie's constancy, her unending domestic labours and her selfless nature. She felt unworthy of Elsie's exemplary life. But her praise also served as an invitation to reciprocate, and in return Elsie wrote of Winifred's courage and her academic successes.

After *The Fellahin of Upper Egypt* in 1927, Winifred published only two short academic papers, in 1933 and 1935. The first briefly described the Egyptian practice of using loaves of bread as harvest gifts, the second, co-authored with Aylward, discussed the use of an ancient hieroglyphic symbol in present-day amulets in Egypt. It was not much to show for all her years of research. Aylward published several books in the course of his career, including six volumes on the Meir tombs and more than sixty academic articles. He might have published more, but he was very self-critical and left behind a stack of detailed, complicated drafts of various studies that he had constantly revised but never completed. Winifred's notebooks from Egypt survive in the archives of Liverpool University, but the manuscripts she was working on do not. We will never know what she might have achieved if she had finished writing up her fieldwork.

In 1934, Aylward became Professor of Egyptology at

Liverpool University, and though the Blackmans were sad to leave Oxford, his new job eased their financial concerns. Winifred became affiliated with Aylward's department, the Institute of Archaeology, whose annual report for 1937 noted that her book on 'Folk medicine of the modern Egyptian peasants' would be published the following autumn, but it never came.

As she entered her late sixties, Winifred must have known that her annual migrations to Egypt would have to end. In the summer of 1939 she returned to England as usual, to look after her mother while Elsie went to stay with Flora for a holiday. Within a few weeks, Britain and France had declared war on Germany. Liverpool braced itself for attack: as one of the country's largest ports, it was a crucial target. While men queued in the streets to enlist, tens of thousands of children were evacuated from the city. Food rationing was introduced in January 1940, and later, clothes, household furnishings and petrol were also rationed. Wardens patrolled at night to enforce the blackout, gas masks were issued, and people were shown how to tape their windows shut in preparation for gas attacks. Council workers dug underground air-raid shelters and put up smaller concrete-and-brick shelters on residential streets. In the summer of 1940, the bombing started in earnest.

The Liverpool Blitz was second only to London's in its ferocity: four thousand people were killed in the bombings, the heaviest loss of life per head of population seen by any British city during the Second World War. The worst attacks came at the beginning of May 1941, when over seven consecutive nights the Germans dropped 870 tons of high-explosive bombs and more than 112,000 incendiary bombs on the city. One thousand five hundred people lost their lives on Merseyside that week. Vast swathes of the city were destroyed, including the nineteenth-century Custom House which housed the Head Post Office, the Central Library, the Liverpool Museum, the Corn Exchange, the Rotunda Theatre, the docks, several railway lines and countless ordinary houses; amongst them, the Blackmans' home, which was destroyed by a direct hit. Winifred and her family lost almost everything: all their furniture and belongings, including Winifred and Aylward's beloved library of Egyptology and their collections of Egyptian artefacts, which had been more than thirty years in the making.

Winifred had not been back to Egypt since the outbreak of war, and her hopes of ever returning were all but extinguished that night along with her possessions; she had lost not one home, but two.

By 8 May 1941, more than seventy thousand people had been made homeless in Liverpool, and only one of twelve 'rest centres' remained standing. People were moved to neighbouring towns and offered food from mobile canteens; many slept in church halls and schools, wrapped in blankets provided by Civil Defence Service volunteers; some even resorted to sleeping in the fields. The Blackmans decided to rent a house across the Wirral peninsula, in Abergele on the north coast of Wales, where they could spend the rest of the war in relative peace and security. That December their mother Anne Mary Blackman died, at the age of ninety-five; friends said that she had never recovered from the shock of losing her home.

Winifred, Elsie and Aylward quietly rebuilt their lives in North Wales. They played bridge and read aloud to each other in the evenings. After his retirement in the autumn of 1949, Aylward returned to Egypt for the first time in ten years, to record tomb inscriptions at Meir. Winifred stayed at home and waited for news in her brother's letters, as she had done thirty years earlier when he first went to Egypt as a young Oxford graduate. Now Winifred was too frail to accompany him; Aylward's departure may have grieved her more deeply than she cared to admit. By the time he saw her again, she had lost her mind.

In June 1950, Aylward was on board the British India liner *Matiana* sailing home from Port Said to Plymouth, when he slipped in his cabin and broke his leg. Still four hundred miles from their destination, the ship's surgeon radioed ahead to arrange for an ambulance to take Professor Blackman to hospital on arrival. Then the *Matiana* received an SOS message, transmitted by the BBC, saying that Elsie Blackman was dying and Aylward was to be taken directly to her bedside in hospital.

Unbeknown to him, the shipping agents in Plymouth, the Port Health Authorities, British Railways staff and Customs and Immigration officials sprang into action to prepare for his arrival. On the night before disembarkation, while the other 168 passengers on board slept in their cabins, Aylward was strapped to a stretcher, lowered by medics into a launch with his four suitcases, and taken into harbour. There, an ambulance was waiting to rush him to the railway station, where he was transferred from the ship's stretcher onto the train's stretcher, to continue his journey to Denbigh in North Wales. But all efforts were in vain. As the newspapers reported next day, Professor Blackman lost his '300-mile stretcher-borne race against time', and arrived on Monday morning to find that Elsie had died. Not only that, but Winifred had been taken to the North Wales Hospital – the Denbigh Asylum – overcome by shock and suffering from a breakdown. She never came home.

The North Wales Hospital, known to locals as Denbigh

Mental, was the largest mental health institution in the region; it housed some fifteen hundred patients, separated into one male and one female wing, with eight medical staff and a team of nurses to look after them. Set in spacious grounds, the three-storey buildings stretched around several courtyards. Denbigh Mental was a formidable Victorian institution in the neo-Gothic style, but it was seen as a 'progressive' hospital where the staff did their best to overcome the problems inherent in old, over-crowded accommodation. It was clean and orderly, and patients were served decent food even if the menus never changed. Some of the more able residents helped to clean the wards and assisted the nursing staff. There was a bowling green, croquet lawn and tennis courts; a library, a hair salon and a shop; plus weekly cinema showings, concerts and regular dances. Some patients were allowed to go on summer picnics, to fetes and on days out at the beach.

It was, however, still a hospital, with beds so closely packed that some patients had to climb in from the bottom of their bed and keep their belongings underneath it. The wards were locked to the patients, and many of the corridors too, so it was easy to hear a member of staff approaching thanks to the distant clank-ing of their keys. There were railings around the courtyards to stop wayward residents escaping. Some had been there for dec-ades, and the elderly like Winifred, who suffered from dementia, seldom returned home.

Elsie had agreed in the last days of her life that Winifred 'should go away', but it must have broken her heart to think of sending her sister to Denbigh. After seventy-five years together, the two women could not carry on alone. Six months after Elsie's death, in December 1950, Winifred died too, of a stroke and 'cardiovascular degeneration'.

Everyone – but everyone – described Elsie Blackman as 'unselfish'. 'She was so faithful and devoted to her loved ones,' one friend wrote after her death, 'an example to us all in unselfishness.' Elsie had stayed at home all her life, running the household for her siblings. Did her unselfishness imply a corresponding vanity in her sister, who spent two decades pursuing her intellectual interests in Egypt at her family's expense? After so many years stretching her family to the limit, relying on them to grant her her freedom, Winifred's world gradually contracted during the last decade of her life. First she left her home in Cairo, then she lost her home in Liverpool; she grieved over her mother's death, and eventually gave up hope of returning to Egypt; then she lost her sister. She had railed against her family at times, but she never left them. She always came back home, and filled her letters with her love and anxious enquiries as to their welfare. Elsie was everything that she could not be, and everything that she still needed. 'I can never say what you are to me,' she wrote in 1939, 'you are just the brightest example in my life.'

One day in February 1923, Anne and Elsie Blackman had written to Winifred in a state of great excitement, to say that Aylward was trying to get her a readership at University College London. It would pay £600 a year and transform their lives. 'My dear,' Elsie wrote, 'if you get it you <u>will</u> be lucky. You will be <u>made</u>. I do hope and pray you will.' Everyone at home was 'very much taken up' with putting Winifred's job application together, sending her telegrams, making copies of her testimonials for each of the twelve men on the selection committee, and talking to the Professor of Archaeology at UCL, Ernest Gardner, who was 'working for all he is worth' on Winifred's behalf. Elsie imagined her sister renting a little flat in London and being self-sufficient.

Living at the time in El Lahun with Saida, the widow of her much loved companion Hideyb, and their children, Winifred was 'quite bewildered' by all the telegrams arriving from home. 'I begin to feel rather nervous about undertaking that Readership,' she wrote to Elsie. 'I do not think I am really good enough for it.' She pointed out that there would be 'crowds' of people better qualified than she was; after all, she did not even have a degree. She could not accept a position that would prevent her annual trips to Egypt in any case. Her work there, she reminded them, was what she had spent years preparing for and she could not miss a single season: the way of life she was recording was constantly changing and would soon be forgotten. Her fieldwork was more important than any job that might keep her in England all year, she added.

When Winifred had the prospect of an academic position with a regular salary, she shrank from it. It was in Egypt, not in England, that she truly felt confident and useful. Her life there could be characterized as an academic indulgence or an elaborate form of escapism, but from a personal point of view it was a triumph. Many Egyptologists at the time were forced into debt. 'The opportunity of work in Egypt without losing money over it,' Aylward had been advised by his tutors early in his career, 'is not to be despised.' Winifred had little money and she had received no formal education, but she had pursued her independence and her intellectual interests with conviction. Her family accepted her unconventional aspirations and she never forfeited their love. Egypt made her happy, and the Blackmans did everything they could to help Winnie hold on to that happiness.

18

First, Last and All the Time

Beatrice Blackwood at
the Pitt Rivers Museum, 1975

When Beatrice Blackwood returned from her second trip to Melanesia in the spring of 1938, she was almost fifty years old. Faced with the prospect of life at the Pitt Rivers Museum, she wrote to a colleague: '[W]ork there is not exactly in my line of interest ... but I suppose I shall come back and settle down to sticking on labels till I get too restless to stand it any longer.' Despite her ambivalence, she has become a legendary figure at the museum, familiar to all those who have followed.

Blackwood had always worked with artefacts in museums. She was an exemplary collector and she gave nearly seven thousand objects to the Pitt Rivers, more than almost anyone else. Artefacts were not just a useful byproduct of her research, they were central to the process. She told her students that, once in the field, anthropologists could begin work on material culture straight away, because people were usually happy to let someone watch them make pottery or carve canoes to find out how it was done. And making things was far from a trivial business. It took up a significant amount of time in non-industrial societies and was imbued with social, spiritual and economic significance. It was also a practical matter that was easy to share from the start. Blackwood had kept notebooks in the field, describing in detail how people made fishing nets, stone tools and other everyday items in the villages where she worked.

She brought this expertise back to the museum, where she catalogued, stored and studied the collections and used them to teach her students. The Pitt Rivers was a busy university department when she returned from New Guinea. The small staff ran courses for students, answered enquiries, hosted visiting researchers and school parties, and managed a constant stream of new acquisitions. But there were only one or two volunteers and a temporary curatorial assistant to help the elderly and ailing Henry Balfour. Blackwood immediately took on almost all of his teaching, as well as the routine work of running the museum, while he went on extended sick leave. Balfour was in his seventies and had been unwell for several years. He died in February 1939.

After Balfour's death, several colleagues suggested Blackwood become curator of the museum. Although she had been acting curator for almost a year and was well qualified for the role, she did not apply. This was partly because she knew that her colleague, Tom Penniman, wanted it, but also because she did not particularly want it herself. 'I really prefer my own subordinate job which leaves me free for expeditions,' she explained to a colleague. 'I like collecting things and seeing them used, but I don't care to be responsible for their safe-keeping in a Museum, nor do I care much about the administrative work which is so large and important a part of a Curator's job.' Penniman, a Rhodes Scholar and fellow graduate of the Oxford diploma in anthropology, became curator, and the two friends worked together to revitalise the museum, which had become 'largely derelict' during the final years of Balfour's long reign.

The Pitt Rivers had unrivalled collections, but it was disorganized and terribly overcrowded: the roof needed fixing, several display cases had to be overhauled, and the heating and drainage systems needed repairs. Meanwhile, the artefacts had to be properly documented. Penniman and Blackwood created a card catalogue with an entry for every object in the collection, each written in duplicate, so that one series of cards could be filed according to the type of object and the other by geographical provenance. This catalogue became Blackwood's main responsibility and she created thousands of cards every year. During the war, when the museum's glass roof prevented the staff from continuing their work after sundown, they would take one of the accessions books, a few packets of index cards and a portable typewriter, and go to work in a blacked-out room in the University Museum next door. By 1963, when Penniman retired, they had created tens of thousands of cards, and Blackwood had typed the majority of them.

It is a wonder she had any time for cataloguing during the war. As well as volunteering for fire-watching, which meant staying up all night on lookout for fires caused by incendiary bombs, she also kept a large allotment and worked as an ambulance driver. Beatrice loved motoring. In the 1920s she had ridden a large motorcycle around Oxford with a sidecar full of books. Later she owned a Baby Austin nicknamed 'Amaryllis', which she drove through Oxfordshire to archaeological digs, academic meetings and friends' houses. It was unusual to see a woman driving herself in her own car, and one of her cousins recalled how curiously independent she seemed when he was a young boy in the 1950s. Once when her car broke down, he remembered, she had fixed the engine long before the mechanic arrived to help.

Driving ambulances required more than mechanical skills. Volunteer drivers during the war were taught first aid, and those who were more experienced learned advanced medical procedures like administering blood transfusions. The Oxford ambulance team drove patients between hospitals and convalescent homes around the city, as well as to outlying prisoner-of-war camps. They worked alone, day and night, with no one to attend to the patient in the back seat. Thanks to her job at the Pitt Rivers, Beatrice was also given a small petrol allowance so she could collect objects donated to the museum and investigate archaeological sites in the locality that were at risk of damage, but she could not run her car as freely as she had in peacetime. She told a friend that it was petrol rationing she found hardest.

Oxford must have seemed a very different place to her after the war. In less than ten years, four of her closest colleagues had died. Her beloved 'chief', Arthur Thomson, Professor of Anatomy, had passed away in 1935 at the age of seventy-seven. They had been great friends. Blackwood's letters to Thomson from the Solomon Islands in 1929–30 are the most natural, honest and humorous of all her surviving correspondence. She wrote to him often, admitted her insecurities and frustrations, and was not above directing the odd barb at the people she had met. Although his letters do not survive, it is clear that he wrote to reassure and encourage her, and worried that she would suffer from the isolation of fieldwork or be in physical discomfort or danger. He was sufficiently impressed by her letters to suggest that she publish them to advertise the work of the department, and although she had reservations, she considered it because she knew that 'it would please you, my very dear Professor and friend'. As a belated birthday present, she sent him a walking-stick carved from coconut wood by an inhabitant of Petats, the Pacific island that she had visited in 1929 – a highly prized item because coconut was so difficult to work. She and Thomson joked and gossiped together, and on the way home from New Guinea she could think of nothing better than having tea with him at the University Museum.

Thomson had died shortly before she left on her second field trip to the Pacific. She must have missed his gentle counsel during her trying months with the Anga.

Soon after she returned to Oxford, just a few weeks after Balfour's death in February 1939, Leonard Buxton died of pneumonia at the age of forty-nine after only four days' illness. Buxton and Blackwood had worked together under Thomson during the 1920s, researching the cranial collections at the University Museum and teaching diploma students. It had been one of her happiest times. They were great allies – she called Buxton 'Bones' – and they shared an acerbic wit. He could be arrogant, but he was a genial and erudite friend. For a time, after his death, Blackwood took on his teaching as well as Balfour's.

In February 1943 R.R. Marett, the last of the old guard, who had nurtured the careers of the women anthropologists he trained at Oxford, suffered a heart attack and died at the university while waiting for a meeting to begin. 'We miss him constantly,' Blackwood wrote, '. . . we could always talk things over with him and be sure of his broad judgment and cheery sane outlook on life'. Like Thomson, Marett had given Beatrice warm encouragement. When he read the draft of her book *Both*

Sides of Buka Passage he had professed himself unable to find a single thing to criticize, calling it a magnum opus and assuring her that her 'scientific fame is secure'. Just a few days before he died, he had written to Penniman: 'Miss Blackwood isn't big enough for all the medals that ought to be hung about her dainty person!'

With many of her closest colleagues gone, an old friend re-entered Beatrice's life after the war. Of the women she knew in her Somerville days, Barbara Freire-Marreco had been no more than an acquaintance, but their friendship flourished in the 1950s when Barbara and her husband Robert Aitken were living in Hampshire. Beatrice took to staying with them at their home in the village of Broughton. They would discuss the latest news in anthropological circles, sharing books and articles, and Beatrice bought them things from the Oxford shops. She helped Robert sort through the ten boxes of notes and pamphlets on ploughs and other agricultural equipment that he had accrued over the years and intended to donate to the Pitt Rivers. When he died in 1965 at the age of eighty-three, Barbara wrote to Beatrice, 'How well we three knew and valued each other!' She confessed that it felt strange not to be able to tell Robert about the funeral service and share all that people had written in his praise.

Beatrice worried about Barbara in her widowhood. She was always so cheerful, but her health was poor and she had little money. She suffered from severe arthritis and propelled herself around the village in a lever-driven tricycle. By the 1960s she was struggling with the stairs at home, and even writing letters could leave her short of breath. Her friends rallied to help – the butcher in Broughton insisted on giving her dinners ready cooked. She died two years after Robert, in 1967. She had told

Beatrice to take her Navajo saddlebag and silver bracelets when she was gone: mementos from a friend, and from another era of anthropology.

Since Barbara Freire-Marreco, Katherine Routledge, Maria Czaplicka, Winifred Blackman and Beatrice Blackwood had embarked on their careers, a great deal had changed in the discipline. Marett, Thomson and Balfour had held sway over Oxford anthropology for more than thirty years, fostering an

Barbara Aitken on her tricycle in Broughton, Hampshire.

interdisciplinary and museum-based ethos for the subject that endured, even when their approach was considered outdated elsewhere. It was Bronislaw Malinowski at the London School of Economics who trained the generation of British anthropologists that rose to leadership positions during the 1930s and 40s. Blackwood saw the merit of Malinowski's 'functionalism' and taught her students to follow his example as a fieldworker, but she believed that his teaching came at the expense of other perspectives that were equally important, including the historical links between different cultures.

To her, the connections between material culture, archaeology, human anatomy and anthropology were powerfully informative, but her younger colleagues regarded such interests as a distraction from the urgent task of understanding the here-and-now of foreign cultures. Though Blackwood advocated intensive fieldwork, she remained at heart a generalist among those younger social anthropologists whose ambitions were more narrowly focused. She had felt these tensions keenly while working with the Anga, particularly when her duty to Balfour to collect objects for the museum impeded her fieldwork. 'All the functionalists will drop on me for coming back without the proper number of marriage classes etc.,' she wrote.

Long after the war, she dreamt of returning to New Guinea. For decades, she bore the disappointment of never working in the uncontrolled territory and the frustration of having had to leave the Anga after only nine months. In 1953 she explained to a colleague, 'I have never ceased to regret that I did not get that last three months, which from previous experience I expected to yield more information than the whole of the first nine.'

Her responsibilities at the Pitt Rivers Museum left her little time to work on the New Guinea material. She did not enjoy writing. She had found *Both Sides of Buka Passage* 'an awful sweat to write'. The process of turning her field notes from the Solomon Islands into a book had simply reminded her of all the things she did not know. It was a 'vicious circle', she explained, because she had to write the book before she could even dream of a second trip to Melanesia, but she needed to go back and fill in the 'glaring gaps' before she could write the book. It had 'dragged on' for years, and she did not relish the thought of attempting another. She joked with a colleague that if she failed to get a publishing contract for her Anga research, '[W]ell, it will save me the trouble of writing up what material I have!'

Blackwood published journal articles and a short guide to Anga technology, but she never wrote a full ethnographic account of her work there. Later scholars would recognize the limitations of her research, and she recognized those limitations too: she had not been able to fully understand Anga social structure because the people had resisted her enquiries: as a consequence, her notes were fragmentary and descriptive, with little theoretical weight. As one reviewer put it, she could describe what the Anga did, but she never fully understood *why* they did it. Her colleagues, however, welcomed what she did write. When E.E. Evans-Pritchard, the pre-eminent anthropologist at Oxford after the war, commented in conversation that *Both Sides of Buka Passage* was 'first class ethnography based on first class fieldwork', she could not hide her surprise or her pleasure at receiving the compliment, but her publication record suggests that she understood what her fieldwork was worth.

Blackwood was recognized for her achievements as a fieldworker when the Royal Anthropological Institute awarded her the Rivers Memorial Medal in 1943. She went on to serve at the highest levels of various academic societies, becoming vice-president of the Royal Anthropological Institute in the late 1950s; she was also involved with local folklore societies in Oxfordshire and continued to join archaeological excavations.

Beatrice Blackwood in later life, *c.*1960.

Meanwhile, daily life was taken up with the practicalities of working at the Pitt Rivers. Like Barbara Freire-Marreco and Winifred Blackman before her, she continued to conscientiously register hundreds of objects. The museum's annual reports record her organizing 'various special catalogues'; documenting individual collections bequeathed to the museum;

working on regional and subject indexes; preparing a 'critical inventory' of four thousand musical instruments for publication; maintaining three card indexes, and updating accession registers. She ran several museum courses, guiding students around the displays, sending them to hunt through the exhibition cases for different specimens, and laying objects out on tables so that they could take a closer look. Her lectures were designed 'to cover the world in one year', and as is often true of those working in museums, her interests remained broad. She knew more about the collections than anyone else: 'She was our database in the days before computers,' one colleague remembered.

Blackwood formally retired in 1959 at the age of seventy, but she carried on coming into the museum as usual. She was made Honorary Assistant Curator in 1966, and in 1974 as she continued to work full time in her eighty-fifth year, her colleagues petitioned for her to be awarded an honorary doctorate. She had no idea, and would no doubt have been embarrassed to know that she had been put forward for such a distinction. The then curator of the Pitt Rivers, Schuyler Jones, wrote in support of the petition, noting all the scholars Blackwood had taught who now occupied distinguished academic positions around the world. *Both Sides of Buka Passage*, he continued, 'ranks with the best', and she had devoted forty years to perfecting the museum's catalogue. 'Correspondence addressed to her from abroad flows into this department in astonishing quantities,' Jones wrote, and her work was well known in North America and South-East Asia.

The principals of Somerville College and St Hugh's warmly supported the application, but the University Council did not award Blackwood an honorary doctorate. Kenneth Kirkwood, Rhodes Professor of Race Relations, expressed his disappointment and hoped that Oxford would find an occasion to publicly acknowledge 'BB's long and dedicated and very modestly remunerated, exceptional and indispensable services'. Meanwhile, Blackwood came into work every day just as she always had.

Around this time, she crashed her Baby Austin and her insurance company asked her to retake her driving test. Blackwood was incensed and refused, preferring instead to walk to and from work. Without her car, however, life became increasingly frustrating and physically demanding, and as winter set in she allowed a colleague to drive her home. She was not used to relying on people's goodwill to take her to work or out in the evenings. Shortly afterwards, one Monday morning, she rang the museum to say she had a cold and would stay at home; two days later she died.

'I am a field worker first, last and all the time, and never shall be anything else,' she had written to Tom Penniman in 1937. The Pitt Rivers Museum had become, in its own way, Beatrice's final field site. She worked there for four decades, surrounded by fragments of her travels. From dance masks to shell ornaments, bark cloth to stone tools, even her photographs and films of the people she lived with in Melanesia: all had been transformed into specimens for teaching purposes. Once, when a researcher wrote to the museum to ask for a copy of one of her publications on the Anga, she sent it to him herself, joking, 'He probably thought I died years ago'.

Blackwood was often the first to arrive at work in the morning and the last to leave at night. She worked quietly in among the artefacts, year after year, and in some ways she became muted like the objects she cared for. She rarely talked about her work with family and friends. One relative remembered: '[F]inding out from her what she did was always difficult. She seemed reluctant to talk about it, as if her work wasn't important or interesting.' At the museum, she worked in the background and avoided telling personal anecdotes about her time in the field. She was too reserved and too busy to spend time chatting about her past. She rarely spoke out in staff meetings, preferring to talk to visitors and students personally and answer any questions in private.

Sometimes, Beatrice Blackwood's fiery side burst through. If she saw somebody mishandle an object or neglect museum protocols she could be 'fiercely sharp', and the transgressor would soon be listening to 'a wrathful lecture delivered with a remarkable economy of words ... a lesson which no one on the receiving end was likely to forget'. When one day she spotted a young member of staff dangling a skull with his finger and thumb hooked through the eye sockets, she let him know 'in no uncertain terms' the error of his ways. Her fury was such that she came back later to apologize to him and explained, in more measured terms, that the bones around the eye were among the most delicate in the human head. On another occasion, she opened the lecture theatre door to find her students throwing paper aeroplanes. There was a split second of silence before Blackwood 'let rip', leaving many of them feeling 'very small indeed'.

These were the two sides to Beatrice in later life: the reticent, conscientious academic who scrupulously avoided attention, and the exacting, energetic woman who could not always contain her passions. Sometimes the objects reanimated her in a way that was startling to those more familiar with her quieter side.

One day she decided to demonstrate the use of a New Guinean bullroarer to a junior colleague. The bullroarer is a ceremonial instrument consisting of a thin slat of wood attached to a long cord that is swung in a circle to create a deep, resonating hum. Heard in the forests of New Guinea, this mysterious object is shrouded in secrecy, and Beatrice had negotiated hard to acquire one. Now, in the early 1950s, she could be found in a yard behind the Pitt Rivers Museum, surrounded by storage buildings and delivery vans, hurling the instrument around her head – to her young colleague's amazement.

[I watched t]he tiny figure of Beatrice whirling the device round and round at arm's length over her head, giving a little dance as she threw herself into the demonstration, and creating the impression that if the wooden blade had been larger she might have risen vertically like a helicopter. The mysterious humming sound was very satisfactorily produced and at the end of this tutorial … somewhat out of breath, but eyes sparkling she said, 'There! Now you know how a bullroarer works and how it sounds.'

19

A Woman Ought Not to Know

Anthropologists Between Worlds

On her way home from the Solomon Islands in late 1930, Beatrice Blackwood wrote that her fieldwork was 'rapidly coming to feel like a cinema show I attended in the past'. She had often felt as though she was 'in the pictures' while in the Pacific, particularly when she first arrived. The thick tropical forest, the white sandy beaches and the palm-leaf huts looked like paradise. It seemed a fantasy world: beautiful, alien, and completely separate from anything she had known before, with its own rules and rhythms – a place where she could become someone new. At the end of her time there, the picture-house lights went up, she sailed away, and that world vanished.

At first, life in industrial society came as a shock. It was hard to remember who she had been before. Arriving in Sydney in October that year, she wrote, 'Australia is wet and cold and miserable and crowded and noisy and I feel like the wild man from Borneo.' As she adjusted to the people, the cars and the shops, and to the museums and universities she visited on her way home, the village of Kurtachi with its rows of huts perched on the forested cliffs of Bougainville Island felt increasingly unreal, as well it might.

She had spent a year living in extreme isolation from her own culture, with little more than a typewriter, a table, a few billycans and a kitten. She had washed herself in an iron bucket and worn cotton breeches every day. She had dispensed medicines to sick children, exchanged sticks of tobacco for stone tools, and listened to stories of love magic and creation myths around a hurricane lamp after dark. She had watched a woman scream for hours, crouching all night while others held her down, before delivering her baby onto a sheath of palm leaves spread on the ground between her knees. She had ventured deep into the bush along with hundreds of men walking single-file through the night, carrying torches and spears, to watch young boys howl in terror as they were ritually killed and reborn during initiation ceremonies that no woman had seen before. She had felt the 'ominous roar' of the bullroarer swelling through the rainforest and had known its power to move those who heard it.

Back in the polished lecture halls of Oxford University, few could imagine the quiet and conscientious Beatrice Blackwood having such visceral encounters. Years later, when she picked up a bullroarer and hurled it around her head to awaken the lost world within her, it was the transformation in Miss Blackwood that astonished her colleague as much as the sound she produced. Suddenly vibrant, dancing, throwing her body forward as though she might take flight, the bullroarer discharged deep energies inside her that were almost inappropriate. After the demonstration, she must have steadied her breath, smoothed down her skirt and tidied her hair before walking back into the quiet, dimly lit galleries of the Pitt Rivers Museum to put the bullroarer safely away in its drawer.

All of the remarkable women in this book escaped their own society in the name of scholarship. To Barbara Freire-Marreco the separation felt slightly surreal. 'I simply cannot realize how far I am from England and all of you,' she had written to her Oxford friends when she first arrived in the pueblos of New Mexico. Within weeks, she declared that she could happily live in a pueblo forever. Daily life in Santa Clara, preserving fruit and trading parrot feathers, was so unfamiliar it had given her the 'scope to live and be a real person' for the first time.

Inevitably, when the moment came to return home, some part of that 'real person' had to be left behind. Katherine Routledge had neared the end of her stay in Easter Island with trepidation. She 'simply daren't think' of leaving the place where her dreams had been filled with beauty, and the intense stillness had brought her peace. She would have to put away her 'knock about clothes' and take her last breath of island air. 'I can't think what it will be to be civilized again,' she admitted to her family. For the rest of her life she held that distant world, those alternative identities, within herself. Years later, on a foggy London day in December, she discussed her travels with a journalist. She told him about being lost at sea for fourteen days while the water rations were running low, and remembered sitting on a coral strand talking to a local woman about the ancient history of the Pacific islands. She announced that she was writing a new book, but she seemed distracted. 'I should like to be back there again', she said, still gazing out of the window.

Fieldwork was more than a job; it was liberation. Winifred Blackman, who likened her life in Egypt to being 'in a dream' or a 'fairyland' and who had never felt so healthy and happy before, returned year after year. Sometimes she was afraid of being too happy, in case something came along to spoil it. She declared Egypt her 'life's work' as though the designation might help secure her future there.

As children, these women could hardly have dreamt of working at the University of Oxford, never mind living in distant and dangerous lands for the purpose of academic research. To become anthropologists, they had to resist powerful social forces that pressed domesticity on them at every turn: the parents who wished they would stay at home or marry; the friends who quietly disapproved of women earning their own living; the professionals who objected to female anthropologists because, as one senior colleague put it, 'there are many things a woman ought not to know'. Most women were educated on the understanding that they would become good wives and mothers. Although they might usefully be employed in secretarial tasks, safely confined in offices, women were thought to be constitutionally ill-suited to the rigours of fieldwork.

Even the Oxford professors who had done so much to champion their research voiced concerns. Robert Marett had advised Katherine Routledge against travelling to Easter Island on her yacht the *Mana*. Fearing that the voyage would be too strenuous, he suggested she take a commercial liner instead, as far as Valparaíso, then join the *Mana* just for the last stretch of the journey. She disregarded his advice.

Winifred Blackman had refused to return home when her faithful servant Hideyb was violently murdered in Egypt. Maria Czaplicka had pressed ahead with her plans to explore Siberia even when Marett's efforts to assemble a team of scientists to accompany her fell through. Beatrice Blackwood doggedly resisted Ernest Chinnery's attempts to alter her travel plans. At Oxford, women were not even allowed to eat dinner at a men's college. On the other side of the world, these 'lady anthropologists' fought hard to prevent men from compromising their ambitions.

Their courage was exceptional. The dangers they faced were considerable: life-threatening diseases, the cruel indifference of the elements, and the hostility of those they wanted to study. Stories of aggression had a particular currency, but the threat was sometimes real. Blackwood knew of several patrol officers and gold prospectors who had been killed in New Guinea. Routledge had suffered sleepless nights with a gun next to her pillow when Angata's rebellion took hold. Winifred Blackman witnessed violent unrest in the villages of Upper Egypt, apparently without fear for her own life. They all accepted danger as part of their autonomy.

None suffered greater physical hardship than Maria Czaplicka. Before embarking on her Siberian trek, she had been warned that no woman could endure the conditions and that she would have to abandon her work. She proved her doubters wrong, braving a world of perpetual darkness, freezing temperatures, fierce storms and limitless snows. No one heard from her for more than six months as she searched for people who were believed to suffer from 'mental perversions' brought on by the extreme environment. In her book *My Siberian Year*, Czaplicka described her own mental perversions as she survived the agony and ecstasy of an Arctic winter. She lost consciousness, spewed blood, starved and hallucinated, and at times her fears and the pressure to succeed incapacitated her.

The isolation of fieldwork could indeed cause intense psychological stress. Routledge wrote of the 'mental and spiritual hunger of those lonely places' where anthropologists worked. Depression, feelings of futility, frustration and self-doubt could haunt you, particularly when working alone. Blackwood suffered severe mental distress at the thought of her professional shortcomings, at times feeling 'imprisoned' in the field. To visit a foreign culture for a few months or a year, studying people who might be unsympathetic or perplexed by your intentions, and then produce a comprehensive assessment of the dynamics of that particular culture's social order, was a hard task. Freire-Marreco, too, regularly referred to her own 'failures' as an anthropologist. She and Blackwood were quick to blame themselves for their inadequacies, as they saw it, believing at times that 'a better man' would have been more successful.

Unlike their male peers, these five women could not realistically expect a professorship or any other permanent university position. Anthropology was a small discipline: there were few jobs and plenty of men to take them. Working in the Trobriand Islands during the war, Malinowski had been driven by the promise of future glory. His field diaries, published posthumously in 1967, revealed that far from living in splendid isolation with his 'natives', he had been intensely lonely and often despondent in the field. In these moments he worked 'with immortality in view', and imagined himself adding letters to his name: FRS, CSI – Fellow of the Royal Society, Companion of the Order of the Star of India – even 'Sir'.

Malinowski was young, unemployed, and had little money at the time. His clear sense of his own destiny was a privilege available only to men.

The field and its freedoms offered women different opportunities. The women in this book wanted, more than anything, to travel far away. Other anthropologists did not necessarily share these longings. Neither Malinowski nor Radcliffe-Brown had particularly enjoyed fieldwork. It was a necessary part of their education that would lead to more orthodox academic occupations; a form of intellectual investment that could be turned into important books, influential theories, and status. By contrast, the Oxford women did not present complex theories. They wrote books reflecting their position in the field: modest and attentive. They tried to be true to their data and its limitations, and their work was respected without being celebrated.

Marett had urged Blackwood to 'let yourself go a little more here and there' when she was drafting *Both Sides of Buka Passage*, but writing up her fieldwork only served to remind her of everything she did not know. She never saw herself as 'master' of the village, as Malinowski had. She and her contemporaries refused – or were unable – to transform the admiration they earned from their colleagues into well-paid, high-status academic jobs. There was no precedent for a senior female anthropologist; there was hardly any precedent for a male one.

At home, Blackwood and her peers earned recognition, and a voice. They worked in a man's world, writing papers, giving lectures and publishing books. They proved that fieldwork in other cultures must be done by women as well as by men if it was to have credibility. This, in itself, was exceptional, and a lasting legacy.

Among the new generation of female anthropologists trained to go into the field during the 1920s and 30s, many of them under Malinowski, were Hortense Powdermaker and Camilla Wedgwood, whom Blackwood had met in the Pacific. Other notable scholars to emerge in the interwar years were Audrey Richards, who worked in Zambia, Uganda and South Africa, and Phyllis Kaberry who did fieldwork in Australia and Cameroon. Lucy Mair worked in Uganda, and Hilda Kuper in Swaziland and South Africa. These women went on to hold university lectureships and readerships. Mair became Professor at the LSE in 1963; Oxford and Cambridge, however, did not award their first female professorships in anthropology until the 1990s.

This later generation of social anthropologists did not look back. The subject underwent a radical shift and the multidisciplinary ethos of the early twentieth century quickly came to seem outdated. Their Oxford predecessors were too easily dismissed as museum collectors, archaeologists or physical anthropologists. Far from being celebrated as female pioneers in anthropological fieldwork, they were almost entirely overlooked by those who followed. Few anthropologists working after the Second World War would have known their work. If they had voiced their common interests it might have been different, but they never formed a coherent group.

Anthropology allowed them to live more fully than they had had reason to hope for growing up. It made a virtue of their peripheral status and conferred on them special insight. They dared to navigate the edges of society and push at the boundaries of what it meant to be a woman.

In March 1914, Katherine Routledge's boat the *Mana* lay in a bay in the Juan Fernández archipelago, a group of tiny islands in the South Pacific Ocean, four hundred miles off the coast of Chile. The deckhouse door was open and Katherine was sitting at her typewriter within, composing a letter to her nieces in England. Across the water, forested mountains rose sharply from the sea, and caves, 'like great halls', cut into the rock below. 'I don't think that you have been yet to Robinson Crusoe's Island,' she wrote to Evelyn, who was sixteen, and her eleven-year-old sister Hilda, 'so perhaps you may like to hear about it.'

Katherine had given a copy of *Robinson Crusoe* to Evelyn for Christmas four years earlier. Now, she described the history of the island, Más a Tierra, and the story of Alexander Selkirk, the marooned sailor who had inspired Daniel Defoe's novel. The girls must have read Katherine's letter in wide-eyed wonder. They had never known a woman like their aunt. That she had lived on the frontiers of British East Africa, writing about the Kikuyu people who lived there, was remarkable. That she had spent a year as the only woman on board a small boat sailing halfway around the world to one of the remotest islands in the Pacific was barely believable. At the age of fifty, Aunt Katherine was writing her own adventure story, and she knew it.

In her letter to the children, Katherine played on the improbability of her situation. This was not, she explained, Robinson Crusoe's island as they had grown to know it, on the hearthrug or in the nursery, or 'where the shrubs are in the corner of the garden'. This was the real thing. The girls might protest that surely there never was a real Robinson Crusoe or a real island, but that, she wrote, would be worse than saying there never was a real Tom the water baby, or a real Alice in Wonderland. Katherine had visited the 'dear little cave' where Crusoe lived, and she had picked her way on a pony up the mountain tracks to his lookout post – 'So that is the end of the matter,' she declared.

The water lapped against the rocks as she wrote. She sketched a picture of the shoreline for them. 'Can you see Crusoe with his umbrella and his goatskin clothes coming out of the cave? I felt as if I could.'

References

I have refrained from using footnotes or citations in the text. However, extensive notes, including sources for all quotations, and a timeline with key dates, are online at www.franceslarson.com/undreamedshores.

Winifred Blackman
Manuscripts and Archives

Bodleian Library, University of Oxford.
    John Linton Myres papers. (Myres 4. Fols. 93–107.)
Garstang Museum of Archaeology, Liverpool University.
    Winifred Blackman papers. (FC 12/1–4.)
    Winifred Blackman photographic archive.
Liverpool University Special Collections and Archives, Liverpool University Library.
    Blackman family papers. (D84 (5 boxes) and D271 (1 envelope).)
Pitt Rivers Museum, University of Oxford.
    Blackman artefact collections, and accession records.
    Letter and press clippings relating to Winifred Blackman. (Manuscript Collections, Misc. MS 1-2.)
    Museum Annual Reports.
Wellcome Archives and Manuscripts, Wellcome Library.
    Winifred Blackman collecting reports for the Wellcome Historical Medical Museum. (WA/HMM/CM/Col/12.)

Publications by Winifred Blackman

Blackman, W.S. 'The Magical and Ceremonial Uses of Fire.' *Folklore*, vol. 27, no. 4, Dec. 1916, pp. 352–77.

—. 'The Rosary in Magic and Religion.' *Folklore*, vol. 29, no. 4, Dec. 1918, pp. 255–80.

—. 'Traces of Couvade(?) In England.' *Folklore*, vol. 29, no. 4, Dec. 1918, pp. 319–21.

—. 'Some Modern Egyptian Graveside Ceremonies.' *Discovery Magazine*, vol. 2, no. 20, 1921, pp. 207–12.

—. 'Some Occurrences of the Corn-'Arūseh in Ancient Egyptian Tomb Paintings.' *Journal of Egyptian Archaeology*, vol. 8, no. 1, Apr. 1922, pp. 235–40.

—. 'Fertility Rites in Modern Egypt.' *Discovery Magazine*, vol. 2, no. 30, 1922, pp. 154–8.

—. 'Festivals Celebrating Local Saints in Modern Egypt – I.' *Discovery Magazine*, vol. 4, no. 37, 1923, pp. 11–14.

—. 'Moslim Saints in Modern Egypt.' *Discovery Magazine*, vol. 4, no. 47, 1923, pp. 283–7.

—. 'Some Modern Egyptian Saints.' *Discovery Magazine*, vol. 5, no. 51, 1924, pp. 67–71.

—. 'Some Beliefs among the Egyptian Peasants with Regard to *'afārīt*.' *Folklore*, vol. 35, no. 2, June 1924, pp. 176–84.

—. 'An Englishwoman in Upper Egypt – I.' *The Wide World*, vol. 52, no. 310, 1924, pp. 271–6.

—. 'An Englishwoman in Upper Egypt – II.' *The Wide World*, vol. 52, no. 311, 1924, pp. 355–60.

—. 'An Englishwoman in Upper Egypt – III.' *The Wide World*, vol. 52, no. 312, 1924, pp. 446–52.

—. 'Sacred Trees in Modern Egypt.' *Journal of Egyptian Archaeology*, vol. 11, no. 1/2, Apr. 1925, p. 56.

—. 'An Ancient Egyptian Custom Illustrated by a Modern Survival.' *Man*, vol. 25, May 1925, p. 65.

—. 'Some Social and Religious Customs in Modern Egypt.' *Bulletin de la Société Royale de Géographie d'Égypte*, vol. 14, 1926, pp. 47–61.

—. 'The Karin and Karineh.' *Journal of the Royal Anthropological Institute of Great Britain and Ireland*, vol. 56, 1926, p. 163.

—. 'A Fertility Rite in Modern Egypt.' *Man*, vol. 26, July 1926, p. 113.

—. 'Sheikhs: The Truth.' *Daily Mail*, 3 October 1926.

—. *The Fellahin of Upper Egypt*. George G. Harrap & Co. Ltd., 1927.

—. 'Some Further Notes on a Harvesting Scene.' *Journal of Egyptian Archaeology*, vol. 19, no. 1, May 1933, pp. 31–2.

—. (with Blackman, A.M.) 'An Ancient Egyptian Symbol as a Modern Egyptian Amulet.' *L'Annuaire de l'Institut de Philologie et d'Histoire Orientales*, vol. 3, 1935, pp. 91–5.

Biographical Sources for Winifred Blackman

Annual report and prospectus of the Institute of Archaeology, University of Liverpool, no. 34, 1937–8, p. 14.

Annual report and prospectus of the Institute of Archaeology, University of Liverpool, no. 35, 1938–9, pp. 12–17.

Anon. 'Surviving Lore of Ancient Egypt. Miss Blackman on her Discoveries.' *The Times*, 13 August 1929, p. 13.

Anon. 'Secret Magic of Egypt.' *Daily Mail*, 14 October 1931, p. 5.

Anon. 'Notorious Witches of Pendle.' *Lancashire Evening Post*, 20 October 1931, p. 4.

Anon. 'Oxford Woman's Research in Egypt: Miss Blackman Interviewed.' *Oxford Times*, 5 October 1928.

Anon. 'Hustle by Injured Professor.' *Western Morning News*, 27 June 1950, p. 1.

Anon. 'Professor Too Late.' *Western Morning News*, 28 June 1950, p. 3.

Bierbrier, M.J. 'Winifred S. Blackman.' *Who Was Who in Egyptology* (3rd revised edition), Egypt Exploration Society, 1995, p. 49.

Blackwood, B. 'Miss W.S. Blackman.' *Nature*, vol. 167, no. 4239, Jan. 1951, p. 135.

Fairman, H.W. 'Aylward Manley Blackman.' *Journal of Egyptian Archaeology*, vol. 42, no. 1, Dec. 1956, pp. 102–4.

Hobley, C.W. '*The Fellahin of Upper Egypt* by Winifred S. Blackman.' *English Historical Review*, vol. 43, no. 171, 1928, pp. 449–50.

Hopkins, N.S. 'W.S. Blackman and Anthropological Research.' In

Hopkins, Nicholas S. (ed.). *Upper Egypt: Life along the Nile.* Aarhus University Press, 2003, pp. 35–47.

Ikram, S. 'Introduction.' In Blackman, Winifred. *The Fellahin of Upper Egypt.* American University in Cairo Press, 2000, pp. v–xiii.

Larson, F. *An Infinity of Things: How Sir Henry Wellcome Collected the World.* Oxford University Press, 2009.

Peet, T.E. 'The Fellahin of Upper Egypt.' *Journal of Egyptian Archaeology*, vol. 14, no. 1/2, May 1928, p. 197.

Sattin, A. *The Pharaoh's Shadow.* Victor Gollancz, 2000.

Spoer, A.M. '*The Fellahin of Upper Egypt* by Winifred S. Blackman.' *Folklore*, vol. 29, 1928, pp. 406–9.

Stevenson, A. '"Labelling and Cataloguing at Every Available Moment": W.S. Blackman's Collection of Egyptian Amulets.' *Journal of Museum Ethnography*, no. 26, 2013, pp. 138–49.

del Vesco, P. 'Jewels from the Nile: The Ethnographical Collection of Winifred Blackman.' *Rawi: Egypt's Heritage Review*, no. 7, 2015.

Beatrice Blackwood
Manuscripts and Archives

Bodleian Library, University of Oxford Archives.
  Beatrice Blackwood staff file. (FA/9/2/90.)
Oxford University Press Archives.
  Papers relating to the publication of *Both Sides of Buka Passage.* (LB 7382.)
Pitt Rivers Museum, University of Oxford.
  Blackwood artefact and photograph collections, and accession records.
  Beatrice Blackwood papers. (Manuscript Collections, 54 Boxes.)
  Museum Annual Reports.
Somerville College Archives, University of Oxford.
  Beatrice Blackwood file.
  College Register entry.
  College Reports.

Publications by Beatrice Blackwood

Blackwood, B.M. 'A Study of Mental Testing in Relation to

Anthropology.' *Mental Measurement Monographs*, Williams & Wilkins, 1927.

—. 'Tales of the Chippewa Indians.' *Folklore*, vol. 40, no. 4, Dec. 1929, pp. 315–44.

—. 'Racial Differences in Skin-Colour as Recorded by the Colour Top.' *Journal of the Royal Anthropological Institute of Great Britain and Ireland*, vol. 60, Jan. 1930, p. 137.

—. 'Report on Field Work in Buka and Bougainville.' *Oceania*, vol. 2, no. 2, Dec. 1931, pp. 199–219.

—. 'Folk Stories from the Northern Solomons.' *Folklore*, vol. 43, no. 1, Mar. 1932, pp. 61–96.

—. (with Buxton, L.H.D.) 'An Introduction to Oxfordshire Folklore.' *Folklore*, vol. 45, no. 1, Mar. 1934, pp. 29–46.

—. 'Treatment of the Sick in the Solomon Islands.' *Folklore*, vol. 46, no. 2, June 1935, pp. 148–61.

—. *Both Sides of Buka Passage: An Ethnographic Study of Social, Sexual, and Economic Questions in the North-Western Solomon Islands.* Clarendon Press, 1935.

—. (with Buxton, L.H.D., et al.) 'Measurements of Oxfordshire Villagers.' *Journal of the Royal Anthropological Institute of Great Britain and Ireland*, vol. 69, no. 1, 1939, p. 1.

—. 'Leonard Halford Dudley Buxton, D.Sc., F.S.A.' *Folklore*, vol. 50, no. 2, June 1939, pp. 204–5.

—. 'Life on the Upper Watut, New Guinea.' *Geographical Journal*, vol. 94, no. 1, July 1939, pp. 11–24.

—. 'Folk-Stories of a Stone Age People in New Guinea.' *Folklore*, vol. 50, no. 3, Sept. 1939, pp. 209–42.

—. 'Crafts of a Stone Age People in Central New Guinea.' *Man*, vol. 40, Jan. 1940, p. 11.

—. 'Use of Plants among the Kukukuku of Southeastern Central New Guinea.' *Proceedings of the Sixth Pacific Science Congress of the Pacific Science Association*, University of California Press, vol. 4, 1940, pp. 111–26.

—. 'Some Arts and Industries of New Guinea and New Britain.' *Man*, vol. 41, July 1941, p. 88.

—. 'Mary Edith Durham.' *Man*, vol. 45, 1945, pp. 22–3.

—. 'Reserve Dyeing in New Guinea.' *Man*, vol. 50, May 1950, p. 53.

—. *The Technology of a Modern Stone Age People in New Guinea*. Oxford University Press, 1950.

—. 'Sir Francis Knowles, Bart.' *Nature*, vol. 171, no. 4358, May 1953, p. 818.

—. (with Danby, P.M.) 'A Study of Artificial Cranial Deformation in New Britain.' *Journal of the Royal Anthropological Institute of Great Britain and Ireland*, vol. 85, no. 1/2, 1955, pp. 173–91.

—. 'Robert H. Lowie.' *Man*, vol. 62, Jun. 1962, pp. 86–8.

—. 'The Classification of Artefacts in the Pitt Rivers Museum, Oxford.' *Occasional Papers on Technology 10*, Pitt Rivers Museum, University of Oxford, 1970.

—. 'The Origin and Development of the Pitt Rivers Museum.' *Occasional Papers on Technology 11*, Pitt Rivers Museum, University of Oxford, 1970.

Biographical Sources for Beatrice Blackwood

Anon. 'Miss B.M. Blackwood: Distinguished Anthropologist.' *The Times*, 2 December 1975.

Gosden, C., and Knowles, C. *Collecting Colonialism: Material Culture and Colonial Change*. Berg, 2001.

Gosden, C., et al. *Knowing Things: Exploring the Collections at the Pitt Rivers Museum, 1884–1945*. Oxford University Press, 2007.

Hallpike, C.R. *The Kukukuku of the Upper Watut: Edited from Beatrice Blackwood's Published Articles and Unpublished Field Notes*. Monograph Series no. 2, Pitt Rivers Museum, University of Oxford, 1978.

Jones, S. 'The Origin and Development of the Pitt Rivers Museum.' (A revised and updated version of Blackwood's 1970 publication.) Pitt Rivers Museum, University of Oxford, 1991.

—. et al. 'Beatrice Blackwood Remembered.' *Friends of the Pitt Rivers Museum 10th Anniversary Newsletter*, pp. 4–6, 1994.

Knowles, C. 'Beatrice Mary Blackwood (1889–1975).' In Petch, A. (ed.). *Collectors Volume 2*. Pitt Rivers Museum, University of Oxford, 1998, pp. 6–13.

—. 'Reverse Trajectories: Beatrice Blackwood as Collector and Anthropologist.' In O'Hanlon, M. and Welsch, R. (eds.).

Hunting the Gatherers: Ethnographic Collectors, Agents and Agency in Melanesia 1870s-1930s. Berghahn Books, 2000, pp. 251–72.

—. 'Blackwood, Beatrice Mary (1889–1975).' *Oxford Dictionary of National Biography*, Oxford University Press, 2004.

Larson, F. 'Did He Ever Darn His Stockings?' Beatrice Blackwood and the Ethnographic Authority of Bronislaw Malinowski.' *History and Anthropology*, vol. 22, no. 1, Mar. 2011, pp. 75–92.

Lutkehaus, N. 'Beatrice Mary Blackwood (1889–1975).' In Gacs, U., et al. (eds.). *Woman Anthropologists: Selected Biographies*, University of Illinois Press, University of Chicago, 1989.

Mimica, J. '*The Kukukuku of the Upper Watut.* By Beatrice Blackwood.' *Oceania*, vol. 51, no. 3, Mar. 1981, p. 226.

Peers, L. 'Strands Which Refuse to Be Braided: Hair Samples from Beatrice Blackwood's Ojibwe Collection at the Pitt Rivers Museum.' *Journal of Material Culture*, vol. 8, no. 1, Mar. 2003, pp. 75–96.

Penniman, T.K. 'Beatrice Mary Blackwood, 1889–1975.' *American Anthropologist*, vol. 78, no. 2, June 1976, pp. 321–2.

—. 'Beatrice Mary Blackwood.' *Oceania*, vol. 46, 1976, pp. 234–7.

Percival, A.C. 'Miss B.M. Blackwood.' *Folklore*, vol. 87, no. 1, 1976, pp. 113–14.

Petch, A. 'Measuring the Natives: Beatrice Blackwood and Leonard Dudley Buxton's Work in Oxfordshire.' Online at http://web.prm.ox.ac.uk/sma/index.php/articles/article-index/364-blackwood-dudley-buxton-and-otmoor.html, 2012.

Simpson, C. 'A Woman of Oxford Lives with the Kukukukus.' In Simpson, C. *Adam with Arrows: Inside New Guinea*. Angus & Robertson, 1953, pp. 64–84.

Wormsley, W.E. '*The Kukukuku of the Upper Watut*: Beatrice Blackwood. C.R. Hallpike, ed.' *American Anthropologist*, NS, vol. 82, no. 4, Dec. 1980, pp. 902–3.

Maria Czaplicka
Manuscripts and Archives

American Museum of Natural History Archives.

Czaplicka correspondence. (Box 52, Folder 17, File 692.)

R.R. Marett correspondence. (Central Archive Collection.)

Bodleian Library, University of Oxford Archives.
    Committee for Anthropology, R.R. Marett correspondence. (DC 1/4, see also DC 1/3/1.)

Lady Margaret Hall, University of Oxford.
    Czaplicka file.
    Helena Clara Deneke memoirs, *What I Remember.* vol. 3. (MPP 3 A 1/3.)

Lucy Cavendish College Archives, University of Cambridge.
    Czaplicka papers collated by Ethel John Lindgren-Utsi. (LCCA EJL 8 (acc. no. A2012/001), Box 8.)

Oxford University Press Archives.
    Papers relating to the publication of *Aboriginal Siberia.* (OP200/10020.)
    Papers relating to proposed publication *Histories & Policies of the Nations – Poland.* (CP70/1002.)

Pitt Rivers Museum, University of Oxford.
    Czaplicka artefact and photograph collections, and accession records.
    Museum Annual Reports.

Royal Geographical Society Archives.
    Czaplicka correspondence. (Cor. Block 1911–1920: CB 7, CB 8 and CB 9; see also JMS/15/121.)

Somerville College, University of Oxford.
    Czaplicka file.
    College Register entry.
    College Reports.

University of Pennsylvania Museum of Archaeology and Anthropology Archives.
    G.B. Gordon correspondence. (LB 12, LB 13, LB 16-18, OD 4/1, OD 8/10.)
    Siberian Expedition papers. (SEH.)
    Czaplicka biographical file and album of press cuttings.
    H.U. Hall biographical file.

Publications by Maria Czaplicka

Czaplicka, M.A. 'Gods of the Australians.' *The Fritillary*, no. 55, Mar. 1912, pp. 22–5.

—. *Aboriginal Siberia: A Study in Social Anthropology*. Clarendon Press, 1914.

—. 'The Influence of Environment upon the Religious Ideas and Practices of the Aborigines of Northern Asia.' *Folklore*, vol. 25, no. 1, Mar. 1914, pp. 34–54.

—. 'The Life and Work of N.N. Miklukho-Maklay.' *Man*, vol. 14, 1914, p. 198.

—. 'Anthropological Work in the Yenisei Valley.' S.S.A. Annual Report, 1915.

—. 'A Year in Arctic Siberia.' *The Wide World*, vol. 37, no. 217, 1915, pp. 52–60; no. 218, 1915, pp. 133–40; and no. 219, 1915, pp. 225–33.

—. 'Tribes of the Yenisei: The Oxford Expedition.' *Times Russian Supplement*, no. 13, 1915, p. 6.

—. *My Siberian Year*, Mills & Boon, 1916.

—. 'A Mujik's Calendar. Russian Saints' Days.' *Times Russian Supplement*, no. 17, 1916, p. 5.

—. 'Fairy-Tales. Russian Folk Stories.' *Times Russian Supplement*, no. 18, 1916, pp. 6–7.

—. 'The Mujik's Marriage.' *Times Russian Supplement*, no. 21, 1916, p. 8.

—. 'Siberia and Some Siberians.' *Journal of the Manchester Geographical Society*, vol. 32, 1916, pp. 27–42.

—. 'The Siberian Colonist or Sibiriak.' In Stephens, Winifred (ed.). *The Soul of Russia*, London, 1916, pp. 123–30.

—. 'On the Track of the Tungus.' *Scottish Geographical Magazine*, vol. 33, no. 7, July 1917, pp. 289–303.

—. 'Kerenski and Korniloff.' *Land and Water*, vol. 70, no. 2892, 1917, pp. 8–10.

—. 'Rights and Limitations of Small Nationalities.' *Land and Water*, vol. 69, no. 2869, 1917, pp. 10–11.

—. 'Russia's Revolutions of 1905 and 1917.' *Land and Water*, vol. 69, no. 2865, 1917, pp. 13–14.

—. *The Turks of Central Asia in History and at the Present Day: An Ethnological Inquiry into the Pan-Turanian Problem, and Bibliographic Material Relating to the Early Turks and the Present Turks of Central Asia*. Curzon Press, 1918.

—. 'A Plea for Siberia.' *The New Europe*, vol. 6, no. 76, 1918, pp. 339–44.

—. 'The Evolution of the Cossack Communities.' *Journal of the Royal Central Asian Society*, vol. 5, no. 2, Jan. 1918, pp. 42–58.

—. 'The War in Arctic Russia.' *The New Europe*, vol. 8, 1918, pp. 172–7.

—. 'Pilsudski, the Polish Leader.' *Land and Water*, vol. 72, no. 2957, 1919, p. 23.

—. 'Poland.' *Geographical Journal*, vol. 53, no. 6, 1919, pp. 376–81.

—. 'Poland of Today.' *Land and Water*, no. 3005, 1919, pp. 10–18.

—. 'Poland of Today. The Polish Premier and His Ministers.' *Land and Water*, no. 3008, 1920, pp. 14, 16, 36.

—. 'Poland of Today. The New Polish Army.' *Land and Water*, no. 3009, 1920, pp. 13–14.

—. 'Poland of Today.' *Land and Water*, no. 3012, 1920, pp. 15–16.

—. 'Poland of Today. Education, Art and Science.' *Land and Water*, no. 3015, 1920, pp. 24–5.

—. 'The Ethnic Versus the Economic Frontiers of Poland.' *Scottish Geographical Magazine*, vol. 36, no. 1, Jan. 1920, pp. 10–16.

—. 'Is Danzig a Free City?' *The New Europe*, vol. 17, no. 210, 1920, pp. 45–8.

—. 'The Samoyed.' In Hastings, J., et al. (eds.). *Encyclopædia of Religion and Ethics*. T. & T. Clark, 1920.

—. 'The Siberians.' In Hastings, J., et al. (eds.). *Encyclopædia of Religion and Ethics*. T. & T. Clark, 1920.

—. 'The Slavs.' In Hastings, J., et al. (eds.). *Encyclopædia of Religion and Ethics*. T. & T. Clark, 1920.

—. 'The Tungus.' In Hastings, J., et al. (eds.). *Encyclopædia of Religion and Ethics*. T. & T. Clark, 1921.

—. 'The Turks.' In Hastings, J., et al. (eds.). *Encyclopædia of Religion and Ethics*. T. & T. Clark, 1921.

—. 'The Yakut.' In Hastings, J., et al. (eds.). *Encyclopædia of Religion and Ethics*. T. & T. Clark, 1921.

—. 'History and Ethnology in Central Asia.' *Man*, vol. 21, Feb. 1921, p. 19.

Biographical sources for Maria Czaplicka

Aitken, B. 'Marie Antoinette Czaplicka.' *Lady Margaret Hall Brown Book*, 1921, pp. 59–62.

Anon. 'Death of Miss M.A. De Czaplicka.' *The Times*, 30 May 1921, p. 8.

Anon. 'Miss Czaplicka.' *Manchester Guardian*, 31 May 1921, p. 6.

Collins, D. 'Letters from Siberia by M. A. Czaplicka.' *Sibirica*, vol. 1, 1995, pp. 61–84.

Collins, D., and Urry, J. 'A Flame Too Intense for Mortal Body to Support.' *Anthropology Today*, vol. 13, 1997, pp. 18–20.

Czaplicka, M.A., and Collins, D. *The Collected Works of M.A. Czaplicka*. Curzon Press, 1999.

Hall, H.U. 'The Siberian Expedition.' *Museum Journal*, vol. 3, 1916, pp. 27–45.

—. 'A Siberian Wilderness: Native Life on the Lower Yenisei.' *Geographical Review*, vol. 5, no. 1, Jan. 1918, pp. 1–21.

Haviland, M.D. *A Summer on the Yenesei*. Edward Arnold, 1915.

Kubica, Grażyna. 'A Good Lady, Androgynous Angel, and Intrepid Woman: Maria Czaplicka in Feminist Profile.' In Bryceson, D.F., et al. (eds.). *Identity and Networks: Fashioning Gender and Ethnicity across Cultures*. Berghahn Books, 2007, pp. 146–63.

—. 'The Shaman's Curse: Maria Czaplicka and her Studies on Shamanism.' *Shaman: Journal of the International Society for Academic Research on Shamanism*, vol. 22, no. 1/2, 2014, pp. 27–56.

—. 'Maria Czaplicka and Her Siberian Expedition, 1914–1915: A Centenary Tribute.' *Arctic Anthropology*, vol. 52, no. 1, Jan. 2015, pp. 1–22.

—. *Maria Czaplicka: Płeć, Szamanizm, Rasa: Biografia Antropologiczna*. Wydanie I, Wydawnictwo Uniwersytetu Jagiellońskiego, 2015.

La Rue, H. 'Maria Antoinette Czaplicka.' In Petch, A. (ed.). *Collectors: Collecting for the Pitt Rivers Museum Oxford*, Pitt Rivers Museum, 1996.

Levin, M. G., et al. *The Peoples of Siberia*. University of Chicago Press, 1964.

Luce, S.B. 'Henry Usher Hall.' *American Journal of Archaeology*, vol. 49, no. 1, 1945, p. 82.

Marett, R. R. 'Marie A. de Czaplicka: Died May 27, 1921.' *Man*, vol. 21, 1921, pp. 105–6.

Vider, J. 'Marginal Anthropology? Rethinking Maria Czaplicka and the Development of British Anthropology from a Material History Perspective'. DPhil thesis, University of Oxford, 2017.

Barbara Freire-Marreco
Manuscripts and Archives

Bodleian Library, University of Oxford.
> John Linton Myres papers. (Myres 1 and Myres 16, various folios.)

Lady Margaret Hall Archives, University of Oxford.
> Freire-Marreco file.

Pitt Rivers Museum, University of Oxford.
> Freire-Marreco artefact collections, and accession records.
> Freire-Marreco papers. (Manuscript Collections, 1 Box.)
> Museum Annual Reports.

Somerville College Archives, University of Oxford.
> Freire-Marreco file.
> College Register entry.
> College Reports.

Publications by Barbara Freire-Marreco

Freire-Marreco, B. 'Notes on the Hair and Eye Colour of 591 Children of School Age in Surrey.' *Man*, vol. 9, 1909, pp. 99–108.

—. 'Anthropology as a Science.' *The New Age*, NS, vol. 7, supplement, 5 May 1910, p. 7.

—. 'The West Riding Teachers' Anthropological Society.' *Folklore*, vol. 21, 1910, pp. 103–4.

—. 'Crosses Cut in Turf after Fatal Accidents.' *Folklore*, vol. 21, no. 3, 1910, pp. 387–8.

—. 'The "Dreamers" of the Mohaveapache Tribe [Abstract].' *Folklore*, vol. 23, 1912, pp. 172–4.

—. 'Tewa Kinship Terms from the Pueblo of Hano, Arizona.' *American Anthropologist*, vol. 16, no. 2, 1914, pp. 269–87.

—. 'A Note on the Kinship Terms Compounded with the Postfix 'E in the Hano Dialect of Tewa.' *American Anthropologist*, vol. 17, no. 1, 1915, pp. 198–202.

—. (with Robbins, W.W., Harrington, J.P., and the School of American

Research in Santa Fe) *Ethnobotany of the Tewa Indians.* Washington Government Printing Office, 1916.

—. (with Espinosa, Aurelio M.) 'New-Mexican Spanish Folk-Lore.' *Journal of American Folklore*, vol. 29, no. 114, 1916, pp. 505–46.

Aitken, B. 'A Tewa Craftsman – Leslie Agayo.' *El Palacio*, vol. 17, pp. 91–7.

—. 'The Burning of the "May" at Belorado.' *Folklore*, vol. 37, no. 3, 1926, pp. 289–96.

—. 'The Game of Ninepins in Castile.' *Folklore*, vol. 38, no. 1, 1927, p. 80.

—. 'Spanish Games and Calendar Customs.' *Folklore*, vol. 38, no. 2, 1927, p. 208.

—. 'The Morning Star Cult in the Southwest.' *American Anthropologist*, vol. 29, no. 4, 1927, pp. 731–2.

—. 'The Miraculous Cure of the "Possessed".' *Folklore*, vol. 41, no. 2, 1930, p. 195.

—. 'Temperament in Native American Religion.' *Journal of the Royal Anthropological Institute*, vol. 60, 1930, pp. 363–87.

—. 'Modern Slab Burials in Northern Castile.' *Man*, vol. 35, 1935, pp. 50–52.

—. 'A Conversation on the Castilian Witchcraft, Poltergeists, Magic and Suggestion.' *Folklore*, vol. 47, no. 1, 1936, pp. 105–7.

—. 'A Classification of Folk-Tales.' *Man*, vol. 47, 1947, p. 30.

—. 'Popular Art in Portugal.' *Man*, vol. 49, 1949, p. 19.

—. 'A Note on Pueblo Belt-Weaving.' *Man*, vol. 49, 1949, p. 37.

—. 'Edgar Lee Hewett, 1865–1946, Sylvanus Griswold Morley, 1883–1948.' *Man*, vol. 50, 1950, pp. 30–32.

—. 'The Game of Knucklebones, "Jugar a las Tabas".' *Folklore*, vol. 62, no. 2, 1951, p. 329.

—. 'On Hoebel's Review of Piddington.' *American Anthropologist*, vol. 53, no. 3, 1951, p. 418.

—. 'A Country Wedding in Austria, 1948.' *Folklore*, vol. 62, no. 4, 1951, pp. 458–63.

—. 'Use of Spanish in Anthropological Literature.' *American Anthropologist*, vol. 54, no. 2, 1952, p. 275.

—. 'Don Luis de Hoyos Sáinz.' *Folklore*, vol. 63, no. 2, 1952, p. 111.

—. 'Luis de Hoyos Sáinz.' *Man*, vol. 53, 1953, p. 40.

—. 'Holy Wells in Surrey.' *Folklore*, vol. 64, no. 2, 1953, p. 350.

—. 'A Note on Eliciting.' *International Journal of American Linguistics*, vol. 21, no. 1, 1955, p. 83.

—. 'Relocalization.' *Folklore*, vol. 70, no. 4, 1959, pp. 546–9.

—. 'The Couvade: Some Observations on an Article Contributed to *Folklore* by Professor Vukanović in September, 1959.' *Folklore*, vol. 71, no. 1, 1960, pp. 44–7.

—. 'Comment on "Can I lend your …?"' *Folklore*, vol. 71, no. 4, 1960, p. 265.

Biographical sources for Barbara Freire-Marreco

Anon. 'Somerville College Research Fellow.' *Common Cause*, 5 Jan. 1911.

Blair, M.E. *A Life Well Led: The Biography of Barbara Freire-Marreco Aitken, British Anthropologist.* Sunstone Press, 2008.

Coote Lake, E.F. 'Barbara Freire Marreco (Mrs Robert Aitken).' *Folklore*, vol. 78, 1967, pp. 305–6.

Crone, G.R. 'Robert Aitken.' *Geographical Journal*, vol. 132, no. 1, Mar. 1966, pp. 172–3.

Houston, J.M. 'Robert Aitken.' *Geography*, vol. 51, no. 2, Apr. 1966, p. 153.

Warrior, C. '"A Small Collection from New Mexico and Arizona": Barbara Freire-Marreco in the Southwestern United States, 1910–13.' *Journal of Museum Ethnography*, vol. 15, 2003, pp. 115–30.

Katherine Routledge
Manuscripts and Archives

Bodleian Library, University of Oxford.
   O.G.S. Crawford papers. (MS. Crawford 1, and uncatalogued correspondence.)
   Committee for Anthropology, R.R. Marett correspondence. (DC 1/4.)
   Oxford University Extension (Dept. of Continuing Education) papers. (CE 3/28/26 and CE 3/22/14.)
Durham County Record Office.
   Pease family papers, including Wilson Pease diary. (D/GP.)
Pitt Rivers Museum, University of Oxford.
   Routledge artefact collections, and accession records.

Royal Geographical Society Archives.

Routledge papers relating to Easter Island Expedition. (WSR.)

Somerville College Archives, University of Oxford.

Routledge file.

College Register entry.

College Reports.

Wellcome Archives and Manuscripts, Wellcome Library.

Ticehurst House Hospital papers. (MS6245/6245/6281/6283; MS6245/6554/6730/6730/3; MS6245/6284/6303/6309/2; MS6245 /6554/6554/6573.)

Publications by Katherine Routledge

Pease, K. 'Some Experiences of South Africa.' In Valentine, E.F. (ed.). *Darlington Training College Magazine*, 1903, pp. 97–102.

—. 'Experiences of an English Worker in South Africa.' *Imperial Colonist*, vol. 2, no. 1, 1903, pp. 3–4; vol. 2, no. 2, 1903, pp. 20–21.

Routledge, K.S. 'Emigration of British Teachers.' *Somerville Students' Association Report*, 1910, pp. 43–5.

—. (with Routledge, W.S.) *With a Prehistoric People: The Akikuyu of British East Africa.* Edward Arnold, 1910.

—. 'The Riddle of Easter Island: First Impressions.' *Spectator*, no. 4493, 8 Aug. 1914, pp. 196–7.

—. 'Easter Island Expedition.' *The Times*, 13 May 1916, p. 5.

—. 'The Bird Cult of Easter Island.' *Folklore*, vol. 28, no. 4, 1917, pp. 338–55.

—. 'Easter Island.' *Geographical Journal*, vol. 49, no. 5, 1917, pp. 321–40.

—. *The Mystery of Easter Island: The Story of an Expedition.* Adventures Unlimited Press, 1919.

—. 'Survey of the Village and Carved Rocks of Orongo, Easter Island, by the *Mana* Expedition.' *Man*, vol. 50, 1920, pp. 425–51.

—. 'The Mystery of Easter Island.' *National Geographic Magazine*, vol. 40, no. 6, 1921, pp. 628–48.

—. (with Routledge, W. Scoresby) 'Notes on Some Archaeological Remains in the Society and Austral Islands.' *Man*, vol. 51, 1921, pp. 438–55.

—. 'The Mysterious Images of Easter Island.' In Hammerton, J.A. (ed.). *Wonders of the Past: The Romance of Antiquity and its Splendors*, G.P. Putnam's Sons, 1924.

Biographical sources for Katherine Routledge

Anon. 'Driven from Home by Burglars.' *Daily Mail*, 14 March 1928, p. 9.

Anon. 'Woman in Locked Mansion.' *Daily Mail*, 2 June 1928, p. 11.

Anon. 'Woman Barricades Her Home.' *Aberdeen Press and Journal*, 2 June 1928, p. 7.

Anon. 'Society Woman in Barricaded House.' *Birmingham Daily Gazette*, 2 June 1928, p. 1.

Anon. 'West End Siege.' *Nottingham Evening Post*, 2 June 1928, p. 1.

Anon. 'Prisoner in Mansion.' *Western Mail*, 2 June 1928, p. 7.

Anon. 'Woman Barricaded in London House.' *The Times*, 4 June 1928, p. 11.

Anon. 'Gaol Threat to Mrs. Routledge.' *Birmingham Daily Gazette*, 4 June 1928, p. 7.

Anon. 'Lady's Lone Fight.' *Western Daily Press*, 14 June 1928, p. 11.

Anon. 'Woman in Locked House.' *Birmingham Daily Gazette*, 14 June 1928, p. 1.

Anon. 'Locked House Woman.' *Daily Mail*, 21 June 1928, p. 11.

Anon. 'Hyde Park Prisoner.' *Daily Herald*, 21 June 1928, p. 1.

Anon. 'Mrs. Routledge Leaves.' *Daily Mail*, 23 June 1928, p. 11.

Anon. 'Left Her Citadel.' *Aberdeen Press and Journal*, 25 June 1928, p. 7.

Anon. 'Woman Bailiff at Mrs. Routledge's.' *Daily Mail*, 26 June 1928, p. 9.

Anon. 'Mrs. Routledge to Argue Her Case Before Judge.' *Daily Mail*, 12 July 1928, p. 19.

Anon. 'Mrs. Routledge.' *Daily Mail*, 18 August 1928, p. 12.

Anon. 'Mrs. Routledge Again.' *Daily Mail*, 9 January 1929, p. 7.

Anon. 'Mrs Routledge Taken to Nursing Home.' *Daily Mail*, 13 February 1929, p. 9.

Anon. 'Mrs Routledge Leaves her Home Prison.' *Nottingham Evening Post*, 13 February 1929, p. 8.

Anon. 'Woman's Protest Sequel.' *Yorkshire Post and Leeds Intelligencer*, 14 February 1929, p. 5.

Anon. 'Woman Hermit Removed. Carried Out on a Stretcher.' *Nottingham Journal*, 14 February 1929, p. 9.

Anon. 'Obituary. Mr Scoresby Routledge.' *The Times*, 1 August 1939, p. 14.

Van Tilburg, J. 'O.G.S. Crawford and the *Mana* Expedition to Easter Island (Rapa Nui), 1913–1915.' *Journal of the Polynesian Society*, vol. 111, no. 1, 2002, pp. 65–77.

—. *Among Stone Giants: The Life of Katherine Routledge and her Remarkable Expedition to Easter Island.* Scribner, 2003.

Additional Manuscripts and Archives

Bodleian Library, University of Oxford.

    Committee for Anthropology papers. (DC 1/1–4.)

    Margaret Deneke papers. (Deneke [uncat.] *War 1914–1918 MD*.)

    Department of Human Anatomy papers. (HA 66/1–3.)

    John Linton Myres papers. (MS. Myres 1–132.)

    Alice Chance, née Carleton, staff file. (FA 9/1/42.)

    Oxford University Museum of Natural History papers. (MU 1–4.)

Cambridge University Archives, Cambridge University Library.

    Alfred Cort Haddon papers. (MS. Haddon 1–1500.)

Exeter College Archives, University of Oxford.

    Marett papers. (box 11–14.)

Lady Margaret Hall, Oxford.

    The Brown Book, Lady Margaret Hall Chronicle.

    Helena Clara Deneke memoirs, *What I Remember*, vol. 3. (MPP 3 A 1/3.)

London School of Economics.

    Raymond Firth papers. (Firth 8/1/36, 8/2/2.)

    Bronislaw Malinowski papers. (Malinowski 7/13, 29/11, 29/14, 29/35, 7/34, 7/38, 33/2–13, 37/17.)

Pitt Rivers Museum, University of Oxford.

    Henry Balfour papers. (Manuscript Collections.)

    Diploma in Anthropology, Register of Students, 1907–1950. (Manuscript Collections.)

Somerville College Archives, University of Oxford.

Published Works

Adam, L. 'In Memoriam: Robert Ranulph Marett.' *Oceania*, vol. 14, no. 3, 1944, pp. 183–90.

Adams, P. *Somerville for Women: An Oxford College, 1879–1993*. Oxford University Press, 1996.

Anderson, M. *Women and the Politics of Travel, 1870–1914*. Fairleigh Dickinson University Press, 2006.

Anon. 'Alice B. Carleton, M.A., M.D.' *British Medical Journal*, vol. 280, no. 6207, Jan. 1980, p. 124.

Anon. 'Arthur Thomson, L.L.D., M.B., F.R.C.S., Emeritus Professor of Anatomy, University of Oxford.' *British Medical Journal*, vol. 1, no. 3867, Feb. 1935, p. 334.

Ardener, S. 'The Social Anthropology of Women and Feminist Anthropology.' *Anthropology Today*, vol. 1, no. 5, 1985, pp. 24–6.

Balfour, H. 'Some Ethnological Suggestions in Regard to Easter Island, or Rapanui.' *Folklore*, vol. 28, no. 4, Dec. 1917, pp. 356–81.

Banner, L.W. *Intertwined Lives: Margaret Mead, Ruth Benedict and their Circle*. Alfred A. Knopf, 2003.

Batson, J. *Her Oxford*. Vanderbilt University Press, 2008.

Bell, M. and McEwan, C. 'The Admission of Women Fellows to the Royal Geographical Society, 1892-1914: The Controversy and the Outcome.' *Geographical Journal*, vol. 162, no. 3, 1996, pp. 295–312.

Benthall, J. 'Oxford Anthropology Since 1970: Through Schismogenesis to a New Testament.' In Rivière, P. (ed.). *A History of Oxford Anthropology*. Berghahn, 2007, pp. 155–70.

Bentley, L. *Educating Women: A Pictorial History of Bedford College, University of London, 1849–1985*. Alma Publishers, in conjunction with Royal Holloway and Bedford New College, University of London, 1991.

Berg, M.L. 'Power, Eileen Edna Le Poer (1889–1940).' *Oxford Dictionary of National Biography*. Oxford University Press, 2004.

Blackwood, B. 'Leonard Halford Dudley Buxton.' *Folklore*, vol. 50, no. 2, Jun. 1939, pp. 204–5.

Brittain, V. *The Women at Oxford: A Fragment of History*, George G. Harrap & Co. Ltd, 1960.

Burke, F. *A Land Apart: The Southwest and the Nation in the Twentieth Century*. University of Arizona Press, 2017.

Bush, J. '"The Right Sort of Woman": Female Emigrators and Emigration to the British Empire, 1890–1910.' *Women's History Review*, vol. 3, no. 3, pp. 385–409.

Caffey, D.L. *Frank Springer and New Mexico: From the Colfax County War to the Emergence of Modern Santa Fe*. Texas A&M University Press, 2007.

Caffrey, M.M. and Francis, P.A. (eds.). *Selected Letters of Margaret Mead*. Basic Books, 2006.

Caine, B. *English Feminism 1780-1980*. Oxford University Press, 1997.

Caton Thompson, G. *Mixed Memoirs*. Paradigm Press, 1983.

Chilton, L. 'A New Class of Women for the Colonies: The Imperial Colonist and the Construction of Empire.' *Journal of Imperial and Commonwealth History*, vol. 31, no. 2, 2003, pp. 36–56.

Chinnery, E. 'Mountain Tribes of the Mandated Territory of New Guinea from Mt. Chapman to Mt. Hagen.' *Man*, vol. 34, Aug. 1934, pp. 113–21.

—. 'The Central Ranges of the Mandated Territory of New Guinea from Mount Chapman to Mount Hagen.' *Geographical Journal*, vol. 84, no. 5, Nov. 1934, pp. 398–412.

Chinnery, S.J. *Malaguna Road: The Papua and New Guinea Diaries of Sarah Chinnery*. National Library of Australia, 1998.

Clarke, L. C. G. 'Professor Henry Balfour, F.R.S.' *Geographical Journal*, vol. 93, no. 6, 1939, pp. 465–7.

Clifford, J. 'On Ethnographic Self-Fashioning: Conrad and Malinowski.' In Heller, T.C., et al. (eds.). *Reconstructing Individualism: Autonomy, Individuality and the Self in Western Thought*. Stanford University Press, 1986, pp. 80–105.

Cooke, A.M. *My First 75 Years of Medicine*, Royal College of Physicians, 1994.

Corney, B.G. *The Voyage of Captain Don Felipe González in the Ship of the Line San Lorenzo with the Frigate Santa Rosalia in Company to Easter Island in 1770–1771.* London, Hakluyt Society, 1903.

Davies, J. and Wilson, J. 'Gendering Oxford: Shirley Ardener and Cross-Cultural Research.' In Bryceson, D.F., et al. (eds.). *Identity and Networks: Gender and Ethnicity in a Cross-Cultural Context.* Berghahn, 2007, pp. 249–58.

Davis, H.W.C. *History of the Blockade.* Her Majesty's Stationary Office, 1920.

Dragadze, T. 'Circumstance, Personality, and Anthropology.' In Bryceson, D.F., et al. (eds.). *Identity and Networks: Gender and Ethnicity in a Cross-Cultural Context.* Berghahn, 2007, pp. 261–2.

Dyhouse, C. *No Distinction of Sex? Women in British Universities, 1870–1939.* University College London Press, 1995.

Ebright, M. *Four Square Leagues: Pueblo Indian Land in New Mexico.* University of New Mexico Press, 2014.

Eggan, F. and Warner, W.L. 'Alfred Reginald Radcliffe-Brown, 1881–1955.' *American Anthropologist,* NS vol. 58, no. 3, 1956, pp. 544–7.

Engel, A.J. ' "Immoral Intentions": The University of Oxford and the Problem of Prostitution, 1827–1914.' *Victorian Studies,* vol. 23, no. 1, 1979, pp. 79–107.

Epstein, M. (ed.). *The Statesman's Year-Book: Statistical and Historical Annual of the States of the World for the Year 1932.* Macmillan, 1932.

Fairman, H.W. 'Aylward Manley Blackman.' *Journal of Egyptian Archaeology,* vol. 42, Dec. 1956, pp. 102–4.

Farnell, V. *A Somervillian Looks Back.* Oxford University Press, 1948.

Fischer, S.R. *Island at the End of the World: The Turbulent History of Easter Island.* Reaktion Books, 2005.

Forster, G. *A Voyage Round the World in His Britannie Majesty's Sloop, Resolution, Volume 1.* Hansebooks, 1777 (2016).

Fortes, M. 'Alfred Reginald Radcliffe-Brown, F.B.A., 1881–1955: A Memoir.' *Man,* vol. 56, Nov. 1956, pp. 149–53.

Gardiner, A.H. 'Francis Llewellyn Griffith.' *Journal of Egyptian Archaeology,* vol. 20, no. 1/2, Jun 1934, pp. 71–7.

Goldberg, E. 'Peasants in Revolt – Egypt 1919.' *International Journal of Middle East Studies*, vol. 24, 1992, pp. 261–80.

Gosden, C. and Larson, F. *Knowing Things: Exploring the Collections at the Pitt Rivers Museum 1884–1945*. Oxford University Press, 2007.

Gosden, C., et al. 'Origins and Survivals: Tylor, Balfour and the Pitt Rivers Museum and their Role within Anthropology at Oxford.' In Rivière, P. (ed.). *A History of Oxford Anthropology*. Berghahn, 2007, pp. 21–42.

Graham, M. *Oxford in the Great War*. Pen and Sword Military, 2014.

Gray, G. 'There Are Many Difficult Problems: Ernest William Pearson Chinnery – Government Anthropologist.' *Journal of Pacific History*, vol. 38, no. 3, 2003, pp. 313–30.

Haddon, A.C. 'A Plea for the Investigation of Biological and Anthropological Distributions in Melanesia.' *Geographical Journal*, vol. 28, 1906, pp. 155–63.

Haddon, A.C., and Quiggin, A.H. *History of Anthropology*. Watts, 1910.

Haines, C.M.C. *International Women in Science: A Biographical Dictionary to 1950*. ABC-CLIO, 2001.

Harbert, N. *New Mexico*. Fodor's Travel Publications, 2004.

Hauser, K. *Bloody Old Britain: O.G.S. Crawford and the Archaeology of Modern Life*. Granta, 2008.

Hays, T.E. 'A Historical Background to Anthropology in the Papua New Guinea Highlands.' In Hays, T.E. (ed.). *Ethnographic Presents: Pioneering Anthropologists in the Papua New Guinea Highlands*. University of California Press, 1992, pp. 1–36.

Herle, A., and Rouse, S. *Cambridge and the Torres Strait: Centenary Essays on the 1898 Anthropological Expedition*. Cambridge University Press, 1998.

Howarth, J. 'Women.' In Harrison, B. (ed.). *The History of the University of Oxford: Volume 8, The Twentieth Century*. Clarendon Press, 1994, pp. 345–75.

—. '"In Oxford but … not of Oxford": The Women's Colleges.' In Brock, M.G. and Curthoys, M.C. (eds.). *The History of the University of Oxford: Volume 7, The Nineteenth Century, Part 2*. Oxford University Press, 2000a, pp. 237–307.

—. ' "Oxford for Arts": The Natural Sciences, 1880–1914.' In Brock, M.G. and Curthoys, M.C. (eds.). *The History of the University of Oxford: Volume 7, The Nineteenth Century, Part 2.* Oxford University Press, 2000b, pp. 457–97.

—. 'The Self-Governing University, 1882-1914.' In Brock, M.G. and Curthoys, M.C. (eds.). *The History of the University of Oxford: Volume 7, The Nineteenth Century, Part 2.* Oxford University Press, 2000c, pp. 599–643.

Hunt, T. and Lipo, C. *The Statues That Walked: Unraveling the Mystery of Easter Island.* Counterpoint, 2012.

Hyam, R. *Empire and Sexuality: The British Experience.* Manchester University Press, 1990.

Inglis, A. *The White Woman's Protection Ordinance: Sexual Anxiety and Politics in Papua.* Sussex University Press, 1975.

Jacobs, E. 'Eileen Power's Asian Journey, 1920–21: History, Narrative, and Subjectivity.' *Women's History Review*, vol. 7, no. 3, pp. 295–319.

Jacobson, D. 'Going Native: Sexual Favours in Colonial East Africa.' *London Review of Books*, vol. 21, no. 23, Nov. 1999, pp. 27–30.

James, E.O. 'Robert Ranulph Marett.' *Folklore*, vol. 54, no. 1, 1943, pp. 271–2.

James, W. ' "A Feeling for Form and Pattern, and a Touch of Genius": E.-P.'s Vision and the Institute 1946–70.' In Rivière, P. (ed.). *A History of Oxford Anthropology.* Berghahn, 2007, pp. 98–118.

—. 'Reflections on Oxford's Global Links.' In Rivière, P. (ed.). *A History of Oxford Anthropology.* Berghahn, 2007, pp. 171–92.

Knightley, L.M. 'Emigration to South Africa.' In Murray, J.H. and Stark, M. (eds.). *An Englishwoman's Review of Social and Industrial Questions*, vol. 34, issue 259, 1903, pp. 220–25.

Kroskrity, P.V. *Language, History, and Identity: Ethnolinguistic Studies of the Arizona Tewa.* University of Arizona Press, 1993.

Kuklick, H. *The Savage Within: the Social History of British Anthropology, 1885–1945.* Cambridge University Press, 1991.

—. *A New History of Anthropology.* Blackwell, 2008.

Kuper, A. *Anthropology and Anthropologists: the British School in the Twentieth Century.* Routledge, 2014.

Larson, F. 'Anthropological Landscaping: General Pitt Rivers, the Ashmolean, the University Museum and the Shaping of an Oxford Discipline,' *Journal of the History of Collections*, vol. 20, no. 1, 2008, pp. 85–100.

—. *An Infinity of Things: How Sir Henry Wellcome Collected the World*. Oxford University Press, 2009.

Larson, F., and Petch, A. '"Hoping for the Best, Expecting the Worst": T.K. Penniman, Forgotten Curator of the Pitt Rivers Museum.' *Journal of Museum Ethnography*, 2006, pp. 125–39.

Leach, E.R. 'Glimpses of the Unmentionable in the History of British Social Anthropology.' *Annual Review of Anthropology*, vol. 13, 1984, pp. 1–24.

Leahy, M.J., and Crain, M. *The Land That Time Forgot: Adventures and Discoveries in New Guinea*. Hurst & Blackett, 1937.

Leonardi, S.J. *Dangerous by Degrees: Women at Oxford and the Somerville College Novelists*. Rutgers University Press, 1989.

Lutkehaus, N. '"She was 'Very' Cambridge": Camilla Wedgwood and the History of Women in British Social Anthropology.' *American Ethnologist*, vol. 13, no. 4, 1986, pp. 776–98.

—. *Margaret Mead: The Making of an American Icon*. Princeton University Press, 2008.

Mackendrick, K. 'John Linton Myres.' *Geographical Journal*, vol. 120, 1954, pp. 541–2.

MacKenzie, C. *Psychiatry for the Rich: A History of Ticehurst Private Asylum 1792–1917*. Routledge, 1992.

Macmillan, H. 'Oxford Remembered.' *The Times*, 18 October 1975, p. 7.

McCarthy, H. *Women of the World: The Rise of the Female Diplomat*. Bloomsbury, 2014.

McCarthy, J.K. *Patrol into Yesterday: My New Guinea Years*. Angus & Robertson, 1964.

Mclean, A. 'In the Footprints of Reo Fortune.' In Hays, T.E. (ed.). *Ethnographic Presents: Pioneering Anthropologists in the Papua New Guinea Highlands*. University of California Press, 1992, pp. 37–67.

Mak, L. 'More than Officers and Officials: Britons in Occupied Egypt, 1882–1922.' *Journal of Imperial and Commonwealth History*, vol. 39, no. 1, 2011, pp. 21–46.

Malinowski, B. *Argonauts of the Western Pacific*. Routledge & Kegan Paul, 1922.

Marett, R.R. 'Presidential Address: Anthropology and University Education.' *Report of the British Association for the Advancement of Science, Section H*. Newcastle-on-Tyne, 1916, pp. 458–67.

—. *A Jerseyman in Oxford*. Oxford University Press, 1941.

Mead, M. *Coming of Age in Samoa: A Psychological Study of Primitive Youth for Western Civilization*. William Morrow, 1928.

—. *Letters from the Field, 1925–1975*. Perennial, 1977.

Michael, P. *Care and Treatment of the Mentally Ill in North Wales 1800–2000*. University of Wales Press, 2003.

Michael, P. and Hirst, D. 'Recording the Many Faces of Death at the Denbigh Asylum, 1848-1938.' *History of Psychiatry*, vol. 23, no. 1, 2011, pp. 40–51.

Mills, D. 'A Major Disaster for Anthropology? Oxford and Alfred Reginald Radcliffe-Brown.' In Rivière, P. (ed.). *A History of Oxford Anthropology*. Berghahn, 2007, pp. 83–97.

Murray, M. *My First Hundred Years*. William Kimber, 1963.

Myres, J.L. 'Henry Balfour, F.R.S., 1863 – 9th February, 1939.' *Man*, vol. 39, May 1939, pp. 77–8.

—. 'Leonard Halford Dudley Buxton.' *Man*, vol. 39, July 1939, p. 11.

Nelson, H. 'Masters in the Tropics.' In Gammage, B. and Spearritt, P. (eds.). *Australians 1938*. Fairfax, Syme & Weldon, 1987, pp. 423–34.

Ogilvie, M., et al. *The Biographical Dictionary of Women in Science: Pioneering Lives from Ancient Times to the Mid-Twentieth Century*. Routledge, 2000.

O'Leary, R.D. *Notes from Oxford 1910–1911: The Journal of a Revered English Professor*. iUniverse, 2015.

Penniman, T.K. 'Robert Ranulph Marett: 13 June, 1866 – 18 February, 1943.' *Man*, vol. 44, 1944, pp. 33–5.

Petch, A., et al. *The Relational Museum Project 2002–2006*. Pitt Rivers Museum Website. (http://web.prm.ox.ac.uk/history)

Powdermaker, H. *Stranger and Friend: The Way of an Anthropologist*. W.W. Norton, 1966.

Radcliffe-Brown, A.R. *The Andaman Islanders*. Cambridge University Press, 1922.

Richling, B. *In Twilight and in Dawn: A Biography of Diamond Jenness*. McGill-Queen's University Press, 2012.

Riedi, E. 'Women, Gender, and the Promotion of Empire: The Victoria League, 1901–1914.' *Historical Journal*, vol. 45, no. 3, 2002, pp. 569–99.

Riley, G. *Taking Land, Breaking Land: Women Colonizing the American West and Kenya 1840–1940*. University of New Mexico Press, 2003.

Rivers, W.H.R. 'A General Account of Method.' In Freire-Marreco, B.W., and Myres, J.L. (eds.). *Notes and Queries on Anthropology*. Royal Anthropological Institute, London, 1912, pp. 108–27.

Rivière, P. 'The Formative Years: the Committee for Anthropology 1905–38.' In Rivière, P. (ed.). *A History of Oxford Anthropology*. Berghahn, 2007, pp. 43–61.

Rogers, P. 'The British and the Kikuyu 1890-1905: A Reassessment.' *Journal of African History*, vol. 20, no. 2, 1979, pp. 255–69.

Rosman, A. and Rubel, P.G. 'Powdermaker's Lesu.' *Journal of Anthropological Research*, vol. 47, no. 4, 1991, pp. 377–88.

Ryan, T. 'Celia Westropp.' *Oxford Medicine: The Newsletter of the Oxford Medical Alumni*. July 2006, pp. 10–11.

—. 'The Development of Dermatology in the Oxford Region.' Available online at www.bad.org.uk, accessed 5 July 2016.

Scargill, D.I. 'The R.G.S. and the Foundations of Geography at Oxford.' *Geographical Journal*, vol. 142, no. 3, 1976, pp. 438–61.

Schwartz, L. *A Serious Endeavour: Gender, Education and Community at St. Hugh's, 1886–2011*. Profile Books, 2011.

Shadle, B. 'Settler, Africans, and Inter-Personal Violence in Kenya, ca. 1900–1920s.' *International Journal of African Historical Studies*, vol. 45, no. 1, 2012, pp. 57–80.

Showalter, E. *The Female Malady: Women, Madness, and English Culture, 1830–1980*. Virago, 1987.

Simpson, C. *Adam with Arrows: Inside New Guinea*. Angus & Robertson, 1954.

Stocking, G.W. 'Gatekeeper to the Field: E.W.P. Chinnery and Ethnography of the New Guinea Mandate.' *History of Anthropology Newsletter*, vol. 9, no. 2, 1982, pp. 3–12.

—. 'From Rousseau to Rivers.' *RAIN*, no. 61, Apr. 1984, pp. 6–8.

—. 'The Ethnographer's Magic: Fieldwork in British Anthropology from Tylor to Malinowski.' In Stocking, G.W. (ed.). *The Ethnographer's Magic and Other Essays in the History of Anthropology.* University of Wisconsin Press, 1992, pp. 12–59.

—. *After Tylor: British Social Anthropology 1888–1951.* University of Wisconsin Press, 1995.

Tate, H. 'Notes on the Kikuyu Tribe of British East Africa.' *Journal of the Anthropological Institute*, vol. 34, no. 1, 1904, pp. 130–48.

—. 'Further Notes on the Kikuyu Tribe of British East Africa.' *Journal of the Anthropological Institute*, vol. 34, no. 2, 1904, pp. 255–65.

Thoden van Velzen, H.U.E. 'Robinson Crusoe and Friday: Strength and Weakness of the Big Man Paradigm.' *Man*, NS, vol. 8, no. 4, Dec. 1973, pp. 592–612.

Thompson, C.A. 'Anthropology's Conrad: Malinowksi in the Tropics and What He Read.' *Journal of Pacific History*, vol. 30, no. 1, Jun. 1995, pp. 53–75.

Tignor, R.L. *The Colonial Transformation of Kenya: The Kamba, Kikuyu and Maasai from 1900–1939.* Princeton University Press, 1976.

—. 'The Egyptian Revolution of 1919: New Directions in the Egyptian Economy.' *Middle Eastern Studies*, vol. 12, no. 3, Oct. 1976, pp. 41–67.

Tobias, H.J. and Woodhouse, C.E. *Santa Fe: A Modern History 1880–1990.* University of New Mexico Press, 2001.

Urry, J. '"Notes and Queries on Anthropology" and the Development of Field Methods in British Anthropology 1870–1920.' *Proceedings of the Royal Anthropological Institute of Great Britain and Ireland*, no. 1972, 1972, pp. 45–57.

—. *Before Social Anthropology: Essays on the History of British Anthropology*, Harwood Academic Publishers, 1993.

Wallis, W.D. 'Anthropology in England Early in the Present Century.' *American Anthropologist*, vol. 59, no. 5, 1957, pp. 781–90.

Wayne, H. 'Bronislaw Malinowski: The Influence of Various Women on His Life and Works.' *American Ethnologist*, vol. 12, no. 3, Aug. 1985, pp. 529–40.

Weaver, J.R.H., rev. Matthew, H.C.G. 'Davis, Henry William Carless (1874–1928).' *Oxford Dictionary of National Biography*. Oxford University Press, 2004.

Wheeler, R. '"My Savage," "My Man": Racial Multiplicity in "Robinson Crusoe".' *ELH*, vol 62, no. 4, 1995, pp. 821–61.

Wilson, C. *The Myth of Santa Fe: Creating a Modern Regional Tradition*. University of New Mexico Press, 1997.

Young, M. '"The Intensive Study of a Restricted Area", or Why Did Malinowski Go to the Trobriand Islands?' *Oceania*, vol. 55, no. 1, 1984, pp. 1–26.

—. 'The Careless Collector: Malinowski and the Antiquarians.' In O'Hanlon, M. and Welsch, R. (eds.). *Hunting the Gatherers: Ethnographic Collectors, Agents and Agency in Melanesia 1870s–1930s*. Berghahn Books, 2000, pp. 181–202.

—. *Malinowski: Odyssey of an Anthropologist 1884–1920*. Yale University Press, 2004.

Acknowledgements

There are several people I want to thank for their help while I was writing this book. Anne Meadows, my editor, for her dedication, her meticulous advice and her belief in this project from the start; Christine Lo and the team at Granta for transforming my work into a beautiful book; and my agent, Patrick Walsh, for being, as always, a key ally and advisor to me. Throughout my research, Jaanika Vider generously shared her knowledge with me, and later she read and critiqued my manuscript. Alison Petch also read the manuscript and gave me the benefit of her considerable expertise. And it is my good fortune that Chris Gosden still provides me with the occasional tutorial these many years later. All the archivists, librarians and curators I have visited have shared their treasures and their wisdom unreservedly. Delving into their collections has been my greatest pleasure while working on this book. I would particularly like to thank Kate O'Donnell at Somerville College; Colin Harris at the Bodleian Library Special Collections; Philip Grover at the Pitt Rivers Museum; and Alex Pessati at the University of Pennsylvania Museum archives, for their time and help. My thanks also to Caroline Bucknell, who warmly welcomed me into her home to talk about her extraordinary great aunt, Katherine. And, of course, to my family – Greger, Mum, Dad – thank you: your faith and your critical powers give me strength. This book is dedicated to my daughters. No one has shown me more about courage and happiness in the face of adversity than they have.

Illustration Credits

Illustration 17 (file D84/3) courtesy of The University of Liverpool Library.

Illustrations 18, 19, 20 and 26 courtesy of The Garstang Museum of Archaeology, University of Liverpool.

Illustrations 21, 22 and 27 from *A Life Well Led* by Mary Ellen Blair courtesy of Sunstone Press, Santa Fe, New Mexico, USA.

Index

Keep in touch with
Granta Books:

Visit granta.com to discover more.

GRANTA

SEVERED

A History of Heads Lost and Heads Found

'Lively, original, important, astounding, well-written:
first class in every way' *Sunday Times*

'Clever, startling, profoundly informative, delightfully
gruesome ... Larson writes like an angel' John Simpson

Over the centuries, heads have decorated our churches,
festooned our city walls and filled our museums; they have been
props for artists and specimens for laboratory scientists, trophies
for soldiers and items of barter. Today, videos of decapitations
circulate online and cryonicists promise us our heads may one
day live on without our bodies. In this extraordinary book
Frances Larson explores our centuries-old fascination with
the severed head and finds a history that is as contentious,
confounding and compelling as ever.

'An elegant history, packed with bizarre and horrifying stories,
fascinating facts and philosophical conundrums'
Independent on Sunday

'Wonderfully original ... it cuts through conventional categories
of science, literature and art'
Richard Fortey, *TLS* 'Book of the Year'

'Scholarly yet sprightly ... its curiosity and intellectual energy
will haunt me – in a good way – for a long time'
Spectator 'Book of the Year'

'Engaging and readable ... a fascinating curio of a history'
The Times